International Trade and Investment Behaviour of Firms

International Trade and Investment Behaviour of Firms

Murali Patibandla

OXFORD
UNIVERSITY PRESS

OXFORD
UNIVERSITY PRESS

Oxford University Press is a department of the University of Oxford. It furthers the University's objective of excellence in research, scholarship, and education by publishing worldwide. Oxford is a registered trademark of Oxford University Press in the UK and in certain other countries.

Published in India by
Oxford University Press
22 Workspace, 2nd Floor, 1/22 Asaf Ali Road, New Delhi 110 002, India

ISBN-13 (print edition): 978-0-19-012686-5
ISBN-10 (print edition): 0-19-012686-8

ISBN-13 (eBook): 978-0-19-099194-4
ISBN-10 (eBook): 0-19-099194-1

Typeset in Adobe Garamond Pro 11/13.5
by The Graphics Solution, New Delhi 110 092
Printed in India by Rakmo Press, New Delhi 110 020

To Pratyusha and Nikhita
My daughters and best friends
and
To all the coincidences of life

Contents

Tables and Figures

Tables

Figures

Preface

During the last four decades, globalization and rapid technological changes and their flows across countries have been important phenomena with significant implications on the world economy, especially the developing world. Several developing and socialist economies that followed long periods of closed-door and import substitution policies started to open their economies to world trade and investments. The countries that established initial conditions in technological, skill, and industrial endowments and in critical income levels are the ones that have been able to achieve a certain degree of economic convergence with the developed world through international trade and investment and technology flows (Spence, 2011). South Korea was the first country that achieved rapid economic growth by adopting export-oriented policies. As is well known, China opened up its economy to international trade and investment in the late 1970s; it achieved extraordinary annual growth rates of 8 to 10 per cent and lifted 600 million people out of poverty to reach the middle-income country stature it occupies at present. India pursued the Fabian socialist policies of inward orientation and import substitution with 'command and controls' from 1950 to the late 1980s. It implemented certain internal reforms in the mid-1980s and initiated major internal and external reforms in the early 1990s. The reforms, in general, resulted in positive outcomes of increased outward orientation and annual growth rates. This was because it possessed a critical level of initial conditions of basic capitalist institutions, industrial and skill base, and entrepreneurial class acquired right from the British Raj and the Fabian socialistic policies after its Independence. In other words, the post-reform outcomes were based on the pre-reform factors.

However, owing to institutional conditions of high transaction costs of doing business, inadequate investments in quality primary and secondary education, and market imperfections, India could not achieve large-scale labour-intensive exports similar to China's. The present government desires to implement 'Make in India' strategies similar to China's 'Made in China' to produce and export labour-intensive goods, and also policies of 'ease of doing business' to reduce transaction costs for investments, both domestic and foreign. Furthermore, in 2019, the finance minister reduced corporate tax from 32 per cent to 26 per cent to provide incentives to domestic and foreign direct investment. However, for these initiatives to succeed, one has to analyse underlying economic and institutional factors that govern international trade and investment of firms at the micro level. This monograph systematically identifies the underlying economic factors of firms' behaviours across industries and, over time, of changing economic and institutional factors locally and globally in general, and more in the context of India.

The monograph is divided into two parts: 1) International Trade Behaviour of Firms: The Pre-reform Era and 2) International Trade and Investment Behaviour of Firms: The Post-reform Era. A portion of the first part draws from my (unpublished) doctoral thesis, 'Firm Size and Export Behaviour', the research for which was done in the late 1980s and the early 1990s and based on which I was awarded a doctor of philosophy degree in 1994 by Jawaharlal Nehru University, New Delhi. At that time, I ignored international investment behaviour as multinational firms were barred in most industries. The second part extends the concepts of the review of theoretical literature, the model, and the empirical analysis of the first part to the post-reform era. Both the parts are interrelated because, as we know, in social sciences, a good study of the past is useful in understanding the present and possible future by systematically relaxing the assumptions and institutional conditions. In the second part, both international trade and international investments are examined because transnational corporations (TNCs) started to play an important role in the market dynamics and corresponding international trade and investment behaviour of firms. International trade and investment are interrelated, as international investment can be a source of expanding international trade and it can also be a substitute for international trade. This interrelationship is examined in the second part. Although India was not able to achieve success similar to China's in flooding the world market with labour-intensive manufactured goods, as the reforms progressed from the 1990s onwards, the Indian economy's global integration started to increase, thereby contributing to output and employment expansion and technology inflows. In a few areas, India was able to leapfrog into exporting skill and technology-intensive services because of prior endowments of skilled manpower with English language skills, which were generated by the import substitutional policies. The following issue is how India can achieve success in deriving maximum benefits from global integration for exporting employment-generating manufactured goods and technology inflows through imports and foreign direct investment. This monograph systematically identifies underlying economic and institutional factors for achieving the above-mentioned objectives.

Murali Patibandla
Indian Institute of Management Bangalore, India

PART 1

International Trade Behaviour of Firms: The Pre-reform Era

1 Introduction to Part 1

During the last forty years, international trade and investments have been a major source of economic growth for several developing economies. The classic examples are the Republic of Korea (South Korea), the Republic of China (Taiwan), the People's Republic of China (China), and other East Asian countries, and to a considerable extent India at present. International trade improves allocative efficiency of limited resources and result in economies of specialization at the global level. International investments by transnational corporations (TNCs) is a major source of technology flows and employment generation and expansion of export sectors in developing economies. Furthermore, emerging economies themselves started producing multinational firms undertaking investments in both developed and developing economies. Developing countries could deliberately adopt export- and TNC-led growth strategies such as those of China. On the other hand, international trade and investment behaviour of firms could be a result of domestic market dynamics, as has been in the case for India.

A brief comparative analysis of China and India in this context is relevant. Both are large and fast-growing developing economies. China generated institutions by combining political communism with capitalism of free markets to achieve high growth rates. India has always been a federal democracy with basic institutions of capitalism. Mao's cultural revolution of the 1970s inflicted heavy costs on the Chinese economy. China opened up its economy to the outside world in the early 1980s. It provided incentives to TNCs to take advantage of its low-cost labour for producing and exporting labour-intensive manufacturing. Its export-led growth strategy resulted in an annual growth rate between 8 to 10 per cent. Private firms were denied property rights until 1998 (Huang, 2002). The TNCs got into joint ventures with the public sector firms to access valuable assets. They did not face competition from local firms in the beginning as there was hardly any significant presence of private sector firms. Later, China started to generate an indigenous entrepreneurial class. In other words, TNCs and exports played important roles in China's growth (Spence, 2011).

India inherited basic institutions of capitalism from the British colonial rule. There has always been the presence of dynamic Indian entrepreneurs, starting from the time of the British rule. After its Independence in 1947, India adopted Fabian socialist policies. Although, it imposed restrictions on the private sector, it did not discourage them. Large private sector firms thrived along with the public sector. However, excessive government intervention resulted in pervasive inefficiencies. Private sector firms realized monopoly profits at the cost of consumers by selling low-quality products (Patibandla, 2006b).

India implemented a few select reforms of industrial delicensing and allowing multinational firms in a few industries through joint ventures in the mid-1980s. India's software industry was the first industry in which multinational corporations were encouraged since the mid-1980s and they played a significant role in the evolution of the industry, especially in increasing India's external orientation and increasing employment and productivity of skilled labour (Patibandla and Petersen, 2002). Major internal and external reforms were implemented in 1991 owing to the balance of payments crisis. The devaluation of the rupee augmented exports. The reforms resulted in the entry of multinational firms into quite a few sectors such as software and services, automobiles, and electronics through joint and greenfield ventures. This, in turn, increased domestic competitive conditions both in the product and factor markets. This improved productivity and scale of firms and consequently led to a decline in monopoly rents and prices, benefitting consumers and workers. Domestic competitive conditions, both in product and factor markets, started to augment international competitiveness of firms in several industries. As the industrial structure evolved, India started producing multinational firms of Indian corporations, investing in overseas markets through cross-border mergers and acquisitions and greenfield ventures (Guillen and Garcia-Canal, 2013).

India is among the few developing economies where the reforms resulted in positive outcomes of increased growth rate and increased international competitive conditions because it possessed a critical level of initial conditions of basic capitalist institutions and industrial and skill base, acquired right from the British time, and the Fabian socialistic policies after its Independence. In other words, the post-reform outcomes were based on the pre-reform factors. India's Fabian socialist policies of the previous policy regime under democracy, despite generating pervasive inefficiencies with institutional controls on the markets, did not destroy the capitalist forces of private property and legal system. Consequently, it led to the emergence of a strong local entrepreneurial class, which became the basis for rapid growth in the post-reform era.

Patterns of international trade of exports and imports are determined by the ability of firms to take advantage of a country's comparative advantage in endowments of technology, labour, capital, and natural resources. Market size, scale economies, product differentiation, firm-level organizational efficiency, and internal and global value chains also play important roles in determining the pattern of trade. In normative terms, international trade between countries improves allocative efficiency of limited factor endowments across nations and thereby increases welfare. International trade also results in economies of specialization (division of labour) and scale economies, and increase in number of differentiated goods available to consumers (Krugman and Obstfeld, 2003).

The classical international trade theories are based on the assumption of perfect competition in which firms and industries are the same. However, organization of industries in structural terms such as degree of competition, number of firms, size distribution, product differentiation, technological differences, organizational factors, and linkages on vertical chains between firms determine the conduct of firms in terms of, for instance, pricing behaviour, technological and organizational efficiency, entry and exit barriers, and domestic versus international orientation. Organization of industries is determined by industry dynamics of the two-way relation between structure and conduct with regard to outcomes. Furthermore, institutional factors such as government policies, transaction and information costs of markets, property rights, and contractual arrangements also determine the structural dynamics.

International trade and international investment are interlinked. International investment could be a substitute for international trade. At initial stages, a firm produces in the home market and exports from home market. After a point, it may set up plants in foreign countries to overcome transport and tariff barriers. A good example of this are the Japanese firms which, in the initial phases of the 1950s and 1960s, undertook exports from home base. At a later phase, they set up plants in foreign countries to overcome tariff and transport barriers and to be close to the customers. International investment may expand international trade. Foreign firms may set up plants in the host market to exploit comparative advantage for their international operations. A good example is India's software industry. A large number of TNCs have entered India's software industry since 1985 to take advantage of low-cost skilled labour for their home and worldwide operations.

India's growth pattern and its internationalization can be observed in two separate time periods: 1950–91 and 1991 onwards. In the first phase, India adopted Fabian socialist policies of excessive government intervention in the functioning of markets and import substitution policies. In most sectors, multinational firms were barred from operating. The Fabian socialist policies in practice were captured by powerful cohesive groups of large-scale corporations who derived monopoly rents at the cost of consumers and workers. At the same time, they generated a large industrial base and led to the presence of a few large and many small- and medium-scale (S&M) firms.

However, most industries remained inefficient compared to international standards. They also generated a sizeable service economy and English-speaking middle class and technical skills, which became an important advantage for the country's ability to generate a comparative advantage in a few technology-intensive industries at a later stage of the post-reform era.

When we talk of firm-level behaviour, we have to consider that one of the dominant characteristics of Indian economy was economic duality of fragmentation of product and input markets (capital, labour, and resources), especially in the pre-reform era. On one hand, there were pockets of sophisticated and well-functioning output, capital, and labour markets of the organized sector and the unorganized markets where a crude form of capitalism prevailed. The economic duality could also be seen in terms of coexistence of different choices of techniques in doing a specific activity. Another dimension of the fragmentation was that the elements of the institutional environment would work in different manners for different agents within the system: large and small firms in an industry faced different transaction and information costs, both in the output and input markets and enforcement of contracts (Olson, 1965; Patibandla, 2006b). This has implications on firms' ability to derive comparative advantage in exports by utilizing labour abundance of the Indian economy. An example of fragmentation of markets in the Indian context was the segmentation of labour and capital markets into the organized and the unorganized. This resulted in large firms having greater access to capital at lower price than its shadow (opportunity costs) price.

On the other hand, S&M firms paid higher price to capital reflecting their opportunity costs in the capital-scarce Indian economy. Labour market segmentation made large firms employ organized labour and pay higher price to labour than S&M firms which, in turn, determine their respective ability to exploit India's comparative advantage in labour-intensive techniques.

Furthermore, many S&M firms functioned as supplier (subcontractor) firms to large firms with unequal bargaining power (Nagaraj, 1984; Patibandla, 1988b). Consequently, S&M firms faced high transaction and information costs in product and capital markets. For example, when S&M firms supplied intermediate goods to large final producer firms, they were made to wait for long periods to get paid for their deliveries by the large firms, which increased scarce working capital costs. So, these firms which faced restrictive market conditions in the domestic market from the leader firms found the export markets less imperfect as everyone from the economically small developing countries in the world markets are price takers. Furthermore, payments for exports were made by letters of credit, which reduced working capital cost significantly.

In the first part of this monograph, we examine the international trade behaviour of large and small firms, referring mostly to the period of the 1980s. In this period, international investment behaviour was ignored as multinational firms did not play a significant role in Indian industries. A reasonably good theoretical framework and empirical analysis of the pre-reforms era should provide predictability of the outcomes of reforms on industrial structure and associated international trade and investment behaviour. The first part set up the basic theoretical and empirical setting to understand the effect of the economic reforms in the second part based on the initial conditions. In the second part, we examine both international trade and international investment behaviour because TNCs started to play a very important role in the industrial structure dynamics and later Indian firms themselves started to undertake overseas investments.

The first part of the study focuses on the industrial structure of distribution of large and small firms in the industrial sector and their corresponding market power, relative bargaining power and interactions in producing output, and generation of employment. It also analyses relative efficiency: both efficiency of technology in converting inputs into output and allocative efficiency of scarce resources of capital, labour and resources in a country with abundant labour supply and the consequent diverse international trade behaviour of firms.

The industrial structure of the roles of large and small firms in technological innovation, utilization of inputs (production efficiency), and employment and income generation were studied extensively (Kamien and Schwartz, 1982; Desai, 1982; Mead, 1984; Page,

1984). For example, small and medium enterprises (SMEs) account for 45 per cent of employment, 40 per cent of gross domestic product, and 50 per cent of exports in India (Dossani and Desai, 2009).

There were a few mostly empirical studies that examined the role of large and small firms in exports and foreign exchange generation, both in the case of advanced countries and developing countries (Glejser, Goossens, and Vanden, 1982; Auquier, 1980; Siddharthan, 1986; Lall and Kumar 1981). Most of them studied issues such as scale economies, technological innovation and research and development (R&D) behaviour, domestic market power, and domestic factor endowment conditions as explanatory factors in the association between firm size and exports.

The issue of firm size and international trade is important in the context of policy choice between capital and labour intensities, increasing returns in technologies, industrial concentration levels, and competitive market structure. This is because market structure in terms of firm size asymmetry (industrial concentration levels) has important implications on the technological behaviour, scale economies, and strategic rivalry between large and small firms and, in turn, on international trade behaviour.

The major objective of the first part of the book is to examine the association between industrial structure in terms of distribution of large and small firms in broadly defined industries and their international trade behaviour, and to identify and analyse the underlying domestic demand- and supply-side conditions governing the association. The analysis of the study concentrates on the domestic demand- and supply-side conditions based on two justifiable assumptions:

1. For the pre-reforms period, India was taken to be a small economy in the world market for manufactured goods, which meant that all the domestic firms were price takers in the world market. In other words, neither large nor small firms from a developing economy could influence world market prices.
2. Domestic and world markets were segmented through partial import protection.

The developments in the analysis of international trade in an imperfect competition framework provide insights into explanation of international trade behaviour by industrial organization factors such as technological innovation, scale economies, product differentiation, domestic market power, and firm-level heterogeneity within specific industries more at the micro level (Linder, 1961; Krugman, 1979, 1987; Lancaster, 1980; Melitz, 2003). These theories show under what conditions these factors would be translated into international trade behaviour. They, in turn, lay theoretical and empirical foundations to systematically identify different economic factors that govern international trade and investment behaviour, which are interrelated.

After a critical review of theoretical literature in Chapter 2, a simple theoretical framework and qualitative behaviour of firms are analysed in Chapter 3 for deriving some of the quantitative and qualitative issues. Chapters 4 and 5 present the empirical testing of the basic underlying hypotheses of Chapters 2 and 3. Some of the assumptions and institutional conditions of the framework are relaxed in the second part to examine international trade and investment behaviour in the post-reform era. The concepts, theories, and empirical exercises are extended in the second part. The empirical analysis for this period is based on large firm-level panel data for a set of manufacturing industries. Many parts of the qualitative issues in Part I are based on an extensive field survey of a sample of firms across the country. The issues are brought forth under three interrelated themes:

1. Domestic industrial structure and international trade behaviour.
2. Domestic industrial structure: scale economies, industrial structure, and international trade behaviour.
3. Industrial structure and technological activity, and associated production efficiency in terms of technical and allocative efficiency of labour and capital utilization.

The issues that have been brought forth under these three themes are utilized in stating the hypotheses in the chapters that follow.

The hypotheses are stated explicitly and tested econometrically in Chapters 4 and 5.

The empirical analysis of the first part is based on a cross-section series data. As Schmalensee (1989) pointed out, the underlying theory of cross-section industry studies was that it was a long-run equilibrium: all variables are endogenous. In the long run, strictly speaking, all variables are endogenous. All variables are determined within the system under consideration. For example, the structure of an industry determines the conduct of large and small firms in terms of entry and mobility; exit barriers and firms' conduct, in turn, could change the structure. Owing to this logic, the best we can expect from the cross-section studies is certain empirical regularities.

The engineering industries that were taken for the study was based on the Standard Industrial Trade Classification (SITC). The field study based on a detailed questionnaire covered a sample of 132 firms belonging to three subgroups of engineering industries, with major emphasis on hand, small, and cutting tools industries located in Delhi, Mumbai, Ahmedabad, Chennai, Bangalore, and Patiala. Out of the 132 firms, 24 were large and the rest were S&M firms. Out of the total number, information for eighty S&M firms was collected through mailed questionnaires. For the rest, direct interviews were conducted across the country.

In Chapter 4, the empirical association between firm size and international trade is empirically verified through estimation of a set of econometric equations. Following this, the other major determinants of firm-level exports that operate through size dimensions such as import intensity and relative factor intensity are examined. An explicit measurement of firm-level scale economies index is measured and its explanation by firm size variable and of exports is tested.

Estimation of firm-level technical and allocative efficiency based on Farrell's (1957) production frontier approach is presented in Chapter 5. The important contribution of this chapter is that relative technical efficiency of firms captures firm-level heterogeneity (Melitz, 2003) in terms of differences in technology (frontiers) and differences in managerial efficiency within specific industries, and its explanation of relative productivity and consequent international trade behaviour of firms. After deriving relative technical efficiency, allocative efficiency in terms of utilization of factors of production in accordance with their relative prices is estimated in order to throw light on firm-level ability to exploit comparative advantage.

2 Review of Literature

The review of theoretical literature of international trade demonstrates different economic factors that determine the pattern of international trade progressively depending on the process and level of development of countries comparatively. This also explains international investment behaviour as theories of international trade are the fundamental basis for international economics and business fields.

Theories of Comparative Advantage

Theories of comparative advantage of international trade available in current literature provide very rich and powerful concepts such as opportunity costs of limited resources of countries and the world economy and show possible benefits of international trade between countries, which could result in improvement in allocative efficiency of limited resources across countries (Krugman and Obstfeld, 2003). However, free international trade should be based on fair trade practices which include three main issues:

1. Fair terms of trade between countries,
2. Absence of dumping and unfair trade practices by countries, and
3. Minimization of negative externalities (environmental damage) and setting up minimum labour standards.

Ricardo's General Equilibrium Theory of Comparative Advantage

In the neo-classical general equilibrium trade theories of comparative advantage, industry and firms are the same due to the assumption of perfect competition: industries consist of a large number of producers and consumers facing similar prices. The model assumes a single factor of production, that is, labour. The theories of comparative advantage remain complete based on the assumptions of perfect competition, and there are no barriers between potentially trading nations. In brief, under the assumption of perfect competition and constant returns to scale, in the Ricardian model trade takes place owing to technological (or production function) differences across nations in the production of tradable commodities. In other words, the extent of the input labour (*L*) that goes into production of goods, say *X* and *Y*, is different in different countries.

The model is set in two goods (*X* and *Y*) and two countries (*A* and *B*). In Adam Smith's theory of absolute advantage of producing both goods in a single country, international trade does not take place if the costs of producing the two goods is lower in one country compared to the other. Ricardo's genius is that even if a country has absolute advantage in producing both the goods, free trade is still beneficial for both the countries. One single production factor, labour, is considered, and it is fixed in both the countries. Owing to differences in technology for producing the goods, the opportunity costs of producing goods is different in different countries. Opportunity cost is defined as follows: given the limited amount of factor of labour in both the countries, it is how much *X* one has to give up producing an extra unit of *Y*. In other words, it is how much of labour one sector has to give up in producing *X* to produce an extra unit of other good, *Y*.

Amount of labour required to produce one unit of *X* and *Y*

ax; ay

$ax\,X + ay Y = L$, L is total endowment of labour in A

Opportunity costs in A in terms of X and $Y = ax/ay$

Opportunity costs in B in terms of X and $Y = ax^*/ay^*$

$(ax/ay) < (ax^*/ay^*)$

$(ax/ax^*) < (ay/ay^*)$

Country A has a comparative advantage in X and country B in Y. After opening up to international trade, country A specializes in producing X by diverting all the limited labour input for producing X and country B diverts all its given level of labour input for producing Y. Country A exports X to and imports Y from country B. It is the other way round for country B. Consequently, allocative efficiency of limited labour across countries improves, which, in turn, increases the bundles of X and Y consumed in both the countries. Free international trade improves consumer welfare in terms of the bundles of X and Y available to consumers in both the countries. It is important to note the assumption that technologies for producing goods X and Y in countries A and B are different. In other words, the amount of labour that goes into producing the two goods is different in the two trading countries.

Heckscher–Ohlin Theory of Comparative Advantage

In Heckscher–Ohlin (H&O) models, production function in terms of technology of producing commodities is similar across nations, but international trade takes place owing to differences in factor endowment of labour (L) and capital (K). Countries differ in magnitude of endowment of L and K. Cost of L is cheaper in a country with larger endowment of L compared to a potentially trading foreign country. This results in differences in relative prices of L and K in the two countries. A country with larger amount of L adopts a labour-intensive production choice and it is the other way round for a country with large amount of K. For example, a country such as India with large amount of L and scarce K, exports labour-intensive goods and imports capital-intensive goods. Free international trade improves allocative efficiency of limited factor endowments of L and K between the trading countries.

In the H&O theoretical framework, the Samuelson–Stolper theorem shows that free international trade between two countries equalizes factor rewards: wages to labour and rate of return on capital.

Free trade expands the output of *X* in *A*; an additional production of *X* requires more labour than capital. Expansion of *X* attracts labour from *Y* sector. *Y* contracts, which releases more capital than labour, as it is capital-intensive. This results in decline in price of capital and increase in the price of labour in *A*. The opposite happens in country *B*.

At the empirical level, Spence (2011) demonstrates that globalization and rapid technological changes and their flows across countries is resulting in a degree of convergence of economic development between the developed and the developing worlds. A few examples for proving the theorem are: Japan since the 1950s; South Korea since the 1960s; and China and India in recent times.

Theories of comparative advantage are set in general equilibrium under the assumption of perfect competition. The focus of this study is to examine micro-level firm-level behaviour. The concept of the relative factor endowments and the technological differences are relevant even at firm-level analysis of the present kind.

Neo-technology and Intra-industry International Trade Theories

The developments in international trade theory in an imperfect market framework analyse international trade by relaxing the assumptions of identical production functions (free flow of technology) across nations, perfect competition, and constant returns to scale, and give importance to demand-side factors in the analysis and accounts for firm-level heterogeneities within industries. A critical examination of these theories can serve to formulate the analytical framework of firms' international trade behaviour.

International trade analysis in an imperfect market framework was initiated in search of explanations to the Leontief Paradox, and later also for Grubel and Lloyd's (1975) findings on intra-industry international trade of nations: exchange in similar but differentiated goods. This disproved the H&O theory's predictions that countries import and export goods that are different in labour and capital intensities.

Leontief (1953) showed by estimating capital and labour ratios for the United States of America's (USA's) exports and imports that the USA, which was capital-abundant and labour-scarce, exported labour-intensive products and imported capital-intensive products. This led to the analysis of human capital and knowledge and skilled labour intensities in production processes of countries. And this led to the question of whether technologies (production functions) of producing a product were isometric across trading nations. Keesing (1966) found that comparative advantage arose out of skilled labour-intensive products. This approach is the application of Fisher's theory of capital in terms of physical, human, and knowledge capital in international trade.

Technology Gap and Product Cycle Theories

Entry of the innovative entrepreneur onto the stage is the crucial aspect of the technology gap and product cycle models. The underlying conditions of these models are that the country where the innovation takes place has favourable capital and labour ratios in terms of physical, human (skills), and knowledge inputs. Second, the flow of technological developments and innovations among countries and firms within the country is not free and instantaneous. As a result of the second condition, the innovating entrepreneur enjoys a temporary comparative advantage resulting in domestic production and exports. Three major works based on the technology gap approach are by Kravis (1956), Posner (1961), and Hufbauer (1970).

The idea of technology gap in Kravis's product availability hypothesis is implicit. International trade takes place because of differences in the availability of certain differentiated products between countries. The differences in the availabilities arise out of technological and product innovations. There are two ways by which technological progress causes comparative advantage: one is by reducing costs and the other is by creating availability of products of new vintages. In

Posner's analysis, technology gap and firm-level factors come more into focus. The model assumes that (two) trading countries have similar factor endowments and identical production functions for the established products. The other very important feature is that the producers of either country do not have the same level of access to new technology. Under the condition, an innovative firm which creates a new product will acquire a temporary comparative advantage in the product over the other country until the imitation lag dissipates. The important firm-level factor of the analysis is the firm-level R&D expenditure, which is crucial for the firm-level comparative advantage not only in terms of initial innovation but also the resultant complementarities (complimentary products) of the innovation. The notable feature of Hufbauer's analysis was that it portended the importance of the role of a country's demand characteristics, market size, and scale economies advantage in international trade.

Vernon's (1966; 1970) elaborate analysis of international trade patterns through product cycle theory not only gave an explanation for Leontief's paradox but also recognized the role of foreign direct investment by multinational firms in international trade. In simple terms, the temporal cycle of a new product's life begins with its birth through innovation and matures through standardization. The precondition that was needed for innovation and standardization to take place in a developed country was equal access given to producers to scientific knowledge and proximity to large markets. In the initial phase, when the price elasticity of demand was low, focus was more on the product characteristics rather than on cost conditions. Once the demand for the product expands, there are increasing tendencies by competitive producers towards standardization of production. As markets develop abroad, a producer from the USA will start exporting. However, after a point, it may be more advantageous to set up production in the foreign markets, not only to make use of low labour costs but also to be closer to the market. The last phase is that the subsidiary may start exporting the product to the parent and other countries. This product cycle might last from five to twenty years for certain manufacturers where the developing countries come into the picture in the last phase. But the relevance of this formulation of the product cycle becomes less germane in the context of recent rapid technological changes taking place within very short intervals. Consequently, the product cycles are getting shorter and shorter with substantial implications on the aforementioned pattern of trade.

The pertinent firm-level factors that can be derived from these models are firm-level innovation and R&D activity and foreign direct investment, which are generally associated with large firms. The other firm-level factor that can be derived is the monopoly power a firm derives out of innovation for a temporary period. The country-specific factors that facilitate the conditions discussed earlier are the size of the domestic market and associated scale economies and the availability of scientific knowledge and skills.

Scale Economies and International Trade

The observation of Adam Smith that 'division of labour is limited by the extent of the market' became the basis of the view that economies of scale and specialization can be an independent cause of international trade. Theoretically, scale economies, especially internal to a firm, are difficult to tackle as they require specification of an imperfect market structure and result in non-convexities and multiple equilibriums under which any generalized framework is problematic.

Scale Economies External to a Firm

To avoid the problem of imperfect market structure, for a long time economies of scale were assumed to be external to a firm to retain the perfect competition assumption intact. External economies are the case where returns to scale are constant at the level of firms and socially increasing returns take the form of economies external to firms. However, these external economies can be positive or negative. In case of the positive economies, cost curves of firms and industry shift downward due to several external reasons such as increase in skills, efficiency improvements in raw material usage, and intermediate product industries. We have to take into notice that the classical trade theory under the assumption of perfect competition assumes that an industry is 100 per cent vertically integrated. This means that firms produce their own raw materials. Presence of firms within an industry specializing in production of intermediate goods and final goods through vertical disintegration results in economies of specialization and consequent external economies at the industry level. However, these economies may not be of equal magnitude for all the industries, in which case the slope of the production possibility frontiers does not give ratio of commodity prices. One simple way this problem could be resolved, as Kemp and Negishi (1970) did, was by assuming that external economies were of equal degree in both the industries in consideration.

External effects can operate from both supply and demand side. If we assume away the demand-side effects, one can introduce the external economies into the production function of a firm or an industry. With external economies, firm-level production can be:

$$Q = f(Y, e), \quad \text{where}$$
$$Q = \text{the output,}$$
$$Y = \text{the inputs,} \quad \text{and}$$
$$e = a,$$

which is the vector of all possible external influences (Helpman and Krungman, 1985) and in case of internationally tradable intermediates (Ethier, 1979).

Elements of 'e' could be industry- and country-specific and could have an international element. Where the external economies are at the industry level, firms' production function is assumed to have constant returns to scale $f(aim) = af(Y, Q)$, where Q is the industry's output subject to increasing returns to scale. The industry's output enters individual firm's production function.

External economies at the industry level may stem from a large industry supporting production of large quantities and variety of intermediate products at lower costs (Helpman and Krugman, 1985). The external economies (or diseconomies) may also arise at the country level in terms of country size, a country's industrial base, and also due to increase in the availability of skills and technology endowments, where Mead's type of externalities, depending on the industrial base, may arise due to interdependence of industries.

Although in the case of external economies at industry level we can retain the competitive market structure assumption and comparative advantage across industries, the concern of the study is whether these external economies have any implications on firm-specific advantages within an industry and in exports. One way to look at it is that a firm can internalize the external economies which would obviously imply market structure to be imperfect. There can be unequal access between firms to certain inputs, certain type of country-specific skilled labour, capital goods, and technology. The unequal access can be a result of factor and product market segmentation of economic duality. Furthermore, firms may follow vertical integration and merger policies to internalize external economies and to achieve monopoly power: the economies in the raw material and intermediate products and in the creation of knowledge capital. Even the country size and the extent of industrial base and product market segmentation may facilitate certain strategic groups of firms to have higher ability to internalize the external economies.

Demand Factors and Scale Economies

So far, the analysis of the previously mentioned theories is mostly concentrated on supply-side factors, although some demand-side considerations are implicit in Kravis's availability hypothesis and Vernon's product cycle theory. Demand factors in terms of nature of domestic and foreign demand, product differentiation, and size of the market have important implications on both static and dynamic learning-by-doing economies of scale which, in turn, have implications on firm-level exports. It is useful to derive pertinent insights from the models which consider these demand factors. In this context, Linder's (1961) contributions bring forth cogent arguments.

According to Linder (1961), exports are an offshoot of manufacturing activities made for the domestic market dictated by the majority tastes. Domestic demand for vertically differentiated products is determined by the per capita income levels and income distributions. A country with high per capita income would tend to produce and export high-quality products. This has been a major advantage of the USA with a large number of middle-class consumers at the time of its industrialization unlike the Western European countries which were segmented from each other until the formation of the European Union. The pattern of international trade in vertically differentiated products requiring nearly identical inputs subject to increasing returns to scale is influenced by the relationship between a country's income distribution and elasticity of demand for quality with respect to income levels. Demand from low-income groups is price-elastic. Therefore, their demand is mostly for low-quality products. On the other hand, demand from high-income groups relates to income elasticity as they demand mostly high-quality differentiated goods. Linder's analysis portended the intra-industry explanation of international trade by saying that more similar the demand structures and income levels of two countries the more intensive international trade could be between these countries.

Like the product cycle theories to some extent, Linder argued that an innovation or creation of a new product was made according to discernible domestic demand needs. Later, the product would be exported to countries with similar demand structure only after saturating domestic demand. The producer acquires an advantageous position (production function) by being in proximity to a large domestic market and certain firm-specific advantages such as technological superiority and managerial skills. Apart from this, the crucial point is that the producer having access to a large internal market will be able to reap economies of scale without having to incur high distribution costs.

In a theoretical model set in Cournot oligopoly market structure, Krugman (1984) showed that access to an economy protected from imports provides an advantage in exports to a domestic firm over a rival in a foreign market. The interesting aspect of the article was that scale economies take the form of static economies, that is, declining marginal costs and dynamic scale economies of 'learning by doing'. Protection of (large) domestic market gives a domestic firm an advantage in scale over foreign rivals, which translates into lower marginal costs and higher market share in unprotected markets. The important condition for the result is the firm-level declining marginal costs. The argument is that protection of the domestic market increases the sales of the domestic firm and reduces the sales of the foreign firm in the home market. Increase in home sales results in lower marginal costs to the domestic firm for a given level of foreign marginal costs. Consequently, this leads to static scale economies advantage of exports for the domestic firm.

Dynamic scale economies can arise out of declining marginal costs of R&D investment. Protection of the home market by increasing the home firm's sales and reducing those of its foreign competitor increases the incentive for domestic R&D at the expense of the foreign firm, which translates into a shift in relative production costs and consequent export advantage to the domestic firm. The form of dynamic scale economies is the learning-by-doing type in which the marginal costs are a decreasing function of cumulative output over time. Protection increases the cumulative output of the domestic firm and reduces the cumulative output of the foreign rival. As a result, it reduces the future marginal costs of the domestic firm and increases its competitive advantage in exports. These dynamic economies of learning by doing can be either internal or external to a firm, but they are internal to an industry or may accrue as a result of the accumulation of manufacturing experience (Stewart, 1984). This type of economy may create cumulative tendencies between countries and firms so that countries or firms that acquire an initial advantage in any area where these learning-by-doing economies are prominent enjoy an increasing advantage over time.

In retrospect, in the above-mentioned theories where demand-side factors play a predominant role, competitive advantage in exports to industries or firms arises across countries due to domestic market size differences, product preference similarities or dissimilarities, and per capita income differences between countries. What is relevant for us is whether these have any implications on these factors not only across countries but also across firms within an industry in the home country. One obvious derivation is that larger firms will be able to attain higher advantage of the large domestic market compared to smaller firms as they can have greater share of the domestic market. Second, if income distribution is highly skewed, it can result in product market segmentation, which can result in distribution of firms on a vertical product differentiation plane (quality differentiation). Consequently, different firms or a strategically sized group of firms in an industry may concentrate on different quality segments that, in turn, can have implications for their respective export behaviour depending on the nature of demand similarities or the extent of representative demand between the trading nations. To illustrate this point, small firms in the Indian industries producing low-quality goods would be able to export these goods to other developing countries based on income similarities or the extent of representative demand.

Intra-industry Trade and Economies of Scale and Specialization

Economies of scale cause international exchange of differentiated goods, and this results in economies of specialization. The two propositions are the basis of intra-industry trade models of imperfect competition. Grubel's (1967) and Grubel and Lloyd's (1975) empirical observations on pattern of intra-industry trade showed that H&O theoretical predictions did not hold as a major part of the world trade was between developed countries of similar factor endowments of labour and capital and in similar but differentiated commodities. Quite obviously, they and the following theories looked for answers in relaxing the H&O assumptions of constant returns to scale and perfect competition (product differentiation).

From these three streams of theoretical developments emerged the following:

1. General equilibrium theories of intra-industry international trade based on Dixit and Stiglitz's (1977) theory of general equilibrium with monopolistic market structure.
2. Partial equilibrium theories based on Cournot strategic rivalry that were called strategic trade policy models to justify government intervention to provide competitive advantage to large domestic large firms in international business. Protection of a large domestic market from imports results in large firms deriving scale economy advantage in exports.

3. 'New' New Trade Theory (Melitz, 2003) which accounts for firm-level heterogeneity in terms of productivity differences and its relation to exports within specific industries.

As mentioned earlier, there can be no generalized theories and outcomes in case of the trade models set in imperfect market conditions of partial equilibrium of strategic rivalry between oligopoly players. This is because predictions of the models depend on the kind of assumptions and market imperfections imposed on the system.

Intra-industry trade between countries of similar factor endowments and technologies can be explained by the presence of firm-level internal scale economies in the production of mostly differentiated products. Gruble and Lloyd's (1975) rigorous empirical studies gave an explanation of the firm-level internal economies of scale and specialization which can be determined by the domestic demand factors, size of the market, and extent of horizontal and vertical product differentiations. Scale economies may arise out of the sources as:

1. size of plants;
2. length of production runs; and
3. size of firms (a firm can have multiple plants).

Scale economies based on size of plants may arise due to presence of indivisibilities (non-separability of tasks in production or teamwork) in capital and skilled labour owing to certain engineering features. The longer production runs may result in lower costs because they require less frequent halts in production to set or adjust machinery and less downtime to move different models or products on production lines. A larger firm may be able to reap the previously mentioned economies if it is specialized and does not produce wider range of goods or models. The firm-level internal economies of scale result in monopoly or oligopoly market structure simply because the number of firms that can produce with profits in an industry with scale economies is limited even if there are no formal barriers to entry. This is termed as natural monopoly where fixed and sunk costs of production are very high and minimum efficient scale can be reached only at a large scale of production.

General Equilibrium Theories of Intra-industry International Trade

Theoretical analysis of internal economies of trade requires specification of market structure based on logistics, such as the number of firms in an industry and market size and elasticity of substitution between the differentiated products. Market size may determine the number of firms that can coexist in a market under scale economies and the consequent market power of individual firms. The extent of elasticity of substitution between goods of an industry determines the interdependency between firms in an industry.

Krugman (1979) utilized Dixit and Stiglitz's (1977) general equilibrium theory of monopolistic competition for explaining international trade between similar countries: similar income levels and relative endowments of factors of production. International trade takes place between similar countries because of horizontally differentiated goods and economies of scale in production. Consumer utility is a function of the number of differentiated goods and price. International trade between identical countries increases number of differentiated goods available to consumers and brings decline in prices owing to extension of the market with limited scale economies at firm-level under monopolistic competition market structure.

Krugman (1979) in a simple model of monopolistic competition market structure showed that internal scale economies can be an independent source of international trade. The article assumed one scarce factor of production—that is, labour—and a number of horizontally differentiated products: each firm producing one of the specifications. The horizontal product differentiation refers to differences in characteristics or features of the products of uniform quality in an industry. The important implication of the later assumption was that the firm-level internal economies are not too high so that a large number of firms can coexist in the industry. Firms can differentiate the products without additional costs. The utility function of the consumers is assumed to be symmetric. All goods are assumed to produce with the same cost functions, with labour used in production being a linear function of output.

$$Li = a + bXi$$

$$a, b > 0$$

where Li is labour used in producing good X and Xi is the output of good 'i'.

The presence of 'a', a fixed-cost component, would imply internal economies in terms of decreasing average costs. Free entry and exit of firms result in normal profit equilibrium (long-run average cost equals long-run average revenue). All goods will be produced in similar quantity and at a similar price. After deriving the pre-international trade equilibrium, the effect of opening up to international trade was taken to be equivalent to increasing market size, which implies that international trade leads to economies of specialization on the basis of the argument that 'division of labour is limited by the extent of the market'.

In the same theoretical framework, in a different article, Krugman (1980) brought forth additional factors such as role of large domestic markets in international trade between countries of similar factor endowments, technology, and incomes. Each differentiated product is produced in only one country for the same reason that each good is produced by only one firm. In this model, international trade occurs because there can be gains from it, as the world economy will produce a greater diversity of goods than a country alone can, offering individuals a wider range of choice. This implies improvement in consumer welfare as consumer utility was taken as a function of a number of differentiated goods available. However, in this model, unlike in the previous one, there is no effect of international trade on the scale of production, and the gains from international trade occur solely through increased product diversity. There is no effect of international trade on scale, as the model assumes, of constant elasticity of demand. Increase in scale can take place if the demand facing individual firms becomes more elastic as the number of firms increase.

In a situation of 'mirror image countries', Krugman shows, similar to Linder's argument, that if the two countries have sufficiently dissimilar tastes, a country will specialize in the industry for which it has the larger home market and each will be a net exporter of the class of goods in which it specializes under the presence of increasing returns.

The same cost functions for all firms are symmetric utility functions. Zero profits, negligible strategic interdependence between firms, costless product differentiation, and internal economies of low and equal magnitude: all these simplifying features of the aforementioned models indicate presence of no explicit firm-specific differential advantages in exports.

In Lancaster's (1971; 1980) model, which emphasized preference diversity as a source of international trade, there could be firm-specific advantages because of horizontally differentiated products entering utility functions asymmetrically (Neo-Hotelling approach) and there are costs of adjustment to firms in differentiating the products.

In the Neo-Hotelling approach, consumers are taken to have extreme preferences for product differentiation: for example, some consumers prefer to listen to classical music and others prefer rock music. When firms compete to attract others' consumers into their basket, all products become similar in equilibrium. Consumers with extreme preferences are worse off in equilibrium. However, as observed in a field study in Bangalore, small firms cooperate to avoid the Hotelling competition equilibrium. Firms could come to an agreement to spread out from the equilibrium point in an equal distance from each other. But in strictly theoretical terms, two firms at the extreme points of the straight line are worse off as they do not have consumers on the right and left side of the distribution of firms.

Lancaster, borrowing from his consumer theory, put major emphasis on product differentiation and preference diversity in a perfect monopolistic competition framework. In this framework, the number and design of goods are themselves equilibrium variables and are not specified as initial data points. Each consumer has a most preferred differentiated good: one consumer likes a red silk tie and another likes a blue silk tie. Lancaster calls it perfect monopolistic competition as it represents the Nash equilibrium of perfectly informed firms facing perfectly informed consumers under conditions of perfect flexibility in choice of specification, with entry of new firms and absence of collusion between incumbent firms. This characterization is closely representative of the market conditions in the advanced countries with consumers with high income levels. In the analysis, the countries are taken to be identical and, in each country, there are two sectors: agriculture and manufacturing. The latter sector produces differentiated goods. Although there is a mention of inter-industry trade, the model concentrates on intra-industry international trade in manufactured goods.

The major feature is the underlying structure with the specification of product differentiation. Pertinent to the objective of the study, Lancaster's analysis has important implications on firm-level factors. Firms are faced with more than one decision variable: price and differentiation of product. The notion of adjustment costs is important before and after international trade. Before international trade opens, different firms may have different levels of potential advantages towards exports depending on their respective product specification and the elasticity of substitution they face. Once international trade opens, some varieties which were previously produced at home may now be produced abroad.

Furthermore, as briefly mentioned in Lancaster's analysis, there can be interaction between H&O comparative advantage of inter-industry specialization and scale economy advantage of intra-industry trade. This is generally approached by specifying two sectors: one sector characterized by perfect competition, constant returns to scale, and a homogenous good (say, agriculture), and the second sector characterized by imperfect market structure of increasing returns to scale and differentiated products (say, manufacturing). The pattern of trade depends on which advantage is dominant.

Dixit and Norman (1984) analyse the intra- and inter-industry possibilities of international trade by characterizing the differentiated industries by Chamberlin's monopolistic competition and numeraire, that is, homogeneous goods industry by perfect competition. The demand side is simplified by assuming homothetic and identical preferences for all consumers with symmetric utility function for the differentiated goods in both countries. The production functions are the same for all firms in the differentiated goods sector for both countries across the two sectors. But there are differences in factor endowments of labour and capital between countries resulting in factor (input) price differentials.

Like Dixit and Norman's model, Helpman and Krugman (1985) derived an international trade structure in a two-sector and two-factor model of interaction between inter- and intra-industry trade. The food sector (*Y*) is characterized by perfect competition and the manufacturing (*X*) by Chamberlin's monopolistic competition with internal economies scale at a small magnitude. Although the conclusions that are derived in Helpman and Krugman's model were like Dixit and Norman's model, the former introduced more rigorous logistics that turn monopolistic competition market structure into oligopoly behaviour in the manufacturing sector.

In Helpman and Krugman's model, a measure of firm-level economies of scale is specified to be:

$$\begin{aligned} O(W,X) &= [C(W,X)/X]/[Cx(W,X)] \\ &= AC/MC \end{aligned}$$

where '*W*' is the product variety, '*C*' costs, and '*X*' output. Analogously to the degree of scale economies, a measure of monopoly power *R*(.) is taken to be the ratio of average to marginal revenue:

$$\begin{aligned} R(.) &= [p/MR(.)]. \\ &= \left[1-\left(\frac{1}{a(.)}\right)\right]^2 -1 \end{aligned}$$

where '*p*' is the price and '*a*(.)' is the elasticity of demand. *R*(.) depends on how one introduces '*a*' into the equation which can be a Lancastrian type of preference where it is greater than 'one'. Under profit maximization condition:

$$MR = C(W, X),\ R(.)/0(W, X)$$

The ratio of degree of monopoly power to the degree of economies of scale equal one plus the mark-up rate on average costs. In the model, in equilibrium the profits are driven to zero due to free entry and exit. As a result, $R(.) = 0(w, x)$.

In the Helpman and Krugman model, conditions isomorphic to the equilibrium conditions in production for a two-sector constant returns to scale economy are derived by treating 'x' as a parameter. The underlying logic is that if 'x' is held constant, output expansion of manufactured differentiated products can be made by increasing the number of firms. With all the firms looking alike with same cost function and level of output, this will generate constant returns at the industry level.

In this analysis of interaction of intra- and inter-industry international trade, firm-level advantages or firm size are neither significant nor explicit. Taking this framework, firm size aspects can be brought in by separating an industry into two strategic groups of firms by vertical disintegration of production process of a product and (or) also by vertical product differentiation, in which the cost or the production function and demand function of the two distinct groups of firms are different. By vertically disintegrating the industry, we can bring in the vertical intra-industry specialization, in which a group of, say, large firms may specialize in the production of final differentiated products under increasing returns and the other group, say, small firms, specialize in a homogenous intermediate product under constant returns. The production of final goods can be capital intensive, and the production of intermediates could be labour-intensive. The inter-industry or vertical intra-industry specialization advantages would be determined by the relative factor endowments of countries in consideration. Second, in case of vertical product differentiation, the two distinct quality products produced by the separate groups of firms may require two different production functions. To illustrate this, higher-quality products may require high R&D expenditure and skilled labour which, in turn, may determine the ability of the separate group of firms to reap the country's comparative advantage in endowment of factors of production. The possibilities of this type of international trade structure and its implications on the issue of firm size and exports in India's case will be discussed in detail in Chapter 3.

In the case of homogenous goods, intra-industry trade can take place due to transport, storage, and selling costs differentials across countries (Gruble and Lloyd, 1975). Similar reasons for international trade can also apply to differentiated final and capital goods. Vertical intra-industry international trade or specialization across nations may involve exchange between countries of certain final products of an industry for the intermediate products used in the industry of different quality on vertical lines. Ethier (1979) showed that intra-industry trade in intermediate goods takes place to exploit economies of specialization for the production of intermediate goods that go into production of the final goods.

Ethier (1979) shows that intra-industry trade is more in intermediate goods than in final goods determined by scale economies and product differentiation factors. He argues that product differentiation in intermediates is more important as tastes for variety implicit in the demand for more specialized machine tools, motors, and control machines may be a higher source of international trade and gains from international trade than the design for variety by the ultimate consumers. As a matter of fact, a major part of the world's trade is in intermediate goods (components) on a global supply chain. A study by the Organisation for Economic Co-operation and Development (OECD) demonstrated that 'intermediate inputs represent 56% of goods trade and 73% service trade' (Miroudot, Lanz, and Ragoussis, 2009). Examples are electronics, semi-conductors, automobiles, garments, and so on, in which different components of a final product are produced in different locations of the globe depending on localized specialization advantages. Global supply chains trade in goods and know-how of improving production processes and assemblies. In the case of India, there was extensive subcontracting activity on a value chain between large final-product producers and component-producing S&M firms. During the pre-reforms era, relative bargaining power rested with large firms; after the reforms improved competitive conditions in the final goods production through entry of multinational firms, the component producers acquired international competitiveness and higher bargaining power in the home market (Sutton, 2004; Patibandla, 2006b).

Market Power: Scale Economies and International Trade

If we go into the models based on monopoly or oligopoly market structures, another important dimension germane to firm-level analysis that could be derived is the firm-level monopoly or market power, which has important implications on firm-level exports. In the earlier discussed models of monopolistic competition, firm-level market power is non-existent because of free entry and exit of firms into an industry. In case of monopolies and oligopolies, apart from the existence of internal economies, the pricing behaviour, market power, and strategic choices of rivalry of firms will have important implications on international trade behaviour. This is crucial especially when firms take the domestic and international markets as segmented and get involved in third-degree price discriminatory behaviour of charging different prices for a product in different countries, depending on price and income elasticity of demand. As a matter of observation, world trade is said to be mostly characterized by price-discriminating oligopolies.

Strategic International Trade Theories and Trade Wars

Trade wars between countries and international oligopolies is a common practice and is pertinent to contemporary issues. Some of the intra-industry trade models show that strategic rivalry of firms itself can be a basis of international trade. Brander and Krugman (1983) analyse price discriminatory oligopoly behaviour leading to reciprocal dumping by countries. The model is based on segmented market approach with applied game theoretic behaviour: each firm perceives each country as a separate market and makes distinct quantity decisions for each country. A price discriminating oligopolistic firm facing a higher elasticity of demand in a foreign market than at home will charge lower price abroad than at home. Japanese oligopoly diversified groups adopted these practices between the 1950s and 1980s. This implies dumping of goods into foreign markets at lower price than long-run average costs in the foreign markets but at higher price in the home market. At present, China is accused of adopting these practices. In essence, the model shows that international trade between two identical countries in similar products may take place because of oligopolistic strategic interaction between large international oligopoly and duopoly firms (one domestic and one foreign) in the absence of any of the usual motivations for international trade:

neither cost differences nor scale economies are necessary. The reciprocal dumping takes place in a simple Cournot duopoly in which the transport cost element of exports plays a crucial role. To illustrate this, Brander and Krugman (1983) specify the cost maximization equation of domestic and foreign firms as follows:

$$\pi = Xp(Z) + X^{*} p^{*}(Z)^{*} - C\left(X + \frac{X^{*}}{g}\right) - F \tag{1}$$

$$\pi^{*} = Yp(Z) + Y^{*} P^{*}(Z)^{*} - C\left(\frac{Y}{g} + Y^{x}\right) - F^{*} \tag{2}$$

'*Z*' is the commodity produced by the two firms. *X* and *Y* are the outputs produced by domestic and foreign firms for their respective domestic consumption. X^* and Y^* are the output produced by the two firms for their foreign consumption. Domestic and foreign country prices are denoted by p and p^* (asterisk represents price for foreign country here). Marginal cost is a constant '*C*' and marginal cost of export is C/g where '*g*' is transport cost.

'*F*' indicates fixed costs. One important point to be noticed in the model is that the profit maximizing choice of *X* and *Y* are independent of X^* and Y^*. There can be a possibility where X^* is independent of *X* in a domestic oligopoly situation. This possibility in the context of the Indian industrial structure will be discussed in Chapter 3.

In the model, the effective marginal cost of delivering exported units is higher than for a unit of domestic sales which is consistent with higher marginal revenue under the maximization of π and π^*. Perceived marginal revenue is equal to marginal costs in both markets. This can lead to a two-way international trade. It is profitable to both firms to do reciprocal dumping as each firm does have a mark-up over cost in its export markets although it is smaller than at home: The free on board (FOB) price for exports is below the domestic price.

Insights from 'New' New Trade Theory

One of the criticisms of Krugman's intra-industry trade theory is that under monopolistic competition all firms are similar except for horizontal product differences. The 'New' New Trade Theory pioneered by Melitz (2003) and his followers accounts for empirically firm-level heterogeneity in technology and productivity within given industries. Melitz's model with US firm-level data for industries showed that within specific industries only a few highly productive firms undertook exports because of high fixed costs involved in the production and marketing for export. The extension of this argument (Helpman, Melitz, and Yeaple, 2004) is that exporting firms' production in the overseas production involves high fixed costs. In other words, only large firms (with high fixed costs) can export. However, as mentioned before, S&M firms play an important role in exports through global supply chains.

This study examines Melitz's hypothesis with firm-level data, especially in Chapter 5. Firm-level heterogeneity in technology and managerial efficiency and associated firm-level productivity (relative technical efficiency) are estimated. Following from this, the association between firm-level productivity and exports is established.

3 Analytical Framework and Qualitative Observations

Theoretical Model

In this chapter, we have developed a simple theoretical model which is used as the basic framework to bring out analytical issues. The model serves the basic purpose at hand, and extension of the model is presented in the second part of the book. To recapitulate, firm size asymmetry refers to imperfect market structure, which in this study is taken to be an oligopoly case with strategic interdependence between firms in the protected home market. The 'structure–conduct–performance' (SCP) approach generally takes industrial structure in terms of number of firms, and degree of concentration of market shares is taken to be exogenously given and observes the conduct and performance of large and small firms (Porter, 1979). Followed by this, there is a widely accepted approach in industrial organization literature that a market structure in terms of firm size asymmetry is an endogenous outcome (Demsetz, 1973). According to this approach, certain firms in an industry grow larger in size because they are more efficient than others. If we assume there are no factor market imperfections, the efficiency differences across firms could be due to random factors, technological innovation, and organizational and marketing efficiency. This study argues that when firms face the protected home market and perfectly competitive export markets, certain aspects of firm-level asymmetric advantages could be specific to the home market, especially when the capital markets are imperfect. We combine the SCP approach and the endogenous approach of firm size asymmetry in bringing out the following theoretical model.

The model is based on two crucial assumptions:

1. India's economy was taken to be a small one in the world market for manufactured goods so that all domestic firms were price takers in the world market.
2. Domestic and world markets are segmented through partial protection of the domestic industry from imports. The model is a typical third-degree price discrimination in which a firm charges higher price in the market with low price elasticity of demand and charges a lower price in a market with higher price elasticity of demand.

These assumptions imply that large firms derived long-run monopoly power in the domestic market but were small players in the world market facing competitive prices (price takers).

Firms were taken to compete strategically à la the Cournot oligopoly model where quantity of output is the decision variable for firms in the domestic market. There were no global internal economies of scale. The domestic demand curve was taken to be downward sloping.

Profit function of firms facing the home and world market is:

$$\pi_i = P(Xi + xi)xi + P^* xi^* - \left(\frac{1}{2}\right)C_i\left(X_i + X_i^*\right)^2 \qquad (1)$$

Where $i = 1, 2, \ldots N$

$$X\_i = \sum_{j+i} x_i$$

x_i are home market sales, x_i^* is export and $\left(\frac{1}{2}\right)C_i\left(X_i + X_i^*\right)$ is the cost function of firm 'i'. P^* is world price and P is home market price.

The first order conditions of profit maximization are as follows:

$$\frac{\partial \pi_i}{\partial X_i^*} = P^* - C_i\left(X_i + X_i^*\right) = 0 \tag{2}$$

$$\frac{\partial \pi_i}{\partial X_i^*} = P(.) + P^*(.)X_i - C_i\left(X_i + X_i^*\right) = 0 \tag{3}$$

Firms maximize profits when,

$$P(.) + P^*(.)X_i = P^* = C_i\left(X_i + X_i^*\right) \tag{4}$$

⇒ Firms maximize profits when marginal revenue of home sales, the world price (the marginal revenue of exports), and marginal costs are equal.

From (2),

$$X_i^* = \left(\frac{P^*}{C_i}\right) - X_i \tag{5}$$

From (4),

$$X_i = \left[\frac{\left(P^* - P(.)\right)}{P^*(.)}\right] \tag{6}$$

$P^*(.) < 0$, $P(.) > P^*$, from this condition X_i is positive.

Firm size in total sales is

$$X_i + X_i^* = {}^{P^*}\!/_{C_i} \tag{7}$$

Firm-level exports in equilibrium are

$$X_i^* = \left(\frac{P^*}{C_i}\right) - P^* = C_i\left(X_i + X_i^*\right) \tag{8}$$

Firm-level export orientation is

$$\left[\frac{X_i^*}{X_i + X_i^*}\right] = 1 - [(P^* - P(.))/P(.)]\left(P^*/C_i\right)^{-1} \qquad (9)$$

From (8) and (9), when there is symmetry in costs, firms are equal in size; and if they export, they export at equal intensity. When *Ci<Cj*, the lower-cost firm will be the larger firm in total sales, and it exports at higher intensity than small firms. Because of the option of exporting, the cost asymmetry does not disturb the equal home market shares between firms unlike in straightforward Cournot oligopoly firms facing a single market where the lower-cost firm will always have higher market share. In this case, exports function as a means of protecting higher home market price. If a large firm in the home market increases total home market sales, it consequently reduces home market price.

In the above-mentioned result, larger firms export at higher intensity. However, the story could be contrary to this result in the case of countries such as India that pursued highly inward-oriented policies. This could be because profits associated with protected home market shares could be proportionately higher than free markets of exports. In such a case, firms would implement strategies aimed mainly at capturing higher home market shares.

In many industries, firms derived relative or asymmetric advantage in sales specific to protected home market especially when capital markets were distorted. This could arise because certain firms were first movers in an industry or because corporate business groups in India already had established brand names and reputation in the home market. This, in turn, helped them to sell in the home market and raise capital with relative ease at lower prices than its opportunity cost. The asymmetric advantages for home market could be numerous. We abstracted them to one example based on stylized facts derived from the field survey.

We take two firms, firms '*i*' and '*j*'. Firm '*i*' is a corporate entity producing automobiles with a nationally known brand name and reputation. Firm '*j*' is an absolute newcomer or a small firm. Since firm '*i*' has an established reputation in the home market, it could sell off its output and raise working capital with relative ease. For firm '*j*' it takes a longer time in selling the output in the home market and, as a result, its interest payment on working capital for home market sales was higher. But in the world market both the firms were equal. Assuming the cost of production was similar for both firms, both would have equal advantage in the world market. Firm '*i*', which had relative advantage in the home market sales, could grow larger in size and would be less export-oriented than the smaller firm '*j*'. In such a case, there would be separate cost functions for home and world market sales. This argument is proved by specifying the profit function in the following way:

$$\pi_i = P(X\_i + xi)xi + P * x(-(1/2)a;xi - (1/2)cix * 2 - \qquad (10)$$

where $I = 1.2....N$

$$xi; \ = Sum\, x;$$

By solving the first order conditions of profit maximization for (10), we obtain:

$$X = (P^* / c) \qquad (11)$$

$$X;=[;P(.)/(a;-P`(.))] \qquad (12)$$

Size of firm 'i' in total sales is:

$$X;+x;=\left[.P\frac{(.)}{a;-P'(.)}\right]+P^*/c; \qquad (13)$$

From (13) it can be observed by assuming '*ci; = cj;*':

If '*a*j < *ai;*', firm '*i*' will have higher home market shares and larger size in total sales. Smaller firm '*j*', which had home market–specific relative disadvantage in sales, would have higher export intensity. There could be differences in '*ci*' and '*cj*', but as long as the differences in '*ai;*' and '*aj;*' were more dominant, larger firms would be less export-oriented.

In order to capture a major share of the protected home market where rate of return was higher than export sales, large firms pursued market share–enhancing strategies aimed mainly at capturing a major part of the home market. The firms that could succeed in this respect were the ones that had higher access to capital and had an established reputation in the home market. As mentioned in Chapter 1, large family-owned business houses which operated in the organized capital markets had access to capital at a lower rate than small firms or unknown new entrants.

Once the industrial structure was established, capital market imperfections would be a source of long-run market power to the large firms. They could effectively block entry and impose mobility barriers on small firms and potential new entrants. The product and factor market structure conditions, in turn, determine the conduct of large and small firms. The conduct in terms of technological rivalry in the home market, and choice of production techniques of factors of production, in turn, had important implications on international trade behaviour of large and small firms.

There were two main reasons why large firms with long-run monopoly power turned out to be inefficient, as Hicks observed: first, low degree of competition is the source of a laid-back life; and second, X-inefficiency of large-scale operations. Leibenstein (1980) argued that large firms were prone to internal organizational inefficiency owing to internal coordination issues arising out of large size. Long-run market power in product markets for large firms allowed them to deviate from comparative advantage. Duality of factor markets which provided capital at cheaper cost than its opportunity cost to large firms made it deviate from utilizing India's comparative advantage in labour intensity. For example, factor market imperfections and segmentation determine the relative factor intensity in production of large and small firms. This, in turn, determines their ability to realize the domestic comparative advantage in relative factor endowment of labour and capital market conditions.

On the other hand, as observed in the field study in Bangalore, a few large firms in certain industries deliberately maintained organizational slack in terms of hiring excess employees than necessary on average. This was because of unpredictable demand for a service: there could be large demand and also decline in demand for the service unexpectedly.

Furthermore, by taking this model as the basic framework, we could apply Porter's (1979) approach of strategically sized groups in bringing forth a few other relevant issues. Small firms that had a relative disadvantage in the home market sales faced large group competition with each other and had to compete with large firms. Small firms that could branch out into exports could be the ones that reached minimum efficient scales and were relatively efficient within the small firms' size group. On the other hand, large firms competed mostly with each other. Within this size group, the firms that could capture higher share of the home market could be the ones who were the home market leader firms and were more aggressive in home market sales.

Figures 3.1 and 3.2 show the firm size distribution (structure) of samples of firms for a few engineering industries. From these graphs,

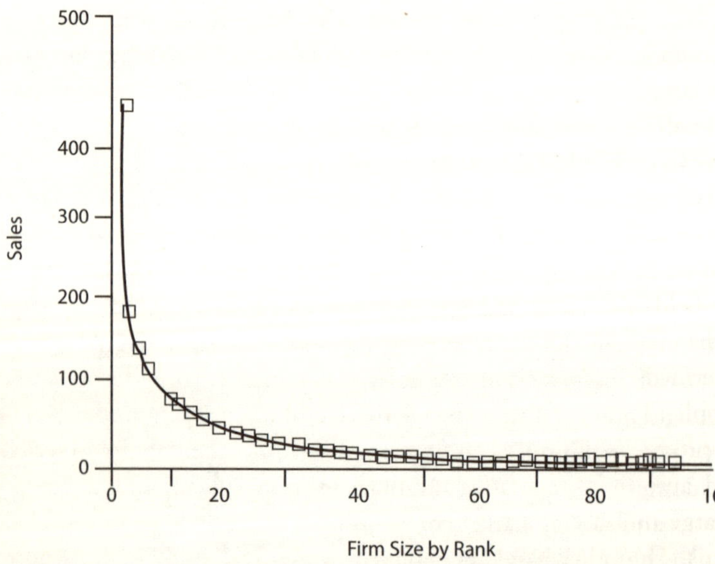

Figure 3.1 Long-tailed Market Structure: Aggregate Engineering Industry Firm Size by Rank (1985/86)
Source: Confederation of Indian Industries.

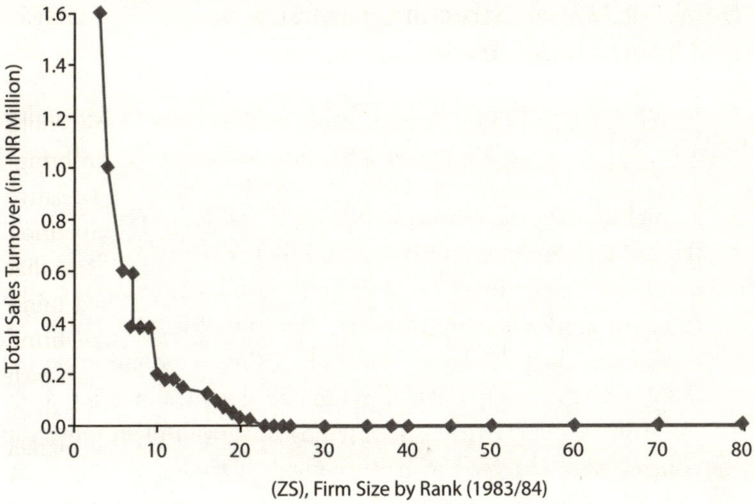

Figure 3.2 Long-tailed Market Structure: Hand, Small, and Cutting Tools Industry
Source: Author's representation.

it could be observed that the size distribution was highly skewed: a few large firms took a major share of the market while a large number of small firms shared the residual. This type of structure was referred to as the long-tailed market structure (Desai, 1982).

In bringing forth the issues for the Indian industry in the following sections, (in certain cases) we deviated from the basic framework so that we did not have to sacrifice certain interesting ideas derived from the field survey. For example, one interesting phenomenon in many Indian industries was subcontracting between large and small firms in intermediate components with incomplete contracts between small supplier firms and large buyer firms on a vertical disintegration chain of production process of a product. In industries such as bicycles and automobiles, a few large firms produced final products while a large number of small firms produced components for the large firms. This had important implications on the export behaviour of small firms which we discuss later. The home market–specific relative disadvantage in sales to small firms was the monopsony squeeze by the large final-product firms.

Domestic Market Structure, Firm Size, and International Trade

In the following section, it is discussed how large firms in the Indian industry derived long-run market power.

1. As mentioned earlier, because of capital market imperfections in the Indian economy, large firms had higher access to capital at a lower price than small firms or (unknown) newcomers, owing to factor market duality in India. The capital market imperfections would help the large firms in blocking entry and imposing mobility barriers on small firms in the domestic market. Even the artificial entry barriers imposed by the government industrial policies were observed to have worked in favour of large firms or family-diversified business houses, owing to large resources at their disposal and political connections with powerful politicians and bureaucrats. In the words of Bardhan (1984: 41), 'The richer industrialists, having better "connections" and better access, got away with the lion's share in the bureaucratic allocations of the licences, thus pre-empting capacity creation and sheltering oligopolistic profits.' The industrial licences would not only be foreclosed by the large firms but the cumbersome procedures of the policies were also observed to have had worked in favour of existing large houses (Hazari, 1986).
2. Even the international trade policies, such as protection based on infant industry arguments, were argued to have benefited large corporations. It was well known that import substitution strategies usually resulted in wide variations in Effective Rate of Protection (ERP) across industries. Tariffs on capital and intermediate goods tended to be lower than those on final production. For example, in case of the Indian automobile industry, the ERP shown by an ICICI study (1985) for 1980/81 showed positive ERP of 8.3 on domestic sales and 29.2 on exports for commercial vehicles and negative ERP of –15.6 on domestic sales and –22 on exports for the auto ancillaries. The production of final engineering products, especially in the heavy engineering industry, was dominated by large oligopolistic firms while the intermediate production was

done mostly by S&M firms. Bruch and Hiemen (1983) showed that the structure of ERP in ASEAN (Association of Southeast Asian Nations) countries benefited large firms more than S&M firms. The industries characterized by higher ERP tended to draw large amounts of the country's resources as the rate of profits and return were generally higher in these industries.

3. A significant amount of domestic market power to large firms arose not only from the final-product markets but also from the input and intermediate product markets: monopsony power. Most of the firms in the engineering industry faced both final and derived demand (the effect of demand for the final goods based on demand for input and intermediate goods) as most of the engineering products were assemblages of several diverse components and intermediate products. This increased the inter-linkages and dependence between firms in the engineering industries. Large firms at the top, both in heavy and light engineering industries, exerted high amount of monopsony market power through their accessibility to scarce inputs and intermediate products achieved through vertical integration, captive supplies, and control of supplier firms. For example, as derived from the field study, in the cutting tools industry, three large firms controlled the supply of carbide, a crucial raw material. The rest of the firms in the industry depended on these three large firms for the supply of the raw material as its import was not allowed.

Table 3.1 shows the degree of vertical integration for a set of firms in the industry. The vertical integration index is generally calculated by dividing value added by total sales of a firm. The index varies between 0 and 1. If it is equal to 1, the degree of vertical integration is 100 per cent (Hay and Morris, 1979).

The problem involved in this measure was that in several cases the annual sales of firms included inventories built up from the previous years' production. In order to reduce the bias, the annual production figures are used in the denominator. In the sample of the top 100 engineering firms at aggregate level, the index was one half (0.5) and was the same across all the firms. Several large firms are multi-product firms and it gives a bias in the estimations. On the other hand small firms are more focused.

Table 3.1 Degree of Vertical Integration, Engineering Firms, 1983/84

Firm Size	1983/84 $\left(\frac{V}{P}\right)$
Top 10 firms	0.44
Top 20 firms	0.49
Top 50 firms	0.46
Top 100 firms	0.45

Notes: V = Value-added
P = Production
V/P = Vertical integration
Production is taken in terms of total sales in value terms.
Source: Confederation of Indian Industry.

4. Large degree of vertical integration was not a necessary condition for large firms to have market power in the input and intermediate product markets. Even the process of vertical disintegration in the form of subcontracting with S&M firms worked in their favour as they had monopsony power in the intermediate goods markets and high degree of bargaining power with incomplete contracts.

As mentioned earlier, subcontracting between small and large firms had been quite extensive in several engineering industries (Nagaraj, 1984). Generally, the intermediate industries were crowded by a large number of small firms selling the intermediate goods to a few large final-product manufactures. The large final-product manufactures could not only reap economies arising out of the vertical disintegration process of supply chain but could also pass on the burden and losses of market fluctuations to the supplier firms, given the low bargaining power of the small firms.

Large firms could have higher access to imports of raw materials and components not only because of large resources at their disposal but also because of institutional factors such as import licences working in their favour (Panchamukhi, 1978). It can be observed from Tables 3.2A and 3.2B that import propensity of the engineering firms in general was high and the imports were highly dominated by large firms. In the domestic market there was premium for imports.

Table 3.2A Share of Top 100 Engineering Firms (INR Crores), 1983/84

	Sales	Exports	Imports	Exports/ Sales (%)	Imports/ Sales (%)
Top 20 firms	10,724.9 (32.0)	150.7 (12.8)	1,454.2 (26.1)	1.40	13.5
Bottom 20 firms	758 (2.2)	19.67 (1.7)	62.80 (1.08)	2.6	8.2
All 100 firms	16,761.5 (50.0)	392.4 (33.0)	2,058.5 (37.0)	2.3	12.2

Notes: Figures in brackets are percentage shares in total engineering industry figures.
Imports refer to imports of raw materials, components, and spares consumed.
Maximum value of sales = INR 3,141 crores.
Minimum value of sales = INR 30.8 crores.
Source: Confederation of Indian Industry.

Table 3.2B Share of 76 (Sample) Firms: Hand, Small, and Cutting Tools Industry (INR Lakh), 1983/84

	Sales	Exports	Imports	Exports/ Sales (%)	Imports/ Sales (%)
Top 20 firms	71,255	2,448	4,358	3.4	6.1
Bottom 20 firms	246	60	0.63	24.0	0.0
All 100 firms	73,533	2,894	4,402	3.9	5.9

Notes: Maximum value of sales = INR 15,922 lakh.
Minimum value of sales = INR 7 lakh.
Source: Field survey.

Higher access to imports could be a source of market power in the domestic market.

Large family-owned business houses realized domestic market power through diversification into multiple products. The import substitution and industrial policies appeared to have encouraged firms to produce a large range of products rather than focus on a few areas (Wolf, 1982). The multi-product strategy by large firms might have been aimed at increasing domestic profitability, risk reduction, overcoming the constraints of licensing policies, and to make captive supplies of inputs and intermediate products. In the sample of top 100 engineering firms obtained, there are quite a few large houses with three to six separate registered firms producing a variety of final and intermediate products. Second, on import substitution cycles, the large houses generally tended to diversify into different branches where ERP was high to reap supernormal profits arising out of a large degree of protection and the advantages of initial entrance. The diversification behaviour of large firms helped them to retain monopoly profits in several single-product lines. Instead of flooding the market with a single product under a high production capacity which might depress the prices, it was more profitable to produce and sell a limited quantity of each of the multi-products.

This observation shows how large firms could derive long-run domestic market power, which was abstracted as 'home market–specific relative advantage' in the theoretical model. This, in turn, would make large firms more inward-oriented than small firms. It was observed that several firms in the industry which were in the best position to export had the least incentive to do so given the relatively secure profitability of domestic sales (Wolf, 1982). So, the most likely outcome could be higher domestic market power: larger the firm size lower was the propensity to export. It can be observed from Tables 3.2A and 3.2B that exports are concentrated more at lower-size categories of firms than at the larger size.

Eighteen out of the twenty-four large firms interviewed in the field study stated that exports were considerably less profitable than domestic sales. It was generally observed that domestic prices of most of the engineering goods were higher than international prices and were sold in international markets at considerable discounts (Nayyar, 1978; Frankena, 1973). However, a noticeable number of large firms did undertake exports, even marginally. Out of the 125 large and medium firms for which data was obtained, 100 had export presence. Some of the reasons for the revealed exports of large firms could be as follows.

As shown in the first part of the theoretical model, the price discriminatory behaviour towards the segmented home and world markets could facilitate protection of domestic market power or high prices. In the field study, three large firms responded that they undertook exports to restrain domestic prices from falling. These firms exported to increase their domestic market power or, in other words, 'home market–specific relative advantage in sales'. One way this could be achieved, under the given demand characteristics of India's economy, was by increasing their access to imported inputs, foreign brand names, and foreign collaborations. Under the import replenishment policies, exports gave firms access to foreign exchange and imported inputs and components. As mentioned earlier, given the nature of domestic demand, where there was higher preference for import-intensive products, increased access to imports increased domestic profitability and market power.

Another way in which exports could increase a firm's domestic market power was by increasing its bargaining power with the government towards acquiring new licences, capacity expansion, and foreign collaborations. Two large firms responded in the field interview that exports were undertaken to improve or retain their lobbying power with the government. Since there was pressure from the government to increase foreign exchange earnings, the firms which had a certain amount of export performance were better off lobbying with the government.

Furthermore, export activity facilitated diversification into new areas and consequent reaping of high profits from initial entrance. Five out of the twenty-four large firms interviewed responded that exports were undertaken even at low profit margins because export activity functioned as a window to the world market conditions and trends which, in turn, helped them grow in the domestic markets. Export activity exposes the firms to new technologies, products, packaging techniques, and advertising methods taking place in the leading world markets. The exposure helped these firms to be first entrants into these new areas in the domestic market. This helped them reap the benefits of initial entrance into new areas and increase their domestic market power.

The revealed exports of large firms could be based on risk-reducing behaviour towards fluctuations in the domestic demand. Firms, in general, might undertake exports in times of domestic recession in order to reduce underutilization of capacity. In times of excess capacity due to domestic recession where no domestic sales were possible at the margin, firms were willing to export at prices lower than the average cost as long as they received something in excess of their marginal (variable) costs in order to recover a part of the fixed costs. India's engineering exports were said to be significantly influenced by domestic recession (Nayyar, 1978).

Four large firms interviewed in the field study responded that long-term export presence was perceived as an instrument of reducing risks due to domestic market fluctuations. Since one could not enter export markets suddenly during times of domestic recession, it was necessary for these firms to have long-term export presence in order to export at larger magnitude during domestic recession. Larger firms could be more prone to such behaviour as marginal changes in domestic demand would have substantial impact on them. Since these firms generally operated with higher fixed costs, they had higher necessity to export in times of domestic recession in order to recover break-even costs.

One more significant cause behind the revealed exports of some large firms was the response mechanism to institutional factors such as government industrial policies. In case of the hand tools industry, several products were reserved for exclusive production by the small-scale sector by restricting the growth of existing capacity of large units and the entry of new large units. The existing large units were not allowed to expand capacity in the domestic market but could expand capacity towards exports. New large firms could be set up if 80 per cent of the production was diverted to exports. Two prominent large firms in the industry responded to the constraint to their growth by augmenting their export orientation.

In case of S&M firms, the relative disadvantage in home market sales arose not only out of the mobility barriers imposed by large firms but also by severe competition pressure they faced in the home market as the market structure was crowded with a large number of them. The latter possibility arose out of easy entry into the small-scale sector due to low fixed costs involved in production, the factor and product market segmentations, and also the government policies. In the light engineering industries (such as diesel engines), the S&M firms generally catered to the price-elastic domestic demand from low-income consumers. As mentioned earlier, in the case of the heavy engineering industry the important feature was the interdependence between a few large final-product firms and the large number of S&M (intermediate products) firms through the vertical disintegration process of production. The production of several intermediate products was reserved exclusively for small-scale industries. The reservation and fiscal incentive policies aimed at the small-scale sector made entry into the component industries easier for small firms. This, generally, resulted in the existence of a large number of small component manufacturers producing intermediates under low ERP for a few final-product manufacturers as mentioned before, in industries such as automobiles and bicycles. As a result, as a generalization, they faced highly competitive conditions in the domestic market (Patibandla, 1988a). Small firms had noticeable levels of revealed exports in many engineering industries as shown in Table 3.3. The share of the small-scale sector in the total engineering exports was about 27 per cent. In industries such as bicycles and parts, diesel engines and parts, and hand, small, and cutting tools, the small firms' share in total exports of the respective industries was significantly high.

A major push factor behind the revealed exports of small firms was the competitive conditions they faced in the domestic market. Under the given characterization of the market structure, small firms faced high competition in selling their products, both in the final light engineering products and the intermediates, owing to high degree of monopsony power of the large final-product firms and barriers to expansion along with mobility barriers in the domestic market. Consequently, relatively efficient small firms were pushed to the export markets by the domestic market conditions they faced. The international markets with infinitely elastic demand or, in other words, price-taking domestic firms in the international markets, became a part of their market segmentation response. The international market for engineering goods was considerably segmented with

Table 3.3 Engineering Exports: Small-Scale Industry (INR Crore)

	1981/82	1982/83	1983/84
Total engineering	318.0 (30.3)	340.0 (27.2)	321.0 (27.4)
Bicycles and parts	26.0 (47.2)	22.0 (55.0)	15.0 (33.3)
Diesel engines and parts	30.0 (37.5)	28.8 (48.0)	21.0 (42.0)
Steel tubes and pipes	6.8 (17.7)	5.1 (17.0)	3.0 (17.6)
Hand, small, and cutting tools	11.3 (23.2)	14.69 (31.2)	15.00 (33.3)
Transmission line towers	1.7 (8.5)	2.38 (8.5)	2.0 (7.1)
Machine tools	7.9 (32.2)	8.6 (30.7)	10.0 (33.3)
Steel structures (fabricated)	10.2 (35.1)	10.2 (34.0)	10.0 (33.3)
EPNS ware	10.9 (49.0)	7.0 (87.0)	9.0 (64.2)

Notes: Small-scale industry was taken as defined by the Union Government prior to 1984.
Figures in brackets are percentage of small-scale industry exports in the total.
Source: CII, 1985.

noticeable markets for low-priced intermediate and finished goods especially in other developing countries. Under the intra-industry and preference similarity arguments, the small firms that catered to price-elastic domestic demand could be in a better position to reap the advantage of representative demand in these markets.

A majority of the small firms interviewed, forty-five out of sixty exporting firms, responded that exports were profitable while, as mentioned earlier, majority of the large firms perceived exports as an unprofitable activity. Most of these firms, however, belonged to the hand, small, and cutting tools industry which had comparative advantage in exports owing to labour intensity of production. Once these firms were able to break the entry barrier into exports, they might have been able to produce at world prices. As mentioned before, several intermediate product industries, such as auto components, dominated by small-scale firms were characterized by low or negative ERP, which implies that domestic prices were lower than import prices. The international markets with infinitely elastic demand where everyone is a price taker became a part of their market segmentation response. Export of small firms is shown in Table 3.3.

To cite an example of the restrictive practices derived from the field interviews, for those products in which small firms were cost- and price-competitive in the domestic market, the multi-product large firms resorted to cross-product subsidization in order to compete with relatively more efficient small firms. The losses incurred in the subsidized products were recovered from the monopoly profits in those products where competition was less.

Furthermore, in case of the component industries, where a large number of small firms competed to sell the intermediate products to the few large final-product firms owing to unequal bargaining power, the large final-product firms passed on the burden and losses of market fluctuations to intermediate product–making S&M firms. In order to overcome the monopsony power of large firms, a few S&M firms appeared to have entered export markets. For example, three small firms interviewed in the field study expanded or were made to expand their production capacity by the large automobile firms in order to cater to the booming market for automobiles. When the market for automobiles declined, these small firms were left without markets or support from the large firms. Two of these small firms went in for exports. Furthermore, a few of the subcontracting small firms responded that they would prefer to sell in export markets because of prompt payments by the overseas buyers through letters of credit. This reduced the cost of working capital. In the domestic markets, these firms faced numerous difficulties in getting payments on time from the domestic purchasers, which resulted in high interest costs and constraints in the availability of working capital.

The other significant reason for the revealed exports of small firms, as mentioned in the case of large firms, was that export activity, in turn, increased a small firm's standing in the domestic market. As observed from the field interviews, a small firm which was relatively successful in the domestic market segments was very much inclined to break into export markets as it would lead to its growth in the domestic market. One intangible benefit appeared to be that export activity by an intermediate manufacturer gave her/his status and brand name as an exporter with respect to the domestic buyer firms. This, in turn, increased the firm's bargaining power in the domestic market.

A couple of small firms in the hand, small, and cutting tools industry responded in the field interview that export activity was undertaken because it made them highly production-efficient, owing to continuous pressure of export markets to be efficient. It induced them to keep upgrading their techniques and technology and achieve higher organizational efficiency. The firm-level dynamic economies of export activity, in turn, augmented a firm's performance in the domestic market.

The large amount of export incentives provided by the government in the form of duty drawbacks, cash compensatory benefits, and import replenishments (see Table 3.4) could be a determinant of revealed exports of firms in general. However, the impressions

Table 3.4 Export Incentives Realized as Percentage of FOB Value of Exports

	Duty Drawback			Cash Compensatory Support		
	1978/79	1979/80	1980/81	1978/79	1979/80	1980/81
Hand tools	3.1	1.7	2.1	9.8	9.7	9.6
Machine tools	1.8	4.5	4.7	19.5	17.8	18.1
Steel tubes and pipes	15.7	15.6	10.3	12.2	12.4	7.1
Castings and forgings	1.3	1.3	2.7	15.0	13.2	12.2
Cables	26.9	22.2	22.9	5.5	10.3	9.9
All engineering products	8.4	5.9	6.8	13.7	13.8	12.7

Source: ICICI (1985).

gathered from the field study about the importance of the export incentives to small firms were mixed. Only about 30 per cent of exporting small firms stated that export incentives played a role in their export decisions. This was because of the high transaction costs they had to incur to avail these government incentives on paper.

One of the important market structure outcomes of export behaviour of small firms was their unrevealed indirect exports. Those small firms which could not break entry and expansion barriers both in the domestic and export markets due to marketing constraints exported through other established, firms, especially the large ones. The large firms which bought the finished and semi-finished products from the small firms could resell them in the domestic and export markets at higher prices.

Apart from the market-structure conditions, there could be several other supply-side factors for the existence of phenomena which were beyond the scope of this study. The incidence of the unrevealed exports of small firms, as observed in the field study, appeared to be quite high in the hand, small, and cutting tools industry. A small firm interviewed in Bangalore which produced carbide tips at a very high quality and cost competitiveness sold considerable amounts of the product to an established large firm with a foreign collaboration. The large firm, in turn, sold these products both in the domestic and international markets at much higher prices with its high marketing budgets and ability to undertake transaction costs of the markets.

Industrial Structure, Technological Activity, and International Trade Behaviour of Firms

As mentioned in the theoretical model, the supply-side conduct of large and small firms in terms of technological activity and relative factor intensity in production was determined by the product and factor market structure conditions in the domestic market. To recapitulate, on the product market structure front, large firms derived long-run market power while small firms faced competitive conditions and mobility barriers in the home market due to capital market distortions and high transaction costs of doing business. On the factor market side, as mentioned before, large firms had access to capital at a price lower than shadow price (opportunity cost) in the labour-abundant and capital-scarce Indian economy. Small firms which operated mostly in the unorganized factor markets paid factor prices more in line with their opportunity costs. These conditions determined the technological activity and organization of production by large and small firms in relation to domestic factor endowment conditions. This, in turn, had implications on these size groups' ability to translate domestic comparative advantage in relative factor endowments of labour and capital into exports.

Firm- and industry-level technological activity that had taken place in the Indian engineering industry between 1950 and 1990 was complex and diverse, which made it difficult to make generalizations. One generalization we could make was that the Schumpeterian 'creative destruction of innovation' of developed country–type of technological activity was more or less absent in India's industries for large firms to achieve the temporary comparative advantage that could be attained through innovation in the world market until the early 2000s. Factors such as the small size of the domestic market, fragmentation of production capacities, and protection from imports of superior international technologies combined with long-run domestic market power appeared to have made innovative R&D with uncertain results an unprofitable activity for the large Indian firms (Lall, 1987).

The costs of importing technology were observed to be lower for the large firms than if they did any significant level of innovative R&D in the home market. As a result, most of the new technologies were imported from the developed countries. A major part of R&D by firms, which was generally very minimal, was observed to be directed towards making marginal adaptations of the imported technology to local conditions. Allam (1988) demonstrated that most firms spent less than 1 per cent of their sales turnover on R&D.

Furthermore, as mentioned earlier, owing to the nature of product and factor market segmentation, government policies, and unequal access to imported technologies, there was significant level of technological distance between strategic groups of firms within given industries. This supports the insights of the 'New' New Trade Theory of heterogeneity of firms within a specific industry. Large firms generally tended to have higher access to imported technology than S&M firms in relative terms in the home market. Small firms, on the other hand, operated with indigenous technology and materials. Out of the 109 small firms in the sample of the field study, only 9 firms used the same kind of imported machinery (generally second-hand) and material while 95 per cent of large firms used the same kind of imported technology and materials. However, as mentioned earlier, most technologies that were imported were of older vintage compared to international standards, and most large firms hardly made efforts at adapting them to domestic market conditions. This caused firms of all scales to operate at different levels of technological frontiers. This, in turn, determined the nature of their technological efforts, capabilities, and activities with implications on their export behaviour.

A major part of the technological activities of large firms could be termed as 'creative importation' and 'not so creative adaptation'. The import behaviour of large firms at the top ladder of the market structure could be a part of their oligopoly rivalry or behaviour towards maximizing or retaining their domestic profits and high market shares. In the early and mid-1980s, partial reforms allowed imports of technology and joint collaboration with multinational firms was made possible which, in turn, facilitated enhancement of advantage in the home market. Second, advertising competition was based on foreign brand names and licences.

If a large firm imported a vintage technology with foreign collaboration and brand name, it was able to increase its market share and profits in the domestic market given higher consumer preference for import-intensive goods. The other large firms in the industry, in order to retain their market shares, followed the strategies of importing technology as a part of their oligopoly rivalry. Furthermore, expenditure or investment on imported technology, and the associated complimentary investment in R&D in adapting the technology was used as an entry barrier by incumbent oligopolies (Katrak, 1985). Imported technology and R&D behaviour were supposed to be complimentary rather than competitive in the Indian industry.

According to Katrak's findings, imported technology in India did result in adaptive R&D efforts, but the complementarity was weaker in case of complex technologies, which might imply that complex technologies were used as they were without much adaptation. If technology imports and associated R&D behaviour by a large firm increased its domestic market power, it reduced its export orientation from the perspective of the market structure argument.

From the supply-side aspects, imported technology, assuming it was superior to the domestic, should put large firms that had higher access to them in a better position to export because the ability to acquire technology should result in high productivity and growth, especially for a catching-up developing country such as India. However, if one observed the technology import and adaptation cycles in India, technology levels of firms lagged far behind the world standards. Most of the new technologies imported were observed to be of older vintage compared to the technologies in the developed countries. According to Desai (1988), many industries which expanded and prospered in India were either insignificant or declining in industrial countries and the firms that produced machinery for them either diversified or declined. The technology that had found large markets in India had often been sidelined in the European firms. This, in turn, reduced export possibilities to a large part of the world market of the developed and middle-income countries based on the product or technology cycle approach.

On the other hand, importation and operation of older technology would not have been a significant constraint in achieving export success if it was combined with domestic factor prices reflecting their true opportunity costs and continuous technological effort in adapting and improving the older technologies. The evidence regarding the nature and extent of technological effort of large firms in adapting and improving imported technologies was mixed (Bell, Ross-Larson, and Westphal, 1984). On one side, the technological progress of Indian firms with imported technology base was observed to be very slow and, in many cases, stagnant. In the beginning of a collaboration or import of technology, the technological effort and the learning process appeared to be high and fast, but in due course it slowed down and the gap between the technology recipient and world standard technology increased (Allam, 1988). The sheltered domestic market was observed to have reduced incentives to undertake substantial technological efforts and cost-saving and quality-enhancing measures (Bhagwati and Srinivasan, 1975). Consequently, export potential in cumulative technological progress and innovation over the older vintage technologies imported tended to be low.

On the other hand, few large firms in the engineering industries that imported technologies had shown technological dynamism in adapting them to the domestic conditions, scale considerations, and demand requirements (Lall, 1987; Desai, 1982; 1988). The technological adaptation and its associated R&D were generally directed towards producing the products relevant to the price-elastic nature of domestic demand and also towards altering or reducing scales to conform to the domestic market size. As a result, the products tended to be of the low-priced, low-quality, and sturdy type. According to Desai (1988), India produced a large volume of sturdy machine tools and other industrial equipment which had passed out of use in the industrial countries twenty years ago.

Consequently, the adaptive solutions made might be unique to the Indian demand- and supply-side considerations and the extent of export possibility got reduced based on the representative demand argument. But there were some industries where firms based on imported technologies achieved international quality and price in the products. A World Bank study (1984) gave the Indian boilers industry as an example of technological dynamism. But this phenomenon was only at a marginal level. As far as the productivity and cost associated with the imported technologies were concerned, it required proper investment choice, continuous technological efforts, and learning by doing. Even if we assumed that the choice of technology under the given information and parameters was made correctly, the costs involved in the beginning were high because of high costs involved in technology transfer and setting up the plants. The cost of technology transfer was observed to exceed 50 per cent of the total cost of a project in developing countries such as India

(Teece, 1976). This could be because the available skills, manpower, and prevalent conditions in the developing countries were different from the developed countries where the technology or the machinery was developed. This, in turn, reduced the possibility of comparative advantage in exports in the beginning.

Generation of comparative advantage with the imported technology required proper choice of technique on the frontiers in accordance with domestic factor (input) prices and movements on the frontiers according to changing conditions as a continuous process of adaptation and further improvements through learning by doing and proper tuning with world market conditions. In case of choice of techniques, firms which operated with imported technologies in India were supposed to use more labour than the extent of labour used for the similar technologies in the developed countries (Lall, 1980). Although it might not have resulted in higher comparative costs since labour in India was cheaper, its implied failure to minimize costs and technical inefficiency.

This result showed that imported technology was being used with more labour than required. On the other hand, imported technology could be changed or adapted towards labour intensity in order to take advantage of domestic relative factor endowments. It was observed that there was practically no evidence of any effort by the large Indian firms to change imported technologies in a labour-intensive direction. The process engineering efforts in production by these firms were towards achieving greater capital intensity and reducing labour intensity. This could be because of labour market policies in India where it was difficult to fire organized labour. Furthermore, despite the abundance of skilled labour, many firms were observed to be weak on the production management requirements of labour-intensive techniques (Lall, 1987). This would imply that productivity within the plant and in terms of efficiency of choice of technique in a macro sense tended to be lower than the potential. This result demonstrated that the large Indian firms operating with imported technology deviated from the country's natural comparative advantage in skilled and semi-skilled labour.

With rapid technological changes in the developed and middle-income countries, the Indian industry and firms in pursuit of catching up with developed economies—like several other developing countries which imported technology on a lagged product or technology cycle—became dependent on imports for technology upgradation in a continuous process. This was especially true in the absence of significant levels of process and product innovation. In such a scenario, there might be technological imports and activity in relation to domestic market success. However, its relevance to exports, especially to the developed countries, was not significant.

On the other hand, there were a few large firms in specific engineering industries which undertook technological efforts and changes without much dependence on the imported technology. These efforts were compatible with the domestic demand- and supply-side conditions of the relative factor prices. One such example, once again, was the bicycle industry. As mentioned earlier, the nature of the domestic demand for bicycles was highly price-elastic. The technological efforts and changes that went into producing the final-product were towards reducing costs and price and making the product sturdy and suited to the Indian conditions. The other industry example was the Indian tractor industry (Desai, 1982). The technological activity and diffusion through inter-firm linkage between the large final-product and small intermediate manufacturers was towards minimizing costs and prices. As a result, the final product that was produced was suitable to the nature of domestic demand but the export potential arising out of the technological activity was not high from the representative demand argument between the domestic and world markets as domestic and export markets demanded different types or quality of products. However, these products could find a market in other developing countries with similar demand patterns and domestic conditions. But these markets were of small size.

In the Schumpeterian world of 'creative destruction', it is only large monopoly firms which are expected to undertake R&D and innovative activity for their ability to internalize costs and benefits of innovation. Empirical evidence shows innovation does take place in S&M firms which do not have monopoly position in the market. Schumpeterian monopoly condition is not necessary if the small firms' innovation is protected from appropriation by intellectual property rights. As a matter of fact, it seems it is the S&M firms which produce major innovations rather the large firms in the USA (Kamien and Schwartz, 1982).

Most of the R&D and innovative activity might be informal in character and mostly undertaken by small firms (Scherer, 1980). The S&M firms might be very effective in the initial stage of innovation where large amount of investment and fixed capital is not necessary in moulding R&D and innovation towards product or process innovation. Apart from this, S&M firms' role in innovation could be very significant in the industries operating with decentralized and vertically disintegrated technologies on separable production processes on a vertical line (Blair, 1972). In vertically disintegrated technologies, S&M firms producing intermediate products could be very effective in process innovations.

In India's case, Katrak's study showed that larger firms undertook proportionately less R&D than smaller ones. Siddharthan (1988b) found a 'U'-shaped relation between R&D intensity (R&D expenditure divided by sales turnover) and firm size for several Indian industries with a sample of firms with sales turnover ranging from INR 10 million to several thousand million. This implied that small firms were as R&D-intensive as very large firms. The explanation that was given for small firms spending a larger proportion of their sales on R&D was that it was owing to the presence of minimum economies of size. However, the nature of R&D done by small firms could be quite different from the large firms. The question, here, would be the implications of the nature of R&D on their exports.

The nature of R&D and product and process innovation by S&M firms could be expected to be very much in line with the nature of domestic demand in which case, as argued in case of the large firms before, the export possibilities would be low under the technology cycle and representative demand approach. However, the major strength of technological activity of these firms was that it fell more in tune with the domestic factor endowments. Small firms, as shown before, were generally said to use the indigenous technologies and factors of production more intensely and effectively. Consequently, they were in a better position to reap the country's comparative advantage in factor endowments more effectively than the large firms operating with imported technologies.

One interesting aspect of some of the engineering industries was that the product or technology innovation cycles and the representative demand arguments in exports which held strongly in the final and differentiated products might not hold to full extent in case of certain equipment and intermediate products. In the production of these products, the technological advancement in the developed countries could be generally towards capital augmenting and labour replacing (on the capital-intensive part of isoquants) since labour was very expensive in these countries. If we assume that the initial technology was the same in both the developed and developing countries, the technological change or advancement in the labour-abundant developing countries was directed towards labour augmenting with minor innovations in the machinery and product characteristics. The firms in these countries would still be able to export to the developed countries under the Heckscher and Ohlin assumption. Although one can apply this argument to both large and small firms, the major determinant factor would be firms' ability to reap the countries' comparative advantage in labour abundance and certain indigenous technological characteristics at every stage and in a continuous process. This argument is illustrated in Figure 3.3. The initial technology in both developed and developing countries is represented by the isoquant QQ_1. The capital-deepening technological changes in the developed countries are represented by the expansion path *OA* and the labour-augmenting technological changes in the developing countries by *OB*.

In such a case, S&M firms which generally concentrate in the production of intermediates and certain equipment might have a relative advantage in adopting the above-mentioned type of technological activity towards exports.

One of the major determinants of the nature of S&M firms' technological activity and efforts was based on the segmented market structure conditions they faced. To recapitulate, small firms, both in the final and intermediate industries, faced severe competitive conditions in the domestic market: price competition among themselves and non-price competition from the large firms, for example, delay in the payment

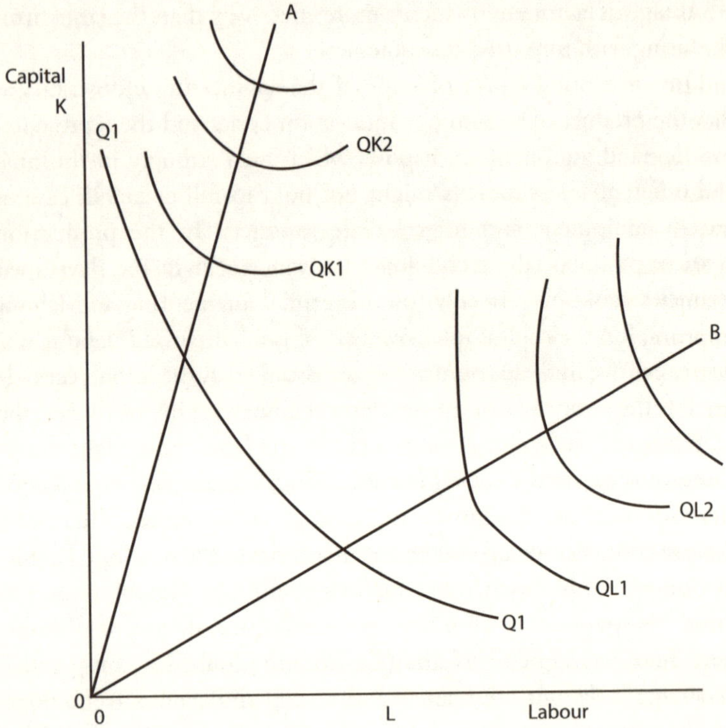

Figure 3.3 Technological Change
Source: Author's representation.

for delivery of components. The efforts of the S&M firms operating mainly with indigenous technology, given their low access to imported technologies, were mainly towards minimizing costs and prices (high degree of X-efficiency). This was because the only way these firms were able to compete and grow was through producing the products at the lowest costs possible. In the process of minimizing costs, both fixed and variable, these firms were able to not only reap the country-specific comparative advantage in the supply side but also generated certain kinds of process and product innovations. The fact that S&M firms in the intermediate industries were able to survive and produce under very low and negative ERP, as shown before, would imply these firms did reap the country's comparative advantage.

As shown in Figure 3.3, this argument could be substantiated by the technological behaviour of two small firms in the cutting tools industry interviewed in the field study. One of them produced carbide tips with a sales turnover of about INR 9 million and the other produced abrasive cloth and other cutting tools with sales turnover of about INR 60 million. Both the firms were managed by technocrat owner–managers, but in the latter's case about three professional managers were employed. In both the cases, the technological efforts and changes were made possible both in the machinery in operation and in improvement in vertical quality product differentiation through high degree of specialization and X-efficiency. The processes of efficiency of small firms was realized in terms of the following stages.

The first stage was the choice of the product to be manufactured. Once the best feasible choice which determined the subsequent efficient operation in relation to the given scale of operation was made, the products sometimes were developed through R&D by bringing in designs from abroad or other firms. In case of subcontracting firms, the required designs of intermediates were taken from the large final-product firms. After developing according to the specified requirements, they were shown to the final-product firms for acceptance and sales.

The second stage was minimizing the installment costs of plant and machinery. From the aforementioned examples, in the former's case, the cost of machinery was reduced substantially by buying second-hand machinery at very low prices and renovating them with new components and parts secured from the domestic and overseas markets. This process not only reduced the overall cost of the machinery by 70 to 80 per cent of new machinery price but also gave scope for innovation in adapting the machinery for the small scale of operation.

The third stage was the minimization of the variable costs along with maximum possible utilization of fixed inputs with high involvement of technocrat owner–managers at every stage of operation. The managers' involvement was generally high due to their ability to survive given the external conditions of mobility barriers and limited access to capital.

In case of small-firm manufacturing, such as manufacture of the carbide tips through the process of learning by doing, some features of the machinery bought from a Swedish firm were changed in accordance with the problems that arose in the production process. These changes, in turn, were taken by the Swedish firm to be added to the subsequent machinery manufactured.

The variable costs of labour were minimized by employing a few permanent skilled labour and temporary semi and unskilled labour. The semi and unskilled labour was a variable input for the small firms as the number varied according to the amount of output produced, unlike in case of large firms where labour was fixed owing to trade unions and government regulations. Second, the labour intensity of small firms had to be observed not in terms of number of workers employed but at the utilization intensity of the employed workers. Most of the small firms, as observed from the field study, made the employed labour work long hours at full intensity by paying low wages compared to large firms.

Furthermore, because of small magnitude of the output produced, the quality control done by the manager who understood the technicalities of the products tended to be high. This process, in turn, helped in upgrading the product quality and changing the product characteristics over a period. So, what came out was a good-quality product at low price. The carbide tips produced by the small firm that was interviewed were not exported directly by the firm due to lack of marketing infrastructure. They were bought at low competitive prices and exported by a large firm with a Swedish collaboration at higher prices under its international brand name.

It has to be taken into notice that this result and characterization was done in view of a model-efficient small firm. A considerable number of small firms turned out to be sick units in the Indian industries due to wrong choice of products, bad financial management, and constraints in the availability of working capital.

The result, as briefly discussed earlier, was an outcome of a high degree of specialization and X-efficiency of the technocrat owner–managers and the resulting learning-by-doing economies. This process facilitated not only the stretching of the machinery to a longer period of economic use but also utilization of domestic resources and inputs at their opportunity costs. The linkage and dynamics of the technological activity, in relation to exports, was more effective for an exporting firm than for a non-exporter. This was because an exporting firm had proper feedback from the changing world market conditions and was able to bring in necessary technological changes and upgradations at the right time to sustain or increase exports. Once the technological upgradations were brought at the right time, the process of stretching the technology would start again.

From the analysis in the preceding sections, it could be observed that an efficient small firm which employed mostly indigenous (or older vintage) technology could have a higher scope to be technically efficient at a point of time in static terms owing to its organizational efficiency. Apart from this, the firm had higher flexibility to move along the frontier in adopting the frontier choice of technique due to the lower complexity of the technologies and because factor inputs such as labour were a variable input to these firms. On the other hand, a large firm operating with imported technologies had higher probability of being technically inefficient from the given frontier if the technology was not properly adapted and if there were technological rigidities and complexities. The technological complexity restricted movement along the frontier in relation to prices of factors of production even if one assumed that the firm was operating on the frontier. This, in turn, resulted in the technology to deviate from the comparative advantage in the domestic factor endowments through loss of degrees of freedom on the choice of techniques (the inputs combinations) on a given technology.

One of the underlying arguments from the preceding analysis was that the firm-level allocative efficiency could be observed in terms of minimizing costs under the relative shadow factor prices in terms of opportunity costs of labour and cost of capital. This also includes allocative X-efficiency within a firm in terms of organizational efficiency. To recapitulate, owing to factor market distortions in the capital and labour markets, large Indian firms that had greater access to formal credit tended to pay lower price to capital and higher price to labour than their opportunity costs at the macro level:

opportunity costs across different sectors of an economy and also between countries with the comparative advantage of international trade argument. This, in turn, made them deviate from comparative advantage of international trade.

On the other hand, as argued earlier, small firms which had lower access to formal credit and share of capital and higher access to unorganized labour paid higher price to capital and lower price to labour in accordance with their opportunity costs—country-level opportunity costs in terms of abundant labour and scarce capital. This, in turn, caused significant differences between the large and small firms in their ability to reap the country's comparative advantage in factor endowments: relative shadow factor prices of labour and capital. From these two arguments, it can be seen that both the technical and allocation efficiency as characterized earlier were not totally independent of each other, being determined by the nature of technology adopted to a considerable extent. Rigidities in adapting technology might not only result in technical inefficiency but also restrict a firm from achieving allocation efficiency.

Some of the arguments presented in this analysis are illustrated through Figure 3.4. The vertical axis represents capital input (*K*) and the horizontal axis represents labour input (*L*). Let the isoquant 'Q_1Q_1' represent the imported technology frontier. The curve *MM* represents the relative factor price line faced by the large firms. *SS* is the shadow factor price line representing the opportunity costs of the factors of production at the country level.

In adapting the imported technology, a large firm could arrive at the isoquant 'Q_2Q_2' by deviating from the original frontier 'Q_1Q_1'. If the firm is at '*a*', the extent of technical efficiency would be '*ab*'. Even if the firm arrives on the frontier 'Q_1Q_1' at point '*b*', provided there are technological rigidities in its adaption, it would be stuck at '*b*' (capital-intensive part), restricting its movement on the frontier. In such a case, the firm may not be able to reach the point '*c*' where its costs could be minimized, resulting in allocative inefficiency to the extent of '*bt*'.

If we take the allocative efficiency in terms of adopting the technical choices subject to the relative shadow price (opportunity costs)

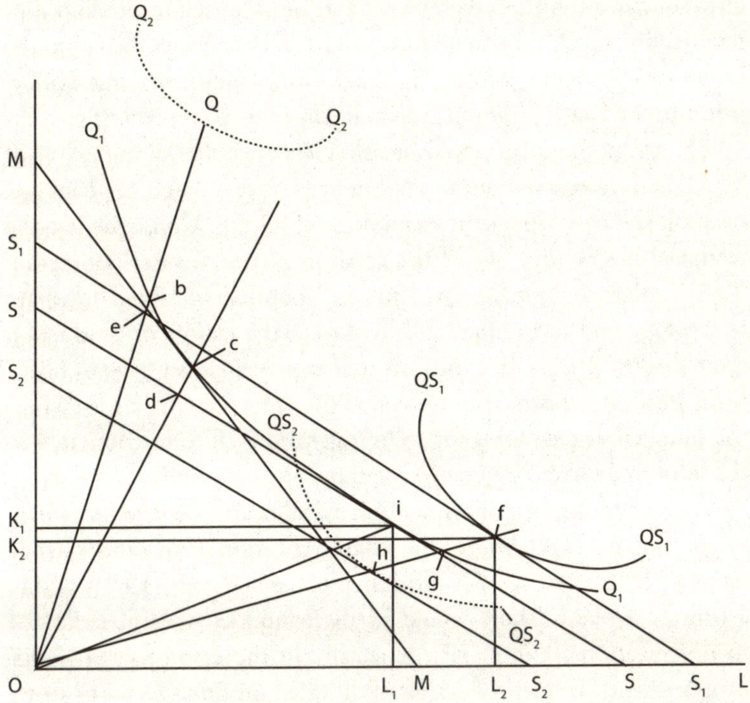

Figure 3.4 Technical and Allocative Efficiency
Source: Author's representation.

line '*SS*', the firm should be at '*e*', at which point it would be able to take advantage of domestic comparative advantage in the endowment of factors of production. In the case of the firm which reaches equilibrium at '*c*', it will have allocative inefficiency in terms of extent of utilization of factors of production at their opportunity costs at the country level to the extent of '*cd*'.

The isoquants 'QS_1QS_1' and 'QS_2QS_2' are taken to represent indigenous or older vintage technology with which S&M firms are assumed to operate. On the isoquants 'QS_1QS_1', under the given technology it operates with, a small firm which pays shadow prices to the factors of production would achieve both technical and allocative efficiency at point '*b*'. But if we take technical efficiency in a relative sense in terms of deviation from the new vintage or imported technology represented by 'Q_1Q_1', the small firm will be technically inefficient to the extent of '*fg*'. At the point '*f*', a small firm which is paying shadow prices to the factor of production and adopting labour-intensive technology and techniques would be using less of capital to the extent of 'K_1K_2' and more of labour to the extent of 'L_1L_2' than if the firm had been on the new vintage of technology of 'Q_1Q_1'. Consequently, the technical inefficiency '*gb*' of the small firm in terms deviation from 'Q_1Q_1' might be compensated by the adoption of labour-intensive technology and techniques and by paying the factors of production their shadow prices. This, in turn, might give an advantage to S&M firms in their exports. The isoquant 'QS_2QS_2' presents a case where the indigenous technology is technically more efficient compared to the imported technology represented by 'Q_1Q_1'.

The other important dimension of allocative efficiency which might not be captured by the characterization here (and quantitatively) is the extent of X-efficiency of Leibenstein (1980) within a firm or a plant. There would be diseconomies of large scale due to organizational complexity, especially in the case of large multiproduct firms. If the production of different products is not properly organized, and if there is lack of coordination between different departments and information flow, or if there is misallocation of duties to employees, it could result in a large degree of X-inefficiency. The factors of production, especially, labour, could be inefficiently utilized in terms of deviations in factor allocations from their opportunity costs within a firm or a plant. This slack in efficiency of a large firm could be not only because of diseconomies of large-scale operations but also due to the market structure conditions. If there is low competition, large firms with long-run market power in the home market would not have incentives and motivation to minimize costs, which, in turn, could result in large degree of X-inefficiency. This was a very important feature of large Indian firms during the pre-reform period.

In this analysis, it can be seen that both the choice of technological frontiers and the choice of technique on a given frontier could be a crucial determinant in a firm's or an industry's ability to benefit from the supply-side factors for international trade advantage. Imported technologies of large firms, if properly chosen, might not be suboptimal but distortions could arise if they were not properly adopted and continuous technological changes were not made. Domestic market distortions, in terms of the existence of market power, protection from imports, the government policies, and factor and product market fragmentations could facilitate large firms even with inefficient choice and operation of technology to be able to reap domestic super-normal profits. But their technological relevance to exports could turn out to be relatively low. For example, it was observed in the case of the textile machinery industry that South Korea produced semi-automatic looms while India produced modern labour-saving equipment although India was relatively a more labour-abundant country. The discrepancy was attributed to the protection of the Indian textile and equipment producers while the Korean industry was export-oriented (Pack, 1981).

Scale Economies and International Trade Behaviour of Firms

The theoretical model assumed non-increasing returns to scale technology in specifying the cost function for analytical abstraction. As discussed in Chapter 2, scale economies both in static and dynamic terms could be major sources of exports, especially for large firms. This section brings forth the issues of whether firms in the Indian industry could realize scale economies and translate them into exports under the existing demand- and supply-side conditions that large and small firms faced in the pre-reform era.

One could argue that, as far as the conventional static scale economies internal to a firm were concerned, they were associated only with large firms or plant size. The dynamic economies, especially of the learning-by-doing type, could be relevant to both large and small firms. However, the incidence and the degree at which these economies could be realized might be related to firm size under specific conditions. In case of external economies, firm size became germane in terms of internalization of externalities. Even the dynamics of external economies in terms of growth of an industry, changing pools of specific inputs, and industrial structure, could be internalized by firms at varying degrees.

The pattern of industrialization that was realized in India, as mentioned earlier, did generate considerable levels of external economies and diseconomies. Under the given industrial structure and the policy regime, most of the benefits of the external economies, both static and dynamic, could be internalized by large firms.

If we look at the input-generated externalities, as shown before, both the vertical integration and disintegration strategies followed by large firms could have facilitated internalization of the economies in the production of raw materials and components. Secondly, the economies of specialization generated by vertical disintegration process through subcontracting between large firms and large number of small supplier firms under the given market structure conditions could be internalized by the large final-product manufacturers (Annavajhula, 1989). As mentioned earlier, the subcontracting process was quite significant in industries such as automobiles and bicycles industries. For example, the bicycle industry in Ludhiana was a notable example of the economies of specialization associated with vertical disintegration. The S&M firms producing the intermediates were generally quite efficient under specialization with labour-intensive techniques. However, these economies of specialization by small firms were generally passed on to the large final-product manufacturers owing to unequal bargaining strength under the given market structure conditions as discussed before.

Furthermore, the dynamic external economies in terms of increasing availability of scientific and skilled manpower through the government's policies of subsidized education could be benefitting the larger firms more than S&M firms. The economies in terms of the increasing pools of specific skills could be internalized by the larger firms as they had greater access to these skilled labour and human capital generated in the country than S&M firms. Apart from this, S&M firms might be training grounds of labour for large firms as workers trained in these medium-scale firms might move to large firms later.

On the other hand, the dynamic increasing returns at the industry level and their internalization might not be very significant. These external economies depend on the industrial base and its growth. Although we assumed that external diseconomies, if any, to be of equal magnitude to firms of all size categories, these diseconomies could be of lower magnitude than larger firms if these firms had greater access to the government-produced raw material, such as access to steel quotas. Although the Indian industrialization process generated a large industrial base, based on Kaldor's law (1966) the accrual of dynamic increasing returns was usually significant when the manufacturing experiences sustained high growth rates. According to Kaldor, technical progress stimulates economic growth in cumulative fashion which, in turn, induces further technical progress, which results in dynamic increasing returns associated with higher rate of economic growth. This, in turn, requires an adequately high and rising level of effective demand: effective demand is different from nominal demand as it accounts for inflation. The significance of these dynamic returns for the Indian industry could be low, given some of the findings on India's industrial stagnation and low growth in effective demand in the country in the pre-reforms era (Ahluwalia, 1985).

Considering the international element of external economies in terms of imports of intermediates and components, if there were any international-level external economies in the production of these intermediates they should be benefitting the large Indian firms more than small firms, given the former's greater access to these imports as shown before. The internalization of external economies by large firms should put them in a better position to export from the supply-side aspects (such as costs of production) and, on the other hand, it might increase domestic monopoly position of these firms with implications on their export orientation.

Economies of Scale Internal to a Firm

In the long-tailed market structure characterized earlier, a few large firms at the top would take up the major market share of the industry. Apart from this, protection from imports given to the domestic industry, especially the final-product manufacturers, gave the large firms access to a big chunk of the domestic market. This should give scope to large Indian firms to reap both static and dynamic internal economies of scale advantage towards exports.

However, the first question as discussed earlier, would be whether the domestic market was large enough to realize any significant economies of scale advantage in exports in the international markets. As argued before, if one took the size of the Indian market in terms of per capita income and income distribution, one could not consider the domestic market large enough to consist of sufficiently large number of consumers' demand for both homogenous and differentiated goods during the 1980s. Apart from this, due to the income distribution characteristics, the market got fragmented with both income- and price-elastic nature of domestic demand patterns. The differentiated consumer goods mostly demanded by small-sized upper income segments tended to be produced on a small scale. This, in turn, reduced scope for firms to have long production runs to realize any significant levels of the internal economies of scale.

On the other hand, there were quite a few engineering industries with a large domestic market. For example, India's bicycle industry was supposed to be the largest in the world. But the major part of the demand for bicycles in the domestic market was from the low-income strata with the demand being highly price-elastic. This implied demand from low-income groups for low-quality-oriented products. So, the bicycles produced for the domestic market reflected the price-elasticity characteristics at low quality while the major part of the world market, especially the developed countries, was income-elastic and was high-quality–oriented. As a result, the firms in the industry, in order to undertake any substantial level of exports, required to differentiate the products produced for exports from the domestic market. This was because the export market required a significantly different type of product from that produced for the domestic market. If a large firm produced different products for the domestic and export markets, production runs would be short or fragmented. As a result, based on Linder's representative demand or preference similarity argument, the large firms in the industry were not be able to realize any significant level of advantage from economies of scale towards exports.

Product market segmentations further reduced scope for scale economies to large firms. A typical illustration for the argument was India's diesel engines industry. A major part of the domestic demand for diesel engines was for those of a highly price-elastic nature, oriented towards low-horse-powered and low-quality engines. The major share of the demand was from the Indian farmers, who were generally highly price-conscious and preferred low-quality and sturdy engines for rough usage. High-quality or sophisticated engines were not relevant to the pattern of usage by the farmers. About 70 per cent of the demand was met by S&M firms, which were generally cost-efficient in producing the low-quality engines at low price. The market was scattered all over the country giving geographical protection to small firms (Desai, 1984). The large firms were generally unable to compete with the S&M firms in this segment of the market of low-quality and low-horse-powered engines.

One of the large firms interviewed in the field study tried to introduce a sophisticated diesel engine into the market with a German collaboration to cater to this segment of the market. But the product was a total failure due to the nature of the domestic demand. As a result, the domestic market for these engines was scattered all over the country and shared by a large number of S&M firms. This did not give scope for large-scale production by few large firms to realize scale economies. The large firms in the industry concentrated on the upper segment of the market (above 20 H.P. engines), mainly catering to industrial and urban demand. A major part of the world demand was for the high-quality engines. The world demand for low-quality and low-horse-powered engines was generally from the other developing countries. However, the magnitude of the domestic demand was too small to realize any scale economies.

The other factor which reduced the scope for internal economies of scale in the length of production runs for the large Indian firms was the nature of their product diversification behaviour. There could be economies of scale arising out of diversification in terms of economies in multi-plant operations and economies of scope related to the production of a diverse range of products for a single large firm or establishment (Panzar and Willig, 1981). However, these economies of scale and scope of multi-product strategy largely depended on the scale of operation, the type of products, and technological 'nearness' between the differentiated products. These economies were realized mostly at a very large scale of operation. For example, the large Japanese firms which follow multi-product strategies operate on a very large scale and realize these economies as they have been highly international-oriented since the beginning of their industrialization in the 1950s. However, the potential of these economies to large Indian firms was not significant since these firms could not operate at a very large scale compared to international standards.

As discussed earlier, large Indian firms prematurely diversified into a large range of products in search of monopoly profits under the import substitution regime of India's Fabian socialist policies till 1991. Consequently, they could not arrive at an efficient scale of operation in any single product line to realize economies of long production runs. Apart from this, the Indian multi-product engineering firms were observed to produce a large variety of less-related products (Desai, 1984). This not only reduced length of production runs but also the scope for economies of specialization in the use of labour and capital equipment, as organization efficiency requirements tended to be high in multi-product operations.

In case of plant-sized economies, it was observed that the industrial licensing and Monopoly Restrictive Trade Practice (MRTP) policies, by restricting establishment and growth of large plants and limiting capacity expansion in production, prevented large firms from attaining the critical plant size required to realize any significant economies of large plant size. This was essentially applicable to those industries in which the existing technology facilitated scale economies only at a very large scale of production. In the case of several of India's heavy engineering industries (such as manufacturing of tractors), most of the large plants were relatively small in comparison to international standards. Until 1992, an MRTP firm was defined to be one with net assets worth INR 25 crore (250 million), which was increased to INR 100 crore (1,000 million) in the late 1980s. The economies of scale, both static and dynamic, in R&D activity in terms of spreading fixed costs of R&D over larger output did not need to be given much importance given the nature and low level of R&D activity in India, which is discussed in detail in the following section.

The incidence and degree of realization of learning-by-doing economies could be lower for larger firms compared to S&M firms given their nature of diversification behaviour and also owing to the organizational aspects. Diversification into multi-products reduced scope-related specialization and increased organizational complexity, which, in turn, reduced the incidence and degree of realization of learning by doing, especially in production. Furthermore, a large firm generally tended to have a large number of separate departments handling separate functions. If these different departments were not properly coordinated, resulting in X-inefficiency, the realization and application of learning-by-doing economies tended to be low.

To illustrate this argument, from the observations made in the field study, on the production floor technicians or engineers were able to realize certain snags and possible improvements in the machinery or products during the production process. However, generally, in large firms these findings had to be referred to R&D or other departments for their approval and application. If these separate departments were not properly coordinated, the realization and application of these learning-by-doing economies would not take place even if they did and it involved long durations. Therefore, the realization of these dynamic economies of cumulative experience in large firms depended on the levels of internal organizational X-efficiency in these firms.

This analysis shows that under the given domestic market and firm-level conditions, large firms experience inability to realize pre-international trade scale economies' advantages towards exports. On the other hand, international trade of exports could function as an extension of the market size, especially for a small economy in international terms, such as India, which, in turn, could lead to scale economies in the form of increased production runs. Recall Adam Smith's argument: 'Division of Labour is limited by Extent of the Market.' But to realize this, the initial condition, as discussed in case of the bicycle and diesel engines industries, was that firms had to produce the appropriate product for the world market, which was determined by the nature of the domestic demand. Most of the final engineering products produced by the large Indian firms might not be appropriate for a major part of world markets while the intermediates produced mostly by S&M firms could find a place in the world market. If the large firms did not have considerable degree of export orientation, realization of economies of exports by these firms tended to be low. On the other hand, increase in production runs and capacity utilization and other dynamics resulting from firm-level exports could be relevant to firms to lower the size characteristics.

As far as the S&M firms were concerned, the most emphatic economies could be in terms of economies of specialization and dynamic economies in cumulative experience and learning by doing. As mentioned earlier, both the economies of specialization and learning-by-doing were highly correlated. A model-efficient small firm, as derived from the field study, generally tended to specialize in a few product lines in which its strength lay. These firms were generally managed by technocrat owner–managers whose involvement in the production process tended to be high, as a result of which they tended to be highly X-efficient. As these firms generally concentrated on a few product lines, they were able to utilize special-purpose machinery fully. It reiterates Dreze's (1960) argument in which firm size is not a crucial determinant of scale economies. Rather, what matters most is the number of items turned out in a given production line. According to Gruble and Lloyd (1975), the most important determinant of productivity or unit costs is not the size of the plant but how production is organized within a plant of a given size. This is especially relevant to multi-product firms. This could facilitate considerable turn-out of number of items from a given production line. High degree of X-efficiency combined with specialization could lead to economies of specialization in terms of lower unit costs. This, in turn, could lead to higher realization of learning-by-doing economies in cumulative experience in the production process, owing to higher involvement of technocrat owner–managers and simpler organizational structure.

To illustrate this proposition, we observed in the field study that a technocrat owner–manager who had understanding of the engineering features of the machinery and technicalities of the product could not only realize the snags that arise and the appropriate solutions but would also be able to take quick decisions in their application. The technocrat owner–managers of small firms, generally, happened to be those who had worked with large firms for a period and branched out on their own. This would facilitate adoption of machinery to changing requirements and possible improvements in their operations and to improve the product quality over a period of time. One small firm in the cutting tools industry, interviewed in Bangalore, was able to bring in additional technical improvements to machinery imported from a Swedish firm. The technical improvement was, in turn, taken by the Swedish firm to be added to new machines manufactured.

These learning-by-doing economies make a firm cost-competitive and, given other conditions, lead to its general growth and growth in specialized areas. This, in turn, could result in a highly productive cumulative experience. The Government of India's policies such as reservation and fiscal incentives discouraged more dynamic and efficient small firms to grow into large size. The fiscal incentives and the reservation policies towards the small-scale sector discouraged efficient registered small firms to grow, as it was more beneficial to remain as a registered small firm. Owing to this reason, the efficient small firms tended to grow by premature diversification into multi-plants (registered under different names) and multi-products, rather than remain in a specialized narrow range. One of the small firms interviewed in the field study controlled six plants registered as small-scale units and achieved growth by this type of diversification. This phenomenon, in turn, dissipated both static and dynamic economies at a very early stage.

4 Empirical Analysis of International Trade and Investment Behaviour of Firms

The econometric exercises of this part of the book were based on cross-section data analysis across firms of different size groups. As Schmalensee (1989) pointed out, the underlying theory of cross-section industry studies was that it was a long-run equilibrium. In the long run, strictly speaking, all variables are endogenous. Because of this reason, the best that one can expect from the cross-section industry studies are certain empirical regularities. This chapter tests for the empirical association between firm size and international trade and goes on to identify and analyse some of the major determinants of this association.

The classification of firms by size and the proposition that their international trade behaviour could be distinct under the specified conditions could imply a large degree of non-linearity in the empirical association between the variables. This becomes germane especially when large and small firms are taken in one sample. This is because, as argued in Chapter 3, the international trade behaviour of large and small firms was not only distinct but also governed by the determinants in differential fashions. As a result, the relationships were not monotonic.

Data

The firm-level data that was used in the following exercises was classified into two broad groups:

1. Firm-level cross-section series data at the aggregate classification level of the engineering industry.
2. Firm-level cross-section series data at the disaggregate level of three subgroups of engineering industries.

The cross-section series data at the aggregate level of the industry was collected for 100 firms for the periods of 1982/83, 1983/84, and 1985/86, based on the company balance sheets from the CEI. As shown in Table 4.1, the sample consists of mostly medium and large firms.

Basic firm-level data for thirty-two firms belonging to steel tubes and pipes industry and twenty firms belonging to the diesel engines and parts industry was collected for 1982/83 from the directory of members of the Association of Indian Engineering Industries (AIEI). In the sample of steel tubes and pipes industry, the sales turnover of firms ranged from a minimum of INR 15 lakhs to a maximum of INR 171.73 lakhs. In the diesel engines sample, it ranged from INR 10.6 to 792.79 lakhs. One of the problems with the diesel engines industry sample was that several firms, especially the large firms, were diversified into producing a wide range of products. The firm-level data was not decomposed for different products produced by a firm. In case of the steel tubes and pipes industry sample, the firms appeared to be specializing in black and galvanized steel tubes and pipes only. Comprehensive firm-level data for 115 firms belonging to hand, small, and cutting tools industry was collected for 1983/84, both from secondary and primary sources. For the reason of completeness of data only seventy-six firms were used in the econometric exercises. As shown in Table 4.1, the size distribution in the sample ranged from very small to very large firms. Out of the seventy-six firms, data for thirty was collected from secondary sources based on the company balance sheets; the rest of the firms' data, especially for the S&M firms, was based on firm-level field interviews. Majority of small firms in the sample, about thirty-five, were in Delhi, Bangalore (Bengaluru), Madras (Chennai), Ludhiana, Jalandhar, and Patiala.

In the sample of seventy-six firms, ten were indirect exporters. The exports of all seventy-six firms were considered. In the hand, small, and cutting tools industry firms were generally diversified into

Table 4.1 Characteristics of Firm Size Measures of the Sample Data (1 & 2)

	Aggregate Industry Sample 1: 1985/86 (INR Lakhs)	Disaggregated Industry Sample 2: 1983/84 (INR 1000)
1. Total sales		
a. Minimum value	4332	640
b. Maximum value	452961	1592206
c. Coefficient of variance	222	261
d. Standard deviation	11.47	395
2. Total capital employed		
a) Minimum value	919	150
b) Maximum value	965502	1137244
c) Coefficient of variance	328	250
d) Standard deviation	77.6	1251
2. Total capital employed		
a) Minimum value	991	203
b) Maximum value	223996	623580
c) Coefficient of variance	226	242
d) Standard deviation	24.9	565
	N=100	N=76

Source: Computed from data collected during field survey.

producing a wide range of products, but mostly within the broad range of the tools industry. A few of the large firms in the sample were diversified into producing products other than the ones that belong to the industry classification. The cutting tools industry produced sophisticated tools such as carbide-tipped and pneumatic tools. The hand and small tools industry produced low-technology products such as spanners, hand hammers, hacksaw blades, knives, reamers, pliers, vices, axes, shovels, band saws, wrenches, and chisels.

A few of the products in the hand, small, and cutting tools industry, such as hammers, chisels, and spanners were reserved for the small-scale sector. As discussed in Chapter 3, the reservation policies resulted in the violation of the basic assumption of the analysis that a firm was set up to cater to the domestic market first and had the option to sell both in the domestic and foreign markets. If some of the large firms in the industry became highly export-oriented because they were not allowed to expand in the domestic market due to the reservation policies, it would mean the elimination of domestic demand pulls on exports. Second, the small firms in the industry would not face much competition from the large firms.

Measurement of Variables

Firm Size Measures

Some of the quantitative measures of firm size that are generally used are as follows:

Total sales turnover (Lall, 1981).
Labour employed (Page, 1984)
Net assets
Total capital employed
Value-added (production value–raw material value)

Each of these measures have limitations and also represent a facet of firm size which is perhaps multidimensional in nature. The following are some of the limitations of each of the measures. Degree of capacity utilization has implications on the measure based on total sales turnover. In times of lower capacity utilization, sales turnover would underestimate a firm's size. Varying degrees of factor intensities, under given technology of an industry, across firms has implications on the size measures based on labour employed, net assets, and total capital employed. A highly capital-intensive firm could be underestimated by the measure of labour employed and vice versa. Varying levels of working and fixed capital employed by firms, depending on the degree of vertical integration or disintegration, has implications on the size measures of value-added and net assets. A firm which is involved mostly in assembling components employs higher working capital and shows low value-added. In such case, the size measures of value-added and net assets underestimate the size of a firm.

Given the limitation of each of the measures, for reasons of reliability, three alternative measures of firm size were used in the econometric exercises. The measures were total sales, total capital employed, and value-added. In the later exercises, among the three measures alternative measures were used in different equations to avoid the possibilities of statistical biases and variables entering both sides of the equations. In the sample of firms of aggregate level of the engineering industry, the firms at the aggregate classification of the industry were taken in one sample for the estimations at the aggregate level. Although it is questionable to use any firm size measure to compare firms across different industries, the aggregate-level exercises were undertaken mostly to derive consistent generalizations.

Apart from the three measures, firm-level domestic market shares were also taken to capture one of the firm size facets, that is, firm-level domestic market power in relative terms. Generally, an imperfect market structure or concentration of market power are measured at industry level in terms of top few firms' market shares and the Herfindahl index which is expressed thus:

$$\left(a.n+\frac{1}{n}\right)$$

a = variance of distribution of market shares
n = the number of firms in the industry

Theoretically, firm-level market power can be taken in terms of positive deviation of a firm's price from marginal and average costs. This assumes that in a perfectly competitive market structure, firms make normal profits with prices equalling average and marginal costs. This is very difficult to measure empirically, given the limitations in the availability of firm-level data. Therefore, the domestic market shares were taken to be a proxy to capture firm-level market power.

Firm-Level Exports (*E*)

Firm-level exports were taken in FOB values. As discussed in Chapter 3, many small firms undertook exports indirectly through marketing

Table 4.2 Matrix of Correlation Coefficients: Size Measures

	Total sales	Value-added
Aggregate Industry Sample: 1985/86		
Value-added	0.97	
Total capital employed	0.93	0.88
Disaggregate Industry Sample: 1983/84		
Value-added	0.78	
Total capital employed	0.97	0.79

Source: Field survey.

houses and other large firms. The value of indirect exports of those small firms in the sample which undertake indirect exports were considered. Please refer to Table 4.2.

Export Propensity (*E/S*)

As defined in Chapter 3, conceptually, firm-level export propensity was taken in terms of a firm's degree of orientation towards export versus domestic market or, in other words, a firm's propensity to export. This can be measured as follows:

S = total sales turnover of a firm in value terms
E = exports of a firm in value terms
$DS = (S - E)$, domestic sales of a firm
$E = (S - DS)$
$(E/S) = 1 - (DS / S)$

Firm-Level Financial Efficiency: Aggregate Industry Sample

Comparative analysis of production efficiency differences across firms is applicable only to the samples of firms representing an industry operating under uniform technological conditions. In the aggregate industry-level exercises, a simple (and rough) measure of firm-level financial efficiency in terms of extent of costs spent for a unit of value-added realized was utilized. Comparative analysis of firms belonging to different industries within the broad classification of the engineering industry is justifiable to some extent, strictly based on the assumption of profit maximization. This would mean that whatever activity a firm does, it aims at equating marginal costs to marginal revenue and price under the assumption of perfect competition. The measures based on this approach can be applied to multi-product firms under the assumption that a multi-product firm equates marginal costs of producing different products in search of maximizing profits (Klein, 1965). This measure is like the measure of scale economies of Christensen and Greene (1976), which will be discussed in Chapter 5. However, cost inefficiency of firms might be a result of differentiable production inefficiencies, such as technical and allocative efficiencies, which will be discussed in the following chapter.

One of the possible drawbacks of this measure or any other measure which takes value-added as output is that it is influenced by the degree of vertical disintegration (subcontracting) of a firm: a highly vertically disintegrated firm which might be almost like a marketing house and does not do much of its own production and mostly procures output from producers and markets them. Consequently, it shows a large sales turnover. Since none of the firms in the data samples had high levels of vertical disintegration and the samples did not show significant dispersion in the degree of vertical integration, the measure should not cause any significant levels of the above-mentioned drawbacks.

The other drawback of the measure was the assumption of perfectly competitive product and factor markets. If firms are realizing different prices for output and pay differential factor (input) prices, it would reflect in the level of the financial efficiency of firms. This is because value-added can be expressed as follows:

P = price of output
Q = quantity of output
R = raw materials in value terms
r is price of capital; w is wage; and K and L are capital and labour.
Value-added = $PQ - R$

Measures of Inputs

Labour

The labour input in production in terms of measuring labour-intensity of production and estimating production functions is generally taken either in terms of total number of people employed or total wage bill. If the skill component of labour in terms of unskilled, semi-skilled, and skilled is not decomposed, both the measures might not be able to give us a complete picture of the extent of the labour input across firms. This is especially true in the context of large degree of labour market segmentation and diversity in the types of labour employed by firms in different size groups. The drawback was more prominent in the measure of total number of people employed. In skill-intensive production processes, the number of people employed would be lower than in the unskilled labour-intensive production processes. Similarly, in case of wage bill, skilled labour and professional people were paid higher wages than unskilled and family labour. Therefore, in such a case, a high wage bill of a firm could be owing to high skill intensity of the production process. In the following exercises, mostly salaries and wage bill were used as the labour input. As discussed in Chapter 3, small firms generally faced the non-unionized labour markets and employed semi-skilled and unskilled labour at low wages. Due to these reasons, the results that were derived with wages as the labour input had to be treated accordingly.

Capital

The most important element of measurement of capital for estimation of production functions is measuring its rental value (current value), as capital investments involve fixed and sunk cost investments. The measurement requires detailed data on the value of fixed capital, the rate of depreciation, age, and the expected lifespan of the machinery. In most of the studies, generally a straight-line depreciation method is used with an assumed lifespan of the machinery (Page, 1984). Most of these estimates are subject to several limitations because firms in an industry employ machinery of different vintages at different levels of depreciation. Due to data limitations, in the present exercises, total capital employed minus depreciation was used as a measure of capital. Total capital employed refers to total investment made by a firm since its establishment. Depreciation figures reported by firms are generally influenced by tax considerations. In order to check for consistency, total capital employed, inclusive and exclusive of depreciation, was utilized alternatively. Therefore, capital was taken in historical costs. Although this measure of capital might not be accurate, since the exercises were at the cross-section series of firms, the measure should capture the extent of capital employed by firms in relative terms in a given sample. This is justifiable especially in capturing relative capital intensity of firms in the given samples.

Imported Inputs and Technology

Firm-level imports of raw materials, components, and spares consumed (inclusive of import duties) were taken to represent the extent of firm-level imported technology. This measure was taken to be a proxy to the extent of imported technologies of firms under the argument that firms which employed higher import-intensive technologies were more dependent on imported inputs and components.

Firm-Level Diversification

The number of products produced by a firm captures only a facet of firm-level diversification behaviour, that is, firm-level multi-product diversification. This measure does not capture a firm's multi-plant diversification to the full extent. This is because, as argued in Chapter 3, firms could diversify into multi-plants within the same products and large houses diversify into multi-products due to the existing industrial policies.

Notations of the Variables

E = exports
S = total sales turnover

DS = (*S* – *E*), domestic sales
(*E/S*) = export propensity or
= export orientation *(1 – (DS/S)*
Z = firm size
ZS = sales as size measure
ZK = total capital employed as size measure
ZV = value-added as size measure
V = value-added
= production – (raw materials + power and fuel)
D = depreciation
LS = salaries and wages as labour
LN = number of people employed as labour
M = managerial remuneration
TK = total capital employed
K = (*TK* – *D*) and *TK* itself as capital measures
IM = imported raw materials, components, stores, and spares consumed
NP = number of products produced by a firm
DSR = domestic market shares
X = (*LS* + *D* + *M*)/*V*, firm-level financial inefficiency
N = number of firms in the sample
DP = dummy variable for the public sector firms
'*0*', for the public sector and '*1*' for the private sector firms
(*LS/V*) = labour intensity
(*K/V*) = capital intensity
(*IM/S*) = import intensity (imports divided by production)

One of the possible major drawbacks of the econometric exercises with ordinary least squares (OLS) estimations for this type of cross-section exercises, where the samples consisted of very large and small firms, was the presence of heteroscedasticity (variance of residuals). This, in turn, causes the parameters estimated to be inefficient. In the cases of the estimations where heteroscedasticity was found to be strong, proper modification of specification of equations or normalization of variables was done in order to reduce heteroscedasticity.

Specification of Equations 1 and 2

Equations 1 and 2 capture the direct relationship between firm size and exports based on domestic market structure arguments.

Equation 1

$$\text{I.i.}\quad E = a + b_1(z) + b_2(z)^2 + b_3(DP) + i$$

$$b_1 \gtrless 0 \qquad b_2 \gtrless 0 \qquad b_3 > 0$$

In this quadratic specification (non-linear) of the association between firm size and exports, we could expect 'b_1' and 'b_2' to be positive. This implies that as firm size increases there is proportionate increase in exports. This would be true if the initial equilibrium of the theoretical model holds for the Indian industry, that a larger firm expands mainly in the export market in order to protect domestic prices such as in the price-discriminating monopoly case. Second, this result could be expected if the assumption of non-increasing returns to scale in the model does not hold for the Indian industry. If larger firms realize economies of scale significantly, they would export at higher intensity.

The alternative hypothesis was that if profits associated with higher home market shares were proportionately higher than in exports, large firms with relative advantage in home market sales capture major part of the protected home market and would be more inward-oriented than small firms. Small firms which faced relative disadvantage in home market sales and mobility barriers in the home market would be more export-intensive.

The sign of the parameter 'b_3' with reference to the public sector firms' dummy variable could be expected to be negative. Although all firms in the industry had the import substitution bias under the existing policy regime, the import substitution bias in the public sector firms was expected to be stronger. This was because the public investment, based on non-profit motive, was based on fostering import substitution in many other sectors. Owing to this reason, the public sector firms in general were expected to play a less prominent role in exports, although certain specific public sector firms such as Bharat Heavy Electrical Limited and Hindustan Machine Tools Limited did undertake exports to a considerable extent.

$$\text{I.ii} \quad (E/S) = a + b_1(Z) + b_2(DP) + i$$

The underlying theory of this equation is like Equation I.i.

It is necessary to note here that the definition of $\left(\frac{E}{S}\right)$ done before is $\left(\frac{E}{S}\right) = 1 - \left(\frac{DS}{S}\right)$. Therefore, conceptually, it refers to degree of export orientation (or propensity to export). The sign of 'b_1' could be negative if large firms were less export-oriented than small firms and vice versa.

Equation 2

$$\text{II.i} \quad E = a + b_1(DSR) + b_2(DSR)^2 + b_3(X) + b_4(IM/S) + b_5(NP)$$

$$\text{II.ii} \quad \left(\frac{E}{S}\right) = a + b_1(DSR) + b_2(X) + b_3\left(\frac{IM}{S}\right) + b_4(NP)$$

The '*DSR*' variable captures one of the dimensions of firm size variable, that is, market shares dimension. Therefore, the expected signs of the parameters associated with the *DSR* variable would be like the parameters of size variable in the previous equation.

The sign of the parameter associated with (*X*), firm-level relative financial inefficiency, was expected to be negative. Relatively inefficient firms were expected to export at lower intensity. However, this association need not be monotonic, as discussed in the theoretical model of Chapter 3, for the different size group of firms. This aspect would be brought out explicitly in the specification of Equation 3.

The sign of b_4 associated with the imports variable was expected to be positive on the grounds that the external economies in the imported intermediates were expected to reduce costs to firms and consequently increase their export-competitiveness. Alternatively, it could be expected to be negative if the imports increase the home market specific advantage for large firms and helped them to increase home market sales at the cost of exports (Patibandla, 1988a). The consumers in the home market had higher preference for import-intensive products with well-known international brand names. A firm which had higher access to imports would be able to capture higher share of the home market and would be less export-oriented.

This argument could be proved by taking a simple theoretical case of a price-discriminating monopolist facing the protected home market and perfectly competitive world market. In this case, exports in equilibrium were expected:

$$E = (P^*/C) - (a - P^*)/2b$$

P^* is the world price. 'C' is costs, 'a' and 'b' are the intercept and slope of domestic demand curve.

$$C = \mathcal{F}\left(\frac{IM}{S}\right), \quad \mathcal{F}' < 0$$

The implication of firm size in the multi-product variable (*NP*) in capturing multi-product diversification might not be direct. This is because, as discussed in Chapter 3, both large and small firms are involved in multi-product diversification owing to various reasons. By taking the variable on its own, the coefficients, 'b_5' in I.i and 'b_4' in I.i were expected to be negative if the large extent of multi-product diversification reduced economies of specialization in production and exports. On the contrary, it could turn out to be positive if there were economies of scope and marketing, and consequent increase in export possibilities.

Results for Aggregate Industry: Sample 1

Tables 4.3, 4.4, 4.5A, and 4.5B show the results obtained for Equation I.i for the aggregate industry sample with total sales turnover, total capital employed, and value-added as firm size measures respectively. Although the results that were presented for sample 1 were for the year of 1985/86, similar exercises were done for periods of 1982/83

Table 4.3 Equation I.i: Aggregate Industry Sample (1985/86): Total Sales as a Measure of Firm Size

I.i	$\text{Ln E} = a + b_1\,(ZS) + b_2\,(ZS)^2 + B_3\,(DP) + i$						
I.i.a.		a	b_1	b_2	b_3	R^2	F
	E	−383	80.5 (5.09)*	−0.74 (4.6)*	586 (3.3)*	0.23	9.9
I.i.b	Ln E	0.76	0.27 (2.28)*	−0.0024 (−1.98)*	1.75 (1.30)	0.05	1.9

Notes: $N = 100$
I.i critical turning point = INR 2,35,227 lakhs
I.i.b critical turning point = INR 2,43,458 lakhs
The figures in brackets are 't' values:
*Significant at 0.025 level.
Source: Based on econometric equations.

Table 4.4 Equation I.i: Aggregate Industry Sample (1985/86): Total Capital Employed as a Measure of Firm Size

I.i	$\text{Ln E} = a + b_1\,(ZK) + b_2\,(ZK)^2 + b_3\,(DP) + i$						
I.i.a		a	b_1	b_2	b_3	R^2	F
	E	−575	16.74 (4.61)*	−0.021 (4.5)*	864 (4.21)*	0.20	8.28
I.i.b	Ln E	0.72	0.04 (1.55)**	−0.000051 (−1.45)***	2.23 (1.40)	0.03	0.94

Notes: $N = 100$
I.i.a critical turning point = INR 3,64,843 lakhs
I.i.b critical turning point = INR 3,67,600 lakhs
The figures in the brackets are 't' values:
*Significant at 0.025 level.
**Significant at 0.05 level.
***Significant at 0.10 level.
Source: Based on econometric equations.

Table 4.5A Equation I.i: Aggregate Industry Sample (1985/86): Value-added as a Measure of Firm Size

I.i $\text{Ln E} = a + b_1 (ZV) + b_2 (ZV)^2 + b_3 (DP) + i$

I.i.a		a	b_1	b_2	b_3	R^2	F
	E	–230	36.6	–0.135	467	0.20	8.0
			(4.5)*	(4.0)*	(2.6)*		
I.i.b	Ln E	0.96	0.13	–0.00055	1.47	0.07	2.4
			(2.61)*	(–2.26)*	(1.74)**		

Notes: $N = 100$
1.i.a critical turning point = R. 115947 lakhs
1.i.b critical turning point = R. 116938 lakhs
The figures in brackets are 't' values:
*Significant at 0.025 level.
**Significant at 0.05 level.
Source: Based on econometric equations.

Table 4.5B Equation I.ii with ZS and DP as Independent Variables

1.ii $E/S = a + b_1 (ZS) + b_2 (DP) + i$

		a	b_1	b_2	R^2	F
A.	E/S	0.611	–0.0003	0.029	0.04	2.28
			(0.59)	(1.7)**		

$$\frac{(E/S)}{ZS} = a\frac{1}{ZS} + b_1 + b_2(DP) + i$$

		a	b_1	b_2	R^2	F
B.	$\frac{(E/S)}{ZS}$	0.066	–0.01	0.003	0.15	8.16
			(3.6)*	(–3.0)*	(0.26)	

Notes: $N = 100$
The figures in brackets are 't' values:
* Significant at 0.025 level.
** Significant at 0.05 level.
B shows the results for Equation 1.ii, corrected for heteroscedasticity.
Source: Based on econometric equations.

and 1983/84. The results obtained were largely similar for all the periods.

The consistent and statistically significant positive and negative signs of the estimated coefficients of b_1 and b_2 of the quadratic terms with respect to three of the size measures support the alternative hypothesis put forward in the specifications. The results indicate that there was a critical firm size above which absolute exports decline as size increases. The major implication of the respected signs of the parameters was that the proportionate increase in exports declines as firm size increases and becomes negative after the critical size level. As shown in Table 4.5B, the sign of the estimated parameters in the equation with export propensity variable (*E/S*) as the dependent variable (Equation 1.ii) were negative in three of the cases of different firm size measures but they were not statistically significant. If one fits a linear curve to a non-linear relationship, R^2 would turn out to be low. In the present case, if there are different clusters of size groups of firms in explaining exports, R^2 would turn out to be low.

As discussed before, in an exercise of this type, based on the cross-section series, heteroscedasticity is a natural outcome (high standard deviation of the residuals in the estimation) which could result in inefficient estimates (but not biased). Heteroscedasticity of errors was tested by segregating the sample into four groups and testing the significance of the variance of the residuals. The variance of the residuals for the groups were quite different from each other.

In general, the results support the hypothesis that domestic market power could be the major factor in explaining firm-level export behaviour under the assumption that larger the firm size higher was its domestic market power, and higher the domestic market power lower would be the export orientation.

The estimated coefficient of b_3 with respect to the public sector firm's dummy variable is positive and statistically significant at large. The result supported the hypothesis that the public sector firms, established with the primary objective of import substitution, were relatively inward-oriented compared to the private sector.

The results estimated for Equation II for the aggregate industry sample are shown in Tables 4.6A and 4.6B. The results for Equation II.i were statistically significant in most cases. In Equation II.i the

Table 4.6A Equation I.ii with ZK and DP as Independent Variables

I.ii $E/S = a + b_1 (ZK) + b_2 (DP) + i$

		a	b_1	b_2	R^2	F
A.	E/S	0.009	−0.000032	0.03	0.04	2.13
			(0.25)	(1.79)**		

$$\frac{(E/S)}{ZK} = a\frac{1}{ZK} + b_1 + b_2(DP) + i$$

		a	b_1	b_2	R^2	F
B.	$\frac{(E/S)}{ZK}$	0.019	−3.66	0.99	0.10	3.8
		(2.05)*	(2.2)*	(1.3)		

Notes: $N = 100$
The figures in brackets are '*t*' values:
*Significant at 0.025 level.
**Significant at 0.05 level.
Source: Computed from data collected during field survey.

Table 4.6B Equation I.ii with ZV and DP as Independent Variables

I.ii $E/S = a + b_1 (ZV) + b_2 (DP) + i$

		a	b_1	b_2	R^2	F
A.	E/S	0.11	−0.000152	0.29	0.045	2.31
			(0.64)	(1.71)**		

$$\frac{(E/S)}{ZV} = a\frac{1}{ZV} + b_1 + b_2(DP) + i$$

		a	b_1	b_2	R^2	F
B.	$\frac{(E/S)}{ZV}$	0.045	−0.006	0.007	0.13	6.93
		(3.37)*	(−3.6)*	(0.99)		

Notes: $N = 100$
The figures in brackets are '*t*' values:
* Significant at 0.025 level.
** Significant at 0.05 level.
Source: Computed from data collected during field survey.

estimated coefficients for b_1 and b_2 with respect to the domestic market shares variables were similar to the one with the firm size variable in Equation I, estimated and subject to similar interpretations. The parameter estimated for b_3 with respect to firm-level relative inefficiency (X) was of negative sign and statistically significant only in case of the semi-log estimations. The result supported the hypothesis of the necessary condition for undertaking exports. As discussed earlier, the causality between (*X*) and (*E*) could be the other way round if there were significant dynamic economies in exports which could possibly be observed in the following chapter.

The coefficient estimated for b_4 with respect to firm-level imports was negative but not statistically significant. This could be due to multi-collinearity between (*DSR*) and (*IM/S*) in the estimation. As established in Chapter 3, there is systematic positive relation between firm size (here *DSR*) and firm-level imports with large firms which had higher access to imports. Furthermore, there could be two countervailing influences operating in the relationship between (*E*) and (*IM/S*). Institutional factors, such as the import replenishment policies which gave access to imports to firms for undertaking exports, impose a positive relation between exports and imports. On the other hand, increased access to imports, as hypothesized, might increase domestic market power and reduce propensity to export which was, to some extent, confirmed by the negative sign of b_4 estimated despite the positive relation imposed by the import replenishment policies.

The following results show the estimated relationship between domestic sales and imports.

$$\text{Log } DS = 8.9 + 0.079 \log (IM)$$
$$(3.0)^*$$
$$R \text{ squared} = 0.08 \quad F = 9.5$$

$$\text{Log } DS = 9.2 + 0.00007\ (IM)$$
$$(8.3)^*$$
$$R \text{ squared} = 0.41 \quad F = 6.9$$

* Figures in the brackets are '*t*' values; significant at 0.01.

It was obvious from these results that firm-level imports explained domestic sales far more significantly than exports.

Table 4.6B shows the results for Equation II.ii with export propensity as the dependent variable. Owing to heteroscedasticity problems, as before, the results are insignificant. The results of the equation, normalized by the (*DSR*) variable in order to correct for heteroscedasticity, as shown in section B of Table 4.6B, were significant to a large extent. The respective signs of the estimated coefficients supported the earlier mentioned observations that export propensity declines as firm size increases.

Results for Industries at Aggregate and Disaggregate Samples: Sample 2

Tables 4.7A, 4.7B, and 4.8A present the results for aggregate industry sample and also show the results estimated for Equation I with the disaggregate industry sample of hand, small, and cutting tools industry. The size distribution in this sample is more skewed than in sample 1, consisting of very large and small firms (see Table 4.1). The results are quite like the results estimated at the aggregate industry level. In addition, the equation estimated (for I.ii) with export propensity (*E/S*) as the dependent variable, without normalization, was statistically significant (with significant 't' and '*F*' values) with negative signs with respect to firm size variable.

The above-mentioned tests indicate the presence of heteroscedasticity in the estimation. However, as expected, it is not significant as in the case of the aggregate industry sample. As before, in order to reduce heteroscedasticity, the equation was re-estimated by normalizing it on both sides by the explanatory variable.

The results confirmed the negative relation between firm size and revealed export orientation and the interpretations made in the case of the results with the aggregate industry sample. As expected, the results were more robust in the present case of the disaggregate industry sample.

Table 4.7A Equation II.i Aggregate Industry Sample: 1985/86

II.i $E = a + b_1(DSR) + b_2(DSR)^2 + b_3(X) + b_4\frac{(1M)}{s} + i$

		a	b_1	b_2	b_3	b_4	R^2	F	Multiple Correlation Coefficient
II.i.a	E	265	1996	−160348	−73	−511	0.14	3.09	0.37
			(3.7)*	(−3.6)*	(−0.55)	(−0.81)			
II. i.b	Ln E	3.7	115	−542	−1.99	−5.57	0.11	2.34	0.33
			(1.96)*	(−1.75)**	(−2.15)*	(−2.6)			

Notes: N = 100 $R^2 = 0.4$

The figures in brackets are 't' values.

* Significant at 0.025 level.

** Significant at 0.05 level.

Source: Computed from data collected during field survey.

Table 4.7B Equation II.ii with DSR as Firm Size Variable

$$E/S = a + b_1(DSR) + b_2(X) + b_3\frac{(1M)}{s} + i$$

		a	b_1	b_2	b_3	R^2	F	Multiple Correlation Coefficient
A.	(E/S)	0.03	−0.036 (−1.36)	−0.008 (−0.68)	0.032 (0.55)	0.02	0.69	0.16

$$\frac{(E/S)}{DSR} = a + \frac{(1)}{DSR} + b_1 + b_2\frac{(X)}{DSR} + b_3\frac{\left(\frac{1m}{S}\right)}{DSR}$$

		a	b_1	b_2	b_3	R^2	F	Multiple Correlation Coefficient
A.	$\frac{\left(\frac{E}{S}\right)}{DSR}$	0.01 (3.7)*	−16.2 (−3.1)*	−0.029 (0.96)	0.037 (3.8)*	0.40	16	0.62

Notes: N = 100 $R^2 = 0.3$
The figures in brackets are 't' values:
* Statistically Significant at 0.025 level.
Source: Computed from data collected during field survey.

Table 4.8A Equation I.i: Aggregate Industry Sample (1983/84): Total Sales as Measure of Firm Size

I.i Ln E = $a + b_1 (ZS) + b_2 (ZS)^2 + i$

		a	b_1	b_2	R^2	F
I.i.a	E	−157	43.3 (6.19)*	−0.0146 (−4.17)*	0.42	27
I.i.b	Ln E	3.6	0.0096 (2.66)*	−0.000003 (−1.67)***	0.13	5.6

Notes: N = 100 R^2 =0.2
I.i.a critical turning point = INR 9,42,465 thousand
I.i.b critical turning point = INR 9,60,000 thousand
The figures in brackets are 't' values:
* Significant at 0.025 level.
** Significant at 0.05 level.
*** Significant at 0.10 level.
Source: Computed from data collected during field survey.

Table 4.8B Equation I.i Disaggregate Industry Sample (1983/84): Total Capital Employed as Measure of Firm Size

I.i Ln E = $a + b_1 (ZS) + b_2 (ZS)^2 + i$

		$\hat{a}$	$\hat{b}_1$	$\hat{b}_2$	R^2	F
I.i.a	E	−157	43.3 (6.19)*	−0.0146 (−4.17)*	0.42	27
I.i.b	Ln E	3.6	0.0096 (2.66)*	−0.000003 (−1.67)***	0.13	5.6

Notes: N = 76 R^2 =0.18
I.i.a critical turning point = INR 1,05,000 thousand
I.i.b critical turning point = INR 8,07,600 thousand
The figures in brackets are 't' values:
* Significant at 0.025 level.
** Significant at 0.05 level.
*** Significant at 0.10 level.
Source: Computed from data collected during field survey.

Table 4.9 Equation I.i Disaggregate Industry Sample (1983/84): Value-Added as Measure of Firm Size

I.i Ln E = $a \quad b_1 (ZV) + b_2 (ZV)^2 + i$

		a	b_1	b_2	R^2	F
I.i.a	E	−423	33.5 (6.5)*	−0.00968 (−4.95)*	0.41	26.1
I.i.b	Ln E	3.5	0.0072 (2.79)*	−0.0000017 (−1.79)**	0.14	6.2

Notes: N = 76 R^2 -015
I.i.a critical turning point = INR 3,52,375 thousand
I.i.b critical turning point = INR 4,10,561 thousand
The figures in brackets are 't' values:
* Significant at 0.025 level.
** Significant at 0.05 level.
Source: Computed from data collected during field survey.

Tables 4.10 and 4.11 show the results estimated for Equation I.i for the sample of the steel tubes and pipes, and the diesel engines and parts industries. Although the parameters estimated for b_1 and b_2 were of positive and negative signs respectively for the two industries, they were marginally statistically significant in case of the semi-log estimations for the diesel engine industry sample only. In case of the steel tubes and pipes industry, as expected, the results were not significant. This could be because, as discussed in Chapter 3, the export relevance of small firms in the industry was minimal. Small firms in the industry were at a disadvantage in exporting because of the nature of the product, which was bulky and, owing to high costs, involved domestic and overseas transportation costs.

Table 4.12 shows the results estimated for Equation II, for the hand, small, and cutting tools industry sample. In comparison to the aggregate industry sample, this estimation of the equation had

Table 4.10 Equation I.i with ZS as Independent Variable

$E = a + b_1 (ZS) + b_2 (ZS)^2 + b_3 (NP) + i$
ZS = firm level sales (normalized)

	$\hat{a}$	$\hat{b}_1$	$\hat{b}_2$	$\hat{b}_3$	R^2
1. E_T	48.9	0.55 (1.88)*	–0.0002 (0.66)	–12.4 –(1.15)	0.25
2. E_D	210.4	1.11 (2.02)*	–0.000039 –(0.54)	–32.4 –(0.86)	0.84

Notes: * Statistically significant at 0.05 level.
1. Steel tubes and pipes industry
N = 32 R^2 = 0.08
   a) Minimum value of Z in the sample = INR 15 lakh
   b) Maximum value of Z in the sample = INR 171.73 lakh
   c) Critical turning point of the quadratic curve estimated = INR 205.25 lakh
2. Diesel engines and parts industry
   a) Minimum value of Z in the sample = INR 10.6 lakh
   b) Maximum value of Z in the sample = INR 792.79 lakh
   c) Critical turning point of the quadratic curve estimated = INR 1,37,500 lakh

Table 4.11 Equation I.i with ZK as Independent Variable

$E = a + b_1 (ZK) + b_2 (ZK)^2 + b_3 (NP) + i$
ZK = firm level capital employed (normalized)

		$\hat{a}$	$\hat{b}_1$	$\hat{b}_2$	$\hat{b}_3$	R^2
1.	E_T	27.6	0.50	–0.00025	–7.48	0.23
		(2.13)*	(1.40)	–(0.75)		
2.	E_D	285.5	0.78	–0.000098	–37.2	0.82
		(1.37)	–(0.84)	–(0.94)		

Notes: * Statistically significant at 0.025 level.
1. Steel tubes and pipes industry
N = 32 firms

a) Minimum value of Z in the sample = INR 3.56 lakh
b) Maximum value of Z in the sample = INR 54.26 lakh
c) Critical turning point of the quadratic curve estimated = INR 3,616 lakh

1. Diesel engines and parts industry
N = 20 Firms.

a) Minimum value of Z in the sample = INR 5.25 lakh
b) Maximum value of Z in the sample = INR 254,76 lakh
c) Critical turning point of the quadratic curve estimated = INR 208,92 lakh

an additional independent variable of number of products (*NP*). The results were quite like the results obtained for the aggregate industry sample but were more statistically significant. In addition, the estimated Equation II.ii, where export-propensity was used as the dependent variable, was statistically significant with significant *F* values and even higher R^2. The higher statistical significance at the disaggregate industry sample shows that heteroscedasticity would tend to be more at the aggregate industry sample where firms belonging to different engineering industries were included in one sample. In such a case, obviously, the external (or residual) effects on the firm's exports would be more random.

The estimated coefficient of the import intensity variable (*IM/S*) was of negative sign and statistically significant. This result supported

Table 4.12 Equation II.i with DSR as Independent Variable

II.i	Ln E =	a	b_1 (DSR)	+ b_2 $(DSR)^2$	+B3()	B4 (x)	+ b_5 (IM/S)	+	+ i	
		a	b_1	b_2	b_3	b_4	b_5	R^2	F	Multiple correlation coefficient
II.i.a	E	2334	5917 (5.8)*	–210 –(4.3)*	–2433 –(0.5)	–3105 – (0.25)	–696 (–1.48)***	0.43	10.6	0.65
II.i.b	Ln E	4.01	0.91 (1.81)**	–0.041 (1.8)**	–1.06 (0.44)	–15 –(2.4)*	–3.25 –(1.09)	0.20	3.66	0.45
II.ii	(E/S) =	a +	b_1 (DSR)	+ b_2(X)	+	b_3 (IM/S)	b_4 (N,P)	+	i	
		a	b_1	b_2		b_3	b_4	R^2	F	Multiple correlation coefficient
	(E/S)	0.37	–0.014 –(1.90)**	–0.22 –(1.84)**		–0.86 –(20.8)*	–0.002 –(0.25)	0.25	5.9	0.36

Notes: The figures in brackets are 't' values

N = 76

* Significant at 0.025 level.

** Significant at 0.05 level.

*** Significant at 0.10 level.

Source: Computed from data collected during field survey.

the argument that under the given domestic market characteristics, firm-level imports and exports could be negatively associated. But this could not be generalized as there was no consistency in the sign of the parameter estimated at the aggregate and disaggregate industry-level estimations.

The estimated coefficient for variable (*NP*) which was taken to capture firm-level multi-product diversification was of negative sign and statistically significant at large. If we go back to Tables 4.11 and 4.12, a similar result occurred with respect to the variable (*NP*) in case of steel tubes and pipes, and diesel engines and parts industries. This result supported the hypothesis that firm-level multi-product diversification would result in the loss of economies of specialization in exports and, in turn, lower exports.

The results obtained for Equations I and II were consistent both at the aggregate and disaggregate industry level. This allowed derivation of some generalizations regarding the primary relationship between firm size and export behaviour. From the result, the major generalizable conclusion is that it was the market structure conditions of the industry which determined the revealed exports of the firms. In a long-tailed market structure of an industry, large and small firms within the industry faced differential market structure competitive pressures. Large firms derived higher domestic market power or home market advantages in sales. Consequently, larger firms, in the absence of scale economies, would be less export-oriented.

Specification of Equation

This equation brings out the possible non-monotonic association between firm-level efficiency and exports through the firm size dimension and introduces the other supply-side determinants of exports that operate through the size variable. To capture the non-monotonic relationships, the equation used 'interactive variables' between firm size and variable, such as relative factor intensities and efficiency.

$$E,\left(\frac{E}{S}\right)=a+b_1(ZS)+b_2(X)+b_3(ZS)(X)+b_4\left(\frac{LS}{V}\right)+b_5(ZS)\left(\frac{LS}{V}\right)$$
$$+b_6\left(\frac{K}{V}\right)+b_7(ZS)\left(\frac{K}{V}\right)+b_8(DP)+i$$

III.1. $$\left[\frac{dE}{d(ZS)}\right]=b_1+b_3(X)+b_5\left(\frac{LS}{V}\right)+b_7\left(\frac{K}{V}\right)$$

III.2. $$\left(\frac{dE}{dX}\right)=b_2+b_3(ZS)$$

III.3. $$\left[\frac{dE}{d\left(\frac{LS}{V}\right)}\right]=b_4+b_5(ZS)$$

III.4. $$\left[\frac{dE}{d\left(\frac{K}{V}\right)}\right]=b_6+b_7(ZS)$$

As briefly discussed in case of Equation II, firm size dimension could cause non-monotonicity in the effect of the various variables on firm-level exports. Equation III captures the possibility of non-linearity in the causality specified. There might be critical turning points in the firm size variable where the effect of the variables, such as firm-level relative efficiency, labour and capital intensity on firm-level exports, and export propensity, changes.

In Equation III.2. If b_2 and b_3 are negative, it implies reduction in inefficiency after a critical point in size and results in proportionately higher exports. This result was expected based on possible scale economies and certain technological advantages of larger firm size in exports. On the other hand, the most likely outcome could be that $b_2 < 0$ *and* $b_3 > 0$ (*or* $b_2 > 0$ *and* $b_3 > 0$). This would mean that after the critically large firm size, the relatively inefficient firms were the ones that were more export-oriented. After the critical point, at a given large size, a relatively inefficient firm would be more export-oriented than a relatively efficient firm of the same size. As a result, the relatively inefficient large firm might be pushed to export markets. This result could be an outcome of the oligopolistic rivalry of large firms in the domestic markets. The possibility of this result could also be observed from the signs of the parameters of b_1 and b_3 in Equation III.1.

In Equation III.3, b_4 and b_5 could be expected to be positive based on the argument that firms of any size that adopt labour-intensive techniques could reap the country's comparative advantage and would be able to export. On the other hand, it could be expected that b_4 is positive and b_5 is negative on the basis of the argument that after a critically large firm size, increase in labour intensity need not result in higher exports if the demand-side factors such as domestic monopoly power neutralizes the supply-side advantage. After the critical size, increase in labour intensity might be counterproductive to exports. This was because increase in labour intensity at very large firm size could result in a large degree of X-inefficiency in labour management and utilization, and consequent decline in overall efficiency and exports. This was necessary to derive consistency in the argument put forward regarding the possible positive relationship between relative inefficiency and exports after the critical turning points in Equations III.2 and III.3, which could be different depending on the effect of (*LS/V*) and (*K/V*) on (*X*).

The signs of the coefficients b_6 and b_7 could be expected to be negative based on the argument that capital-intensive techniques result in the deviation of production processes from the country's comparative advantage. Increase in capital intensity at any firm size should cause decline in a firm's ability to reap the country-specific comparative advantage. But on the other hand, b_6 could be positive and b_7 negative on the basis of the argument that certain level of capital intensity was necessary for a firm to be able to export. This implied that a threshold size of technological sophistication was necessary to produce the exportable products on a vertical product differentiation plane.

The results for Equation III for the aggregate industry sample (1985/86) are as follows:

$$\text{III.a}\quad \text{E} = -194 - \underset{(2.0)^*}{2.9(ZS)} - \underset{(1.9)^*}{1830(X)} + \underset{(1.79)^*}{893\left(\frac{LS}{V}\right)} - (0.067) - \underset{(2.0)^*}{(1.03)(0.5)}$$

$$+\underset{(2.06)^*}{159\left(\frac{K}{V}\right)} + \underset{(0.21)}{106(ZS)(X)} + \underset{(0.8)}{149(ZS)\left(\frac{LS}{V}\right)}$$

$$-23(ZS)(K/V)+652(DP)$$

$$-(2.3)^{*} \quad (1.47)^{***}$$

$$R^2 = 0.26F = 4.09$$

Multiple correlation coefficient = 0.51

$$\text{III.b} \quad (E/S) = 0.028 - 0.0057(ZS) - 0.516(X)$$

$$(1.4) \qquad (3.02)^{*}$$

The results for Equation III for the aggregate industry sample (for 1985/86) are as follows:

$$\text{III.a} \quad \text{E} = -194 - 2.9(ZS) - 1830(X) + 893(LS/V)$$

$$-(0.067) - (1.03) \qquad (0.5)$$

$$+159(K/V) + 106(ZS)(X) + 149(ZS)(LS/V)$$

$$(2.06)^{*} \qquad (0.21) \qquad (0.8)$$

$$-23(ZS)^{*}(K/V) + 652(DP)$$

$$-(2.3)^{*} \qquad (1.47)^{***}$$

$$R\,squared = 0.26 \quad F = 4.09$$

$$Multiple\ correlation\ coefficient = 0.51$$

$$\text{III.b} \quad (E/S) = 0.028 - 0.0057(ZS) + 0.516(X)$$

$$(1.4) \qquad (3.07)^{*}$$

The turning point of the curve = (5.84 ∗ 4332)

(*ZS*)*k** = INR 25,335 lakh.

The statistical significance of the coefficients whose values were significantly different from zero of the interactive terms reconfirmed the non-monotonicity (non-linearity) hypothesis regarding the relationship between firm size and exports. The critical turning points of the relationships estimated with respect to (*X*), (*LS/V*), and (*K/V*) were at a close range (5.27, 5.46, and 5.84). It is important to keep in mind here that the sample consisted of only large and medium firms: the size distribution ranging from a minimum of INR 43 crore to a maximum of INR 4,529 crore. But it was interesting to take into notice that $(ZS)1^* < (ZS)K^*$, which will be discussed later.

The result of Equation III.b.2 could be interpreted thus: until the firm size of INR 228 crore sales turnover, increase (or decrease) in firm-level inefficiency results in lower (or higher) export propensity. The estimated relationship between (*ZS*) and (X) in the same sample is as follows:

$$\log X = -0.37 - 0.10 \log(ZS) + 0.63(DP)$$
$$\qquad\qquad (1.47)^{***} \qquad\qquad (3.47)^{*}$$

R squared = 0.14, *F* = 7.9, *N* = 100.
Figures in brackets are 't' values.
*Significant at 0.025 level. ***Significant at 0.10 level.

After the critical firm size of INR 228 crores sales turnover, increase (or decrease) in firm-level inefficiency results in higher (lower) export propensity. In other words, after the critical size, among the large firms, the firms which were more inefficient were more export-oriented than the relatively more efficient ones at a given size.

This result could be explained by the argument regarding the possibility of the outcome in the export behaviour of large firms as a result of their oligopolistic behaviour in the domestic market. As discussed in Chapter 3 and in this chapter, the relatively efficient large firms could be market leaders in the domestic market and would be able to impose the domestic market shares on the relatively inefficient large firms. The relatively inefficient large firms, which had to accept their domestic market shares determined by the leader firms, might be pushed to undertake exports. This possibility might arise because at the imposed domestic market shares, the relatively inefficient large firms might end up with higher excess capacity. The excess capacity, in turn, might allow these firms to undertake exports at prices just covering variable costs. The export activity, in turn, might enable these relatively inefficient large firms to compete in the domestic market (at a later stage) by facilitating fuller capacity utilization and resultant lower average costs, and by giving more access to imports. However, this was a possible dynamic outcome of export activity, which will be observed in the following chapter.

The result of Equation III.b.3 for the labour-intensity variable, implied after the critical size of INR 23,681 lakh sales turnover, shows that increase in firm-level relative labour intensity among the firms within the size group would result in lower export propensity. This result supported the argument that at a very large firm size, relatively higher labour intensity did not necessarily lead to higher exports. Relative higher firm-level labour intensity did not necessarily mean higher firm-level comparative (advantage) efficiency in exports. What matters might be the type of labour that was chosen and the extent to which it was utilized in determining a firm's ability to reap the country's comparative advantage. Second, the supply-side factors which determined relative advantages in exports were less significant at very large firm size group in determining their relative export orientation. At this size group, it would be the relative domestic market power which was the principal determinant of revealed exports. Apart from this, as discussed in Chapter 3, large firms might be highly X-inefficient in management of labour and consequently it could result in lower ability to realize the relative advantage in relatively higher labour intensity.

The result of Equation III.b.4 was like the previous result. But the noticeable aspect of the result was the critical turning point in firm size. *(ZS)K** was the highest of all at INR 253 crore sales turnover. Until the firm size of INR 253 crore, increase in capital intensity was contributing positively to export propensity, and negatively after the critical point. The noticeable aspect of the results was that *(ZS) k** > *(ZS)1** was counterintuitive. In this sample (consisting of only medium and large firms), relative capital intensity was contributing positively to export propensity than a larger firm size in the case of the relative labour-intensive variable. This result can be explained by two possible reasons: (*i*) there might be scale advantages in relative capital-intensive operations or (*ii*) the capital-intensive factor could be causing exports due to excess capacity possibilities. As discussed in

Chapter 3, higher the capital intensity higher would be the possibilities of excess capacity owing to domestic demand fluctuations. Excess capacity in the large firms could be a result of domestic oligopoly rivalry also. Consequently, higher the excess capacity among the large firms higher their need to export (possibly at variable cost pricing) to achieve fuller capacity utilization. On the other hand, the result is counter to India's comparative advantage in labour intensity but not capital intensity.

Disaggregate Industry Sample of 1983/84

Unlike the case of the aggregate industry sample, the disaggregate industry sample for hand, small, and cutting tools industry consisted of very large and small firms (see Table 4.2), which had significant implications on the critical turning points.

Second, to recapitulate, the aggregate industry sample consisted of firms belonging to a wide variety of engineering industries and, as a result, the heterogeneity in the type of labour and capital employed and the technological conditions across firms would be very high. In the present case of the disaggregate industry sample, the degree of heterogeneity is a lot lower, which gave higher reliability to the interpretations of the results. Apart from this, in the present case, the variable (*X*) and the variables (*LS/V*) and (*K/V*) could be expected to be highly correlated.

Although the efficiency aspects at the disaggregate industry level will be empirically examined more rigorously later in this book, the results with the variable (*X*) in the present case should help us to observe the reliability of the results from the aggregate industry sample. As expected, in the estimation of Equation III for the present sample, the variable (*X*) caused multi-collinearity. In order to avoid the multi-collinearity problem, the result with (*X*) was estimated separately.

$$\text{III.b}\quad (E/S) = 0.38 - 0.0083(ZS) - 0.359(X)$$

$$-(1.98)^{*} - (2.0)^{*}$$

$$+0.0014(ZS)(X)$$

$$(1.61)^{***}$$

$R\ squared = 0.17 F = 5 N = 76$

The figures in the brackets are 't' values.

*Significant at 0.025 level.

***Significant at 0.05 level.

$$D(E/S)/d(X) = -0.359 + 0.0014(ZS)$$

The critical turning point, $(ZS)x^{*}$ = INR 1,641 lakhs.

The signs of the parameters were like the results obtained for the aggregate industry sample. As expected, the turning point of *(ZS)x** is far lower than the previous case. This result indicated that until the firm size of INR 16.4 crores sales turnover, firms which were relatively more efficient were able to export at higher propensity. After the critical size, it was the relatively inefficient firms which were more export-intensive. This result reconfirmed the argument regarding the implications of domestic market structure on the export behaviour of different size groups. The firms below the critical size faced highly competitive conditions in the domestic market. As discussed in Chapter 3, the S&M firms within the size group which adapted to the domestic conditions by being efficient producers tended to branch out into the export markets for their survival and growth. On the other hand, above the critical size, the firms within the size group which were relatively more efficient could achieve higher domestic market power. Consequently, their propensity to export would decline. As observed earlier, the relatively inefficient producers within the size group would be pushed to export markets by the domestic market leaders.

III.a $E = 1190 + 26.5(ZS) + 3169(LS/V) - 830(K/V)$

$$(4.0)^{*}(0.64) - (1.46)^{***}$$

$$-147(ZS)\ (LS/V) + 27(ZS)\ K/V)$$

$$-(9.7)^{*} \qquad (11.6)^{*}$$

$R\ squared = 0.80\ F = 58$

Multiple correlation coefficient = 0.8

$$\text{III.b} \quad (E/S) = 0.34 - 0.0005(ZS) - 0.606(LS/V)$$
$$-(1.83)^{**} - (2.76)^{*}$$
$$+ 0.016(K/V)$$
$$(0.65)$$
$$+ 0.0001\,(ZS)\,(LS/V) + 0.000005\,(ZS)\,(K/V)$$
$$(1.55)^{***} \qquad (0.056)$$

$R\ squared = 0.18 \quad F = 32 N = 76$

Multiple correlation coefficient = 0.43

The figures in the brackets are 't' values.

* Statistically significant at 0.025 level.

** Significant at 0.05 level.

*** Significant at 0.10 level.

In the preceding results, the estimated parameters associated with capital intensity variable were statistically significant only in Equation III.a, where the absolute exports were the dependent variable. In contrast, the estimated parameters associated with labour intensity variable were significant only in Equation III.b, where export propensity was the dependent variable. This could be because given the size distribution in this sample, which consisted of both very small and large firms, the specification of the equation was incomplete. There might be a certain threshold size that firms had to reach in order to export. Very small firms, which operated unsophisticated technology might not be able to produce the exportable products (vertically differentiated products within an industry). This would mean two critical turning points in the specification. In order to test this argument, the equation was re-specified to capture the possible turning points. Before going into the results of the re-specified equation the following analysis gives a brief interpretation of the statistically significant part of the results presented earlier.

$$\text{III.a.4.d} \quad (E)/d(K/V) = -803 + 27(ZS)$$

$$\text{The turning point } (ZS)k^{*} = (307 * 640)$$
$$= \text{INR } 196.7 \text{ lakh}$$

$$\text{III.b.3.d} \quad (E/S/d(LS/V) = -0.606 + 0.001(ZS)$$

$$\text{The turning point } (ZS)1^{*} = (606 * 640)$$
$$= \text{INR } 3{,}878 \text{ lakh}$$

The signs of the estimated parameters in the above results were opposite to those obtained in case of the aggregate industry sample. This could be, as argued earlier, because of the significant difference in the firm size distributions in the two samples.

The results indicated that the capital intensity factor was contributing negatively to absolute exports until the critical size of INR 2 crore sales turnover. After the critical firm size, it was positively associated with exports. The positive association could be explained in a straightforward manner. Because the dependent variable was absolute exports, capital intensity was operating as the scale effect. Obviously, the absolute exports of larger firms would be more than smaller firms.

The labour intensity variable was negatively associated with export propensity until the critical size of INR 38 crore and positively above the critical size. The explanation for the result could be derived from the way labour intensity was measured. As discussed earlier in this chapter, labour was taken in terms of salaries and wages paid rather than number of people employed. The salaries and wages measure put the composition of skilled and unskilled labour into a single basket. Skilled labour and professional employees are generally paid higher wages than unskilled labour and family members employed (in relation to intensity of man-hours put). As a result, higher wages and salaries billed would imply either higher content of skilled labour or larger number of unskilled labour. Based on the argument, the result could be interpreted as that among the S&M firms below the critical size, the comparative (advantage) efficiency in exports across firms might be in unskilled labour intensity or, in other words, the relative advantage was with respect to labour paid at lower wage rate.

After the critical size, the relative advantage among the firms in the size group could be in skilled labour intensity.

But in case of the results with the aggregate industry sample, it was argued that at a very large firm size there would be negative economies in labour intensity owing to organizational complexity, which was not shown by this result. This might be captured in the estimation of the re-specified equation, the results for which are as follows.

$$\text{III.b}\quad (E/S) = 0.33 + 0.00016(ZS) - 0.616\,(LS/V)$$

$$(0.34) - (2.67)^{*}$$

$$+0.034(K/V) + 0.0031(ZS)(LS/V)$$

$$(1.32) \qquad\qquad (1.6)^{***}$$

$$-0.00122(ZS)(K/V)$$

$$-(2.15)^{*}$$

$$-0.0000032(ZS)^{**}2(LS/V)$$

$$-(2.08)^{*}$$

$$+0.00000096(ZS)^{**}2(K/V)$$

$$(2.2)^{*}$$

R squared = 0.24 F = 3.08 N = 76

Multiple correlation coefficient = 0.49

The figures in brackets are 't' values.

*Statistically significant at 0.025 level.

**Significant at 0.05 level.

***Significant at 0.10 level.

The results of the preceding equation were statistically far more significant than the previous results with higher F and T values and R squared. This equation was estimated with absolute exports also as the dependent variable. Since it was statistically less significant it was not presented.

The statistical significance and the respective signs of the estimated parameters supported the argument regarding the possible two turning points in the non-monotonic relationships. The partial derivatives with respect to the variables and the critical turning points are as follows:

$$\text{III.b.3.d} \quad (E/S)/d(LS/V) = -613 + 0.003(ZS) - 0.0000032(ZS)^{**}2$$

The turning point at the minimum.

$$Min(ZS)1^{*} = (483 * 640) = \text{INR } 3{,}091 \text{ lakh}$$

The turning point at the maximum.

$$Max(ZS)1^{*} = (487 * 640) = \text{INR } 3{,}118 \text{ lakhs}$$

$$\text{III.b.4.d} \quad (E/S)/d(K/V) = 0.034 - 0.0012(ZS) + 0.00000096(ZS)^{**}2$$

The turning point at the minimum.

$$Min(ZS)k^{*} = (12.4 * 640) = \text{INR } 79.5 \text{ lakh}$$

The turning point at the maximum.

$$Max(ZS)k^{*} = (1264 * 640) = \text{INR } 7{,}958 \text{ lakh}$$

The signs of the parameters and the critical turning points of the curves estimated were subject to very interesting implications. From Equation III.b.3 it can be seen that increase in labour intensity until the firm size of INR 3,091 lakh sales turnover resulted in lower export propensity. Between the firm sizes range of INR 3,091 lakh and INR 3,110 lakh, increase in labour intensity was positively associated with export propensity. And after the critical size, it was again negatively associated with export propensity. The results implied that comparative (advantage) efficiency in labour intensity appears to be most effectively utilized at the firm size of INR 31 crore sales turnover. Second, the explanation for the negative association below the firm size of INR 30.9 crore sales turnover could be derived, as before, from the way the labour was measured. The firms below the critical size may have had comparative (advantage) efficiency in employing labour at lower wages and skills. Furthermore, within this size group those firms which were able to realize more value-added for a rupee spent on labour input were able to export at higher propensity than the others. As argued in Chapter 3, small firms which were run by owner-managers and family members tended to put intensive effort and tended to be highly X-efficient. As a result, these firms realized higher output for given levels of inputs and would be able to produce exportable products in a cost-efficient manner. As far as the negative association after the critical size of INR 31 crore was concerned the explanation of X-inefficiency in the utilization of labour at larger firm size might be more valid than the unskilled and low-cost labour argument put forward in case of the small firms. This was because larger firms were generally run by professional managers and employed organized and skilled labour at higher wages.

In case of Equation III.b.4, results indicated that until the firm size of INR 79.5 lakh, increase in capital intensity was positively associated with export propensity. This result supported the technological threshold size argument in relating firm size and exports. Capital intensity variable captures the technological level of a firm and the size dimension. The firms within the size group below the critical size of INR 79 lakh which operated with lower capital intensity tended to operate with outdated and crude technology and as a result might not be able to produce exportable products.

Between the firm size range of INR 79.5 lakh and INR 7.985 lakh export propensity and capital intensity were negatively associated. In this size range, comparative advantage in lower capital-intensive production processes was in operation. These results suggested that after reaching the technological threshold size, firms which operated with lower capital-intensive techniques were able to export more effectively. Above the critical size of INR 7,985 lakhs, increase in capital intensity, within the size group, was contributing positively to exports. This could be because the firms within the group which were more capital-intensive might have certain technological advantages in exports. On the other hand, as argued in case of the results of Equation II and with respect to (X) in Equation III, the larger firms which were more capital-intensive might be more prone to excess capacities due to domestic oligopoly rivalries and also domestic demand fluctuations. Consequently, these firms would tend to branch out into exports.

The notable outcome of these results was that there was a technological threshold size which firms had to reach to be able to produce exports and to be effective exporters. Second, under the existing conditions there appeared to be a size range where the domestic comparative advantage in relative factor endowments was effectively reaped. But one of the puzzling aspects of the results was that between the firm size range of INR 79 lakh and INR 3,091 lakh sales turnover, increase in both capital and labour intensity was negatively associated with export propensity. One possible explanation for this could be that the efficiency factor in the size group might be the most predominant determinant of exports. In other words, those firms within the size group, which derived maximum output at lowest possible expenditure on the inputs, capital and labour, could be the most effective exporters compared to other firms belonging to all size groups. The efficiency aspect will be examined explicitly in the next chapter.

Possible Generalizations

The results for Equations II and III were consistently similar, both at the aggregate and the disaggregate industries levels. The generalizable observation was that exports declined proportionately as firm size increased and after a critical large firm size, the relationship was negative. But the results of Equation III showed that this relationship operated only after a critical technological minimum threshold size was reached by firms. Although the concept of the critical minimum size was generalizable, the critical size observed in the results was not. This was because the critical size was established with the sample of firms belonging to a specific light engineering industry. The basic explanatory factor for the non-monatomic relationship between firm size and exports was derived from the domestic market structure argument.

Scale Economies, Firm Size, and Exports: The Empirical Analysis

This section tests for the significance of scale economies in explaining exports explicitly. The firm-level data that was used was based on the CEI's annual publication of data for top 100 engineering firms.

Table 4.13 Characterization of Firm Size Measures; Sample 3: Time Series Data of the Aggregate Industry (INR Lakh)

	1978/79	1983/84
1. Total sales		
a. Minimum value	1,180	3,300
b. Maximum value	67,100	1,34,000
c. Coefficient of variance	140	133
d. Standard deviation	8.46	6.3
2. Total capital employed		
a. Minimum value	220	420
b. Maximum value	54,800	99,600
c. Coefficient of variance	180	149
d. Standard deviation	39.4	38.9
3. Value-added		
a. Minimum value	326	931
b. Maximum value	28,921	55,027
c. Coefficient of variance	138	195
d. Standard deviation	15.4	16.2

Notes: N = 71

* (c) and (d) are the parameters of the normalized measures.

Source: Confederation of Indian Industries.

From this source, time series data for the six-year period of 1978/79 to 1983/84 was collected for a cross section of seventy-one firms. The basic features of this data are shown in Table 4.13.

Measurement of Variables

Firm-level scale economies index is measured based on Christensen and Greene (1976).

$SE = [1 - 8 \; log \; C / 8 \; log \; V]$

$8 \; log \; C$ = change in costs in natural logs

$8 \; log \; V$ = change in value added in natural logs

$SE > 0$ = presence of positive scale economies

$SE < 0$ = diseconomies of scale

Costs (C) = salaries and wages + capital costs at the present value
Capital cost at present value = *TK X Dr X R*
TK = total capital employed
Dr = depreciation rate
R = bank lending rate of interest

Change in costs and value-added for each firm are taken between the years of 1981/82 and 1983/84.

ZKz = firm size variable based on total capital employed for the base period of 1981/82
ZK4 = firm size variable for 1983/84
CVL = cumulative value-added for six years from 1978/79 to 1983/84. This variable is taken to capture dynamic economies of learning by doing
CIM = cumulative imports of raw materials, components and intermediates from 1981/82 to 1983/84. This variable is taken to capture external economies in imports of intermediates
(IM)-1 = firm-level imports of intermediates in the year 1982/83. In explaining exports, firm-level imports variable is taken with one-year (backward) time log
E = firm-level exports in the year 1983/84
DP = dummy variable for public and private sector firms as defined before

The average value of SE index for the sample is 0.057 with a standard deviation of 5.97 and variance of 35.7. The maximum value of the index is 16.2 and the minimum value is −17.4.

The following equation was estimated to observe the explanation of *SE* by variables of firm size (*ZKz*), cumulative value-added (*CVL*), and cumulative imports (CIM). All the variables were taken in natural logs. Therefore, the estimated coefficients provide elasticities.

$$\text{IV.1} \quad SE = 23.5 + 0.66 \log(ZKz) - 2.5 \ \log(CVL)$$
$$(3.0) \quad (0.65) \qquad\qquad (-2.68)$$

$$+0.11 \log CIM - 1.01(DP)$$
$$(0.52) \qquad\qquad (-0.43)$$

$R\ squared = 0.14 \quad F = 2.45 \quad N = 71$

Figures in the brackets are 't' values:

*Significant at 0.01 level.

The estimated coefficient associated with firm size variable was statistically insignificant and its value of elasticity was less than one. Larger size of firm did not appear to lead to higher level of scale economies. The other startling result was that estimated coefficient associated with the cumulative value-added variable was statistically significant and of negative sign. The negative sign of the coefficient implied there might have been no dynamic economies but rather negative dynamic economies in the Indian industry in cumulative growth. In order to double check this result, cumulative production variable was used instead of *CVL*, but the results were the same. This result could be interpreted on the basis of the Kaldor–Verdoorn law that if the overall industrial sector and effective demand in the system did not grow at a sustained rate, it would not provide much scope for the learning economies.

The estimated coefficient associated with cumulative imports variable was statistically insignificant and its value was far less than one. There was no proof that higher access to imported inputs leads to lower costs.

The following Equation IV.2 tests for the explanation of firm-level exports by firm-level relative scale economies, firm size (ZK4), and firm-level imports variable (with a time lag).

$$\text{IV.2} \quad \log E = 1.57 - 0.11(SE) + 0.53 \log(ZK4)$$
$$(1.08) \quad (-2.2)^{*} \qquad (1.56)^{**}$$
$$+0.10 \log(IM)t - 1 + 1.12(DP)$$
$$(1.31) \qquad\qquad (1.28)$$

$R\ squared = 0.18 \quad F = 3.4 \quad N = 71$

Figures in brackets are 't' values:

*Significant at 0.01 level

**Significant at 0.10 level

In these results, the estimated coefficients associated with the explanatory variables of scale economies and firm size were statistically significant. The negative sign of estimated coefficient of *SE* implied that firms with relatively lower costs exported at lower intensity. This sample of firms consisted mostly of large firms. Within the size group of large firms, as heuristically argued in Chapter 3, relatively efficient firms were able to be more aggressive in the home market and capture higher home market share and were relatively less export-oriented. The estimated coefficient (the elasticity) associated with firm size variable was less than one which implies proportionate increase in exports declined as firm size increased. This result provided further support to the results of Equations I and II. As before, the estimated coefficient associated with the import's variable was statistically insignificant. There was no significant association between firm-level exports and imports.

5 Empirical Analysis of Technical and Allocative Efficiency of Firms and International Trade Behaviour

As argued in Chapter 3, the firm-level efficiency differentials were not only in terms of firm-level utilization of inputs but also in terms of adopting the optimal choice of techniques in accordance with the domestic factor endowments and technological conditions. The present chapter explicitly brought forth the firm-level technical and allocative efficiency variables to empirically examine their effect on firm-level exports.

The exercises with regard to technical efficiency (total factor productivity) tested for insights of the 'New' New Trade Theory (Melitz, 2003) by accounting for heterogeneity in technology and managerial efficiency across firms within specific industries and their implications on productivity and consequent international trade behaviour. The exercises with respect to firm-level allocative efficiency (AE) captures firm-level ability to utilize India's comparative advantage in exports, given the factor market imperfections discussed before.

Measurement of Technical and Allocative Efficiency: The Methodology

The firm-level relative efficiency measures were derived following Farrell's (1957) production frontier approach. Farrell's original approach in measuring technical efficiency (TE) was a non-parametric one where a technology envelope or frontier was derived from observed (scattered) technical coefficients of capital and labour ratios for given output levels.

As shown in Figure 5.1, the scattered observations cause the *K* and *L* combinations employed by different firms to produce a unit of output under the existing technology of an industry. Observations below the isoquant are not technologically feasible. The observations

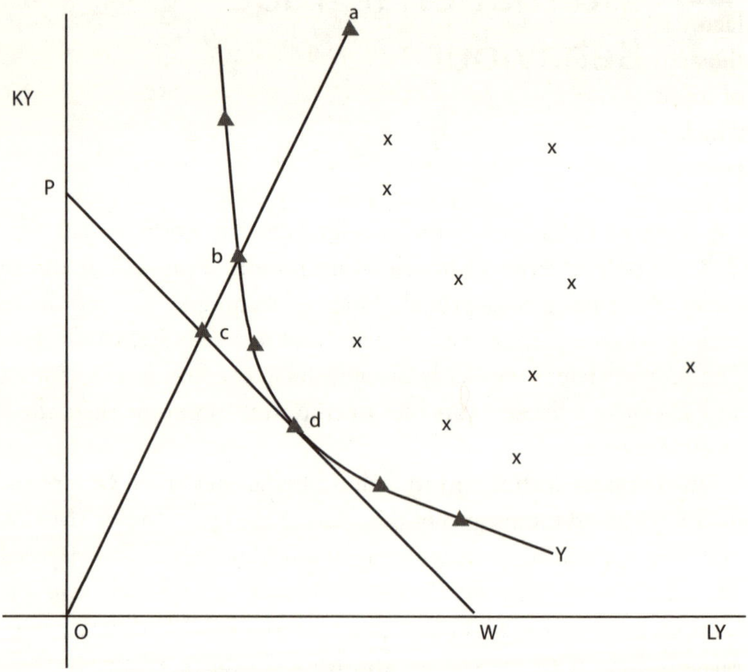

Figure 5.1 Allocative and Technical Efficiency

Notes: K = Capital employed
L = Labour employed
W = Wage rate
P = Price of capital
Y = Output

$ob / oa = TE$

$oc / ob = AE$

Source: Author's representation.

above the frontier indicate the presence of technical inefficiency. By taking the derived isoquant, one could derive firm-level AE under the constraint imposed by the factor price line 'wr' on cost minimization. Based on the Figure 5.1:

Nishimizu and Page (1982) and Little, Majumdar, and Page (1987) argued that the concept of TE is similar to the concept of total factor productivity. The difference between actual output and potential output was equivalent to the difference between total factor productivity that was based on the best practice and that of the actual practice of a firm. The potential output for a given level of inputs was determined by the most efficient firms in the industry which lie on the frontier. Figure 5.2 illustrates the argument. The points *a*, *b*, and *c* are three levels of outputs realized by a given level of inputs, with *a* being the potential or the maximum output that

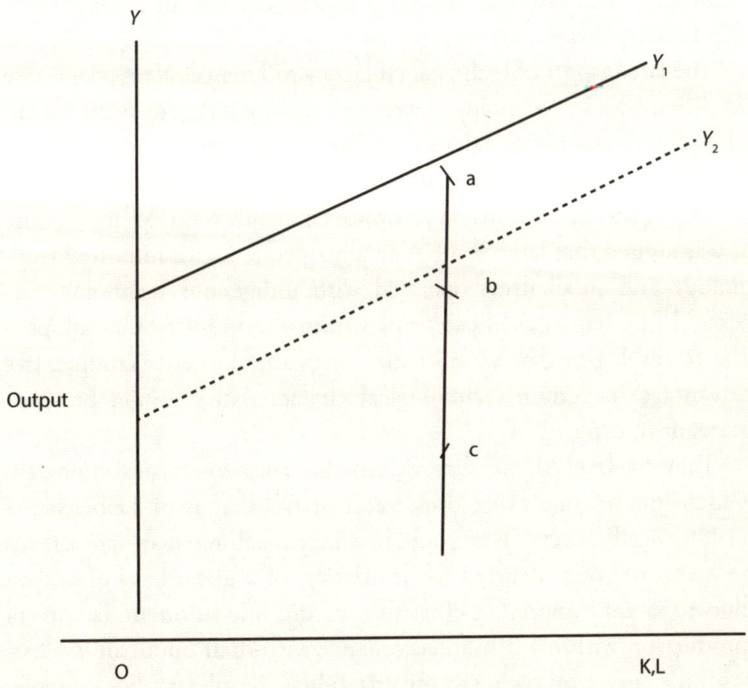

Figure 5.2 Two Technology Frontiers in an Industry
Source: Author's representation.

can be realized. Y_1 and Y_2 can also be taken as two different levels (or vintages) of technology of, say, firms A and B. If both firms are on their respective frontiers, the technical efficiency differences between the two firms can be taken to be only due to technology differences or distance between the firms. The TFP or TE differences between firms in an industry could be taken as consisting of both differences in technical efficiency (*ac*) and differences in technological levels (*ab*). Therefore, the TE measure is a relative measure across firms in an industry. Thus, if the usual assumption of homogenous technology across firms in a sample fails and firms in an industry operate with different levels in terms of the vintage or types of technology as shown in Figure 4.2, *a* and *b* represent points on two different technology frontiers.

The estimated TE measure captures the technical efficiency differences across firms not only due to excess use of inputs under a given technology but also the efficiency differences due to technological gap between firms.

The later aspect of technical efficiency differences across firms due to differences in technology levels adopted by different firms within an industry was highly relevant in this context, especially in explaining exports. The technology difference across different size groups of firms and its implications on technical efficiency was relevant because it was argued that large firms generally operated with imported technology and small firms operated with indigenous technology. As argued in Chapter 3, those firms within the industry that adopted the technologies that were in tune with the domestic comparative advantage in certain technological characteristics should be more relevant to exports.

The firm-level AE measure was based on the neo-classical approach, which ignores one other dimension of AE that is of Leibenstein's (1980) X-efficiency. There could be efficiency differences across firms in terms of costs incurred for realization of a given level of output due to organizational X-efficiency in the allocation of factors of production within a firm in accordance with their opportunity costs within a large firm owing to organizational complexity. For example, employees might have differences in their opportunity costs within a firm determined by their respective aptitudes and motivations. The management which realized these aspects and allocated functions according to the aptitudes of the employees might be able to realize higher output for a given level of inputs than a firm which did not realize these X-efficiency factors. Empirically, it is difficult to segregate the extent of firm-level X-efficiency as it requires information regarding issues such as motivation of managers and labour. Relative X-efficiency across firms could partly reflect in the TE measure as this is relative.

Estimation of Technical Efficiency

The production relation between inputs and outputs was taken to be purely technological. A given technology of an industry determines the extent of inputs required to produce a given level of output (technical efficiency). It also determines the possible combinations of inputs on a frontier to produce a unit of output (AE). Farrell's estimation of the efficient isoquant was non-parametric in approach, in the sense that he simply constructed the free disposable convex hull of the observed input–output ratios by linear programming techniques. No functional form was imposed on the data but constant returns to scale were assumed. Aigner and Chu (1968) were the first to apply Farrell's approach to parametric estimation. The principle advantage of the parametric approach was its ability to characterize frontier technology in a simple mathematical form and to accommodate non-constant returns to scale. The disadvantage could be that it imposes structure on the frontier that may be unwarranted (Forsund, Lovell, and Schmidt, 1980; Porcelli, 2009).

Even though a functional production form may be imposed on the frontier, in this analysis TE was taken to be determined purely by the technological relationship between inputs and outputs. The production relation, in simple terms, could be expressed as

$$Y = (X : B) + u$$

where Y is a vector of output observations, X is a matrix of input observations, B represents the parameters, and u represents the one-sided error. The one-sided error term forces $Y \le f(x)$.

In general estimations of production functions, u is specified to be normally, independently, and identically distributed with zero mean and finite variance. Frontier estimations, from the preceding specification, takes u to have a negative expectation, indicating presence of technical inefficiency in production. The crucial aspect of the estimation of TE is the specification of the distribution of u which, in turn, determines the possible efficient econometric estimators.

The frontier is called deterministic if all the observations must lie on or below the frontier and stochastic if observations can be above the frontier due to random events. In case of the deterministic frontier, the technical inefficiency (the negative expectation of the error) is purely due to managerial failure to arrive at the efficient frontier. In case of the stochastic function, a firm could be technically inefficient due to reasons beyond its control (Porcelli, 2009).

The one-sided error component in the preceding specification would imply the frontier is deterministic. If we impose the Cobb–Douglas production form on the earlier specification, it can be specified as

$$Y = f(X)e**(-u)$$

$$\text{Log } Y = \log[f(X)] - u$$

where $u \geqq 0$ and thus $0 \leqq e^{-u} \leqq 1$ and where log $[f(X)]$ is linear in the Cobb–Douglas case. It is assumed that the observations u are independently and identically distributed and X is exogenous, independent of u. Any number of distributions for u can be specified. Afriat (1972) specified a two-parameter beta distribution for e^{-u} and proposed that the equation could be estimated by maximum likelihood method which would mean a gamma distribution for u (Richmond, 1974).

As suggested by Richmond, the Cobb–Douglas specification can be estimated by OLS by a simple modification. If we let w be the mean of u, we can write:

$$\text{Log} Y = (\gamma - w) + w\sum_{i=1}^{n} \gamma 2 \log Xi - (u - w)$$

where the new error term has zero mean.

The error term satisfies all the usual properties except normality. The equation could be estimated by OLS to obtain the best linear unbiased estimates. The estimated residuals could be used to correct the OLS constant term. One of the possible drawbacks of this method in measuring technical inefficiency for individual observations is that some of the residuals might still end up above the estimated frontier. One way this problem could be resolved is that the constant term could be corrected by shifting it up until no residual was positive and one was zero and take deviations of rest of the observations to estimate TE. This is illustrated in Figure 5.3. The Y axis represents output and X axis represents inputs; a is the estimated constant and a^* is the corrected constant. All the observations except one (c) lie below Y^*. The deviations of the observations from Y^* can be measured to estimate firm-level TE.

The specification as mentioned earlier is a deterministic frontier. A composite error or a two-sided error specification leads to a stochastic

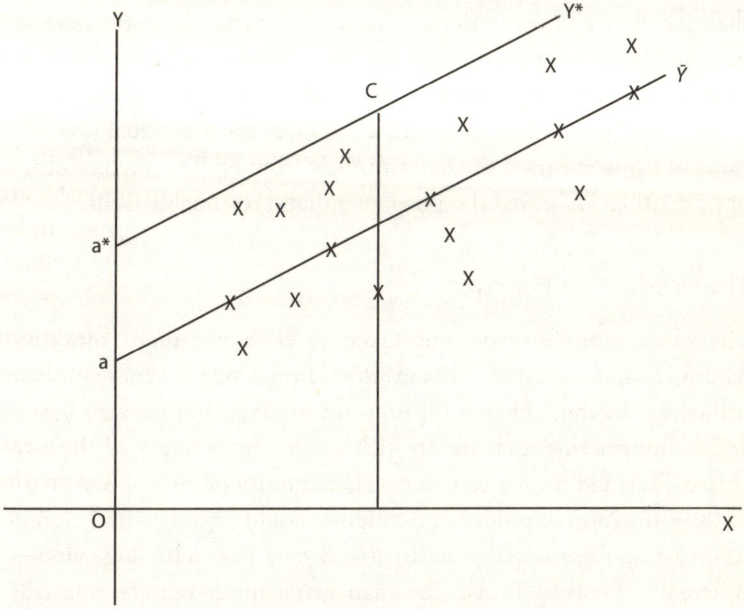

Figure 5.3 Technical Efficiency Owing to Technology Distance
Source: Author's representation.

element in efficiency in the sense of systematic efficiency differences between production units and random differences (Aigner, Lovell, and Schmidt, 1977; Meesen and der Broeck, 1977; Broeck et al, 1980; Porcelli, 2009).

The specification of stochastic frontier can be

$$Y = f(X)\exp(v - u).$$

The error consists of the symmetric components which were assumed to be independently and identically distributed. The error component u was assumed to be distributed independently of v. The symmetric component permits the random variations of the frontier across firms and captures the effects of measurement error; other statistical 'noise' and random shocks are beyond the control of the firms.

The major defect of the stochastic frontiers is that it is not possible to decompose individual residuals into their two components and so it is not possible to estimate technical inefficiency for each observation (Forsund, Lovell, and Schmidt, 1980). Broeck et al. (1980) observed that 'the choice between deterministic and stochastic frontiers must be made based on the information about the quality of the data or how the data are generated and, above all, the purpose of the study'. Since our objective is to estimate TE indices for individual observations of firms, we used the deterministic frontier. This methodology of estimating TE served the purpose at hand reasonably well.

The Production Function

The production function was taken to be a two-input function: labour (L) and capital (K). The extent of firm-level efficiency could be influenced by the omission (or non-measurement) of relevant inputs and by measurement errors. In such a case, the accuracy of the estimated TE could be questionable. A fair amount of the residual factor in the estimation of production function could be due to omission of information regarding the managerial inputs and technology vintage differences between firms. The managerial input reflects especially on the degree of X-efficiency in a firm. Since the managerial and vintage factors were built into the theory and the objective here was to measure relative efficiency indices across firms, the two-input production functions should serve the purpose to a large degree.

As far as the choice of the functional forms is concerned, the most appropriate form for the exercise is the trans log production function due to its relative merits in capturing the underlying functional relationships, especially in this case where the sample consisted of firms with a large degree of size distribution. The Cobb–Douglas functional specification was also used in such cases where the size distribution of firms in a sample was not large. Expressing in logarithms, the trans log case takes the form

$$\text{Log}Y = \log a + bl\log L + b2\log K + b3\log ½(\log L)^{**}2$$
$$+b4½(\log K)^{**}2 + b5(\log L * \log K) + u.$$

The form reduces to Cobb–Douglas if the parameters b_3, b_4, and b_5 are zero and insignificant. In our case, the trans log function was more appropriate than Cobb–Douglas as it imposes fewer a priori restrictions on the properties of the underlying technology. The basic limiting properties of Cobb–Douglas form are as follows:

1. The elasticity of substitution between L and K is constant and equal to 1.
2. The output elasticity (*dlogY/dlogL*) is constant (so are the factor shares).
3. It imposes the homothety conditions. The optimal factor proportions are independent of scale.

Where the sample consisted of firms with large size or scale differences, as in this case, it was highly likely that these conditions failed to hold. The trans log function relaxes these conditions. The output elasticity with respect to inputs are as follows:

$$(d\log Y / d\log L) = b1 + b3\log L + b5\log K$$

Under the producers' equilibrium:

$$(d\log Y / d\log L) = (wL / pY) : (d\log Y / d\log K) = (rK / py)$$

w is the wage rate and r is the price of capital and p is the price of output.

When *(dlogY/dlogL) and (dlogY/dlogK)* > 0, the value shares of the respective factors increase as the quantity of the inputs increases at constant factor and product prices, holding all other inputs constant. In contrast when the output elasticity is less than 0, the opposite holds true. As a result, the factor shares are also variables, depending on the scale. Consequently, the elasticity of substitution between the inputs is variable with the changes in the scale: the parameters b_3, b_4, and b_5 provide the information on the curvature of the function and the elasticity of substitution. In case of the Cobb–Douglas form, the function is mutually dual, that is, both the production and cost functions belong to the same group of functional form. But the trans log functions are not mutually dual. Since both the trans log and Cobb–Douglas functions are linear in parameter and non-linear in the variable, OLS can be applied in estimating the functions (Kmenta, 1971; Aigner, Lovell, and Schmidt, 1977).

Estimation of Allocative Efficiency

As mentioned earlier, firm-level AE was observed in terms of choosing the optimum point on the frontier determined by the relative input prices (the factor price line). By taking the production frontiers approach, Schmidt and Lovell (1979) decomposed technical and allocative efficiencies. They assumed that departures from minimum cost were a result of both technical and allocative inefficiencies. Since a frontier cost function standard alone cannot define the two components, they employed a stochastic frontier production function and the necessary conditions for a cost minimum to identify both technical and allocative inefficiency. They took the variations in output attributed to technical inefficiency and introduced a composite stochastic disturbance structure. Violations of the necessary conditions were modelled by a symmetric disturbance and explained allocative inefficiency of utilization of labour and capital in production of output. The production parameters were estimated by maximum likelihood techniques. The estimated parameters were then substituted into the necessary conditions of the equations and the residuals from these equations were used to estimate allocative inefficiency. The merit of this methodology was that it could estimate both TE and AE simultaneously and AE for each observation (Kopp, 1981).

Schmidt and Lovell specified, based on the Cobb–Douglas functional form, a stochastic production frontier as

$$\text{Log}Y = \log a + \sum_{i=1}^{n} \gamma i \log Xi + (v - u).$$

Log Y is bounded from above by the stochastic frontier. The TE relative to the frontier is given by *u*. The firm is assumed to be allocatively efficient in the sense that it makes no mistakes in selecting the cost-minimizing factor proportions of labour and capital which are given by the solution to:

$$\text{Log}\, X1 - \log Xi = Bi, \quad i = 2......n$$

where $Bi - \log(pi\gamma 1 / p1\gamma i)$ and $pl\ ..P2\ ....pn$ are the input prices.

From this, stochastic factor demand frontiers were derived. *Log Xi* was bounded from below by the factor demand frontiers. Based on these, the cost function was derived. The cost function was bounded from below by the stochastic cost frontier. With AE assumed, a firm could be above its cost frontier only by being below its production frontier.

Allocative inefficiency was measured on the basis that the firm seeks to minimize costs of producing its desired rate of output subject to a stochastic production frontier constraint. In measuring AE, presence of technical inefficiency is allowed. Allocative inefficiency was modelled by permitting the cost-minimizing conditions which define the least cost expansion path, which, in implicit form, fails to hold exactly. The errors in choosing the cost-minimizing factor proportions then correspond to the disturbances. The specification of the production frontier is

$$\text{Log}Y = \log a + \sum_{i=1}^{n} \gamma i \log Xi + (v - u)$$

$$Log\ X1 - \log Xi = Bi + ei. \quad i = 2.....n$$

where, as before, $Bi = \log(pi\gamma 1 / p1\gamma i), v \sim N\ (0, \sigma_u^2)$, u is the absolute value of a $N(0,\ \sigma_u^2)$ variable, and *ei* represents the amount by which the first order conditions fail to hold and represents the extent of allocative inefficiency.

As before, in case of TE, from the previous equation, the factor demand equations and the cost functions were derived with added term *ei*. The residuals of the cost-minimizing conditions could be taken as *e*, which enabled to estimate the extra cost due to allocative inefficiency for each observation.

Unlike in Schmidt and Lovell, the methodology adopted for our purpose estimates TE and AE separately. As discussed earlier, technical efficiency was estimated based on a deterministic production frontier. The extent of firm-level relative technical inefficiency was determined by the extent of the deviation of the input use from the most efficient technological frontier. Although production functional forms were used, TE was taken to be determined purely by technological relationship between inputs and outputs and factor prices were taken to have no role to play.

Subsequently, in order to estimate allocative inefficiency, all the firms in the sample were assumed to be technically efficient, which could be achieved by pushing all the firms to be on the frontier. The extent of the technical inefficiency for each firm was the difference between the output that could be realized by being on the production frontier and the actual output. The extent of the difference was added to the output of all firms in the sample to remove technical inefficiency in the sample.

$$Y \sim I = Yi + Qi.$$

To estimate allocative inefficiency (at each data point) *Y~* was introduced into the trans log cost function which takes the form

$$\log C = \log a + b1 \log Y \sim + \; b2\ ½(\log Y) \sim^{**}\ 2 + b3 \log w$$
$$+ b4 \log r + b5(\log w * \log r) + b6(\log Y \sim * \log w)$$
$$+ b7(\log Y \sim * \log r)$$

Firm-level AE indices could be derived by minimizing costs (C) subject to $Y\sim$. The factor prices enter the optimization through the cost function. The objective function to be minimized is

$$\text{Min} \sum\nolimits_{1}^{N} \log C.$$

The right side of cost function specified is subject to

$$Ci \geq Ci(Y \sim i).$$

The residuals in the minimization programme were taken to be the firm-level indices of AE. In other words, the difference between the estimated and the actual costs was taken to be the extent of firm-level AE.

$$AE = (Cai \,/\, Cei)$$

where '*Cai*' is firm-level actual cost and '*Cei*' is the firm-level estimated cost.

If (*Cei*/*Cai*) < 1, it would imply presence of firm-level allocative inefficiency.

Factor (Labour and Capital) Prices and Systematic Allocative Efficiency (AEii)

The AEii that was considered in this context was different from the pure firm-level AE discussed earlier. The relative factor prices determine AE. In competitive market conditions factor prices, given exogenously, are same for all the firms. But if the factor markets are highly distorted and segmented, different firms in the industry might have not only unequal access to the inputs but would also pay differential prices to the factors of production of labour and capital.

As argued in Chapter 3, owing to the factor market segmentation in the Indian economy, large and small firms in an industry had differential access to the inputs and pay different prices to the factors of production. Our objective is to examine firm-level AEii in relation to exports (comparative advantage) rather than the absolute AE of firms with respect to their respective factor price lines. The firms which choose the optimal techniques of production based on the opportunity costs (prices) of factors of production would be closer to the domestic comparative advantage in relative factor endowments. In highly distorted factor market conditions, the relative opportunity cost prices at the country level would represent the country's comparative advantage in relative factor endowments. So, the allocative efficient point on the frontier determined by the factor price line closely representing the relative shadow factor prices (opportunity costs at the country level) would be the appropriate one to estimate firm-level AEii in relation to exports.

This argument is illustrated in Figure 5.4 (X-axis represents labour and Y-axis represents capital and corresponding relative prices). The

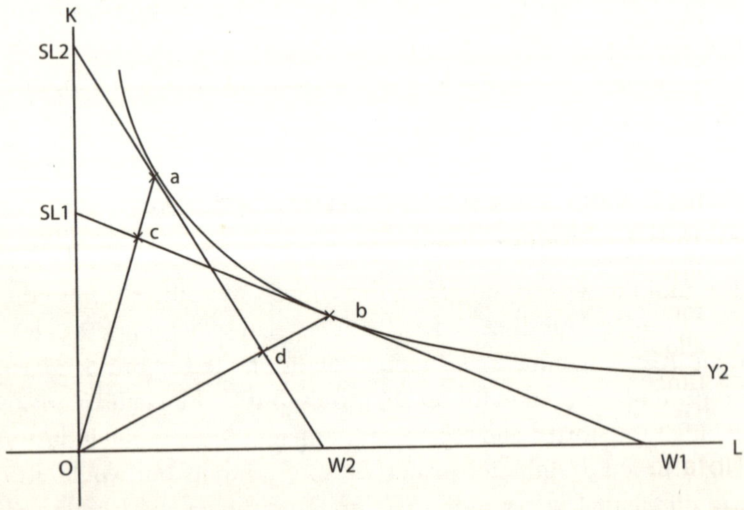

Figure 5.4 Allocative Efficiency

Source: Author's representation.

factor price lines SL_1W_1 and SL_2W_2 represent two segmented factor markets. If the large firms had higher access to capital at a lower price, one could take SL_2W_2 as the factor price line faced by the large firms. Let us take the factor price line SL_1W_1 to represent relative opportunity cost prices of inputs faced by small firms. So, the point *b* represents the AEii. A large firm which faced the factor price line SL_1W_1 could be firm-level allocative efficient at the point *a* based on its factor price line. But the firm will be systematically allocatively inefficient to the extent of *ac/oa*, based on the relative shadow factor price (opportunity costs) line.

The AE was estimated based on two approaches:

1. AEi: In this approach the price of capital was taken to be the bank lending rate of 12 per cent. Large firms of the organized sector generally had access to capital at this rate. If one takes the share capital of the large public limited companies into account, the price of capital to the large firms might be even lower. The wage rate was taken to be the average wage rate of firms in the sample. In this approach the factor prices were the same for all firms in the sample. In this case, AE was estimated by linear programming.
2. AEii: In a capital-scarce and labour-abundant Indian economy, the shadow (opportunity cost) price of capital was generally observed to be a lot higher than the bank lending rate. In this approach, the price of capital was taken to be 21 per cent, which was closer to its shadow price and was the rate at which small firms obtained capital. Majority of small firms covered in the field study reported that they paid interest rate ranging between 18 to 24 per cent. The wage rate was taken to be variable across firms in the sample in terms of total wage bill divided by the total number of workers employed by each firm. Firm-level allocative indices were measured by estimating the trans log cost function by OLS.

Notation of the Variables

TE = firm-level relative technical efficiency
T/E = (I/TE), firm-level relative technical inefficiency

AEi = firm-level AE measured with interest rate of 12 per cent and an average wage rate of the sample
AEii = systematic allocative efficiency measured with interest rate of 21 per cent (shadow price) and the variable wage rate
ZS = firm size, with total sales turnover as size measure
IM/S = firm-level import intensity
VK = vintage or age of machinery in years
EXM = experience of managers in years
EXL = experience of permanent labour in years
SL = skill intensity of labour
Wages/Value-added = (number of skilled labour * wage rate of skilled labour)/value-added
YEX = number of years of a firm in export activity

The industry at disaggregate subgroup level that was taken for the exercises is hand, small, and cutting tools industry. The sample used was based on Sample 2 as discussed in Chapter 4. The sample consisted of seventy-six large and small firms (see Table 4.2), out of which forty-one firms were S&M firms. For the sub-sample of forty-one S&M firms, apart from the quantitative data, qualitative information was also collected from the primary sources. The additional information for the forty-one firms covered managerial and employees' experience, vintage of machinery, number of years in export activity, skilled and unskilled labour, wages, and interest rate paid.

Specification of Equations and Results

$$V.I.E.\left(\frac{E}{S}\right) = a + b_1(ZS) + b_2(TE) + b_3(AE) + b_4(ZS)(TE)$$
$$+b_5(ZS)(AE) + ib_2;\ b_3$$

If one ignores the interactive terms, b_2 could be expected to be positive under the implication that higher the relative technical efficiency higher the exports and export propensity. As mentioned in Chapter 4, in the case of (*X*) the causality between exports and TE could be the other way round if one takes the dynamic effects of the export activity itself. This was because, as mentioned earlier, the measure reflected relative efficiency differences due to technological differences between firms. As discussed in Chapter 3, firms which adopted the technology that facilitated realization of higher total factor productivity based on the specific domestic indigenous technological conditions or features should be in a better position to export. If this technology was the one that determined the efficient production frontier, the positive relationship between exports and TE (measured) was straightforward. It was argued in Chapter 3 that the technological differences between firms was based on firm size groups. As a result, firm size variable became a crucial determinant of the nature of causality between (*E/S*) and TE. Apart from this, the relationship between firm size, efficiency, and exports could be governed by the domestic market structure conditions as discussed in Chapter 3. These aspects were captured by the interactive terms. The interactive terms show the size group at which the comparative efficiency reflected by TE is realized in the revealed exports.

It was established in Chapter 4 that revealed exports of different size groups were governed mostly by the market structure conditions. So, the causality between TE and exports could change depending on the firm size factor, which reflected firm-level domestic market power. For example, among large firms which had oligopoly rivalry for domestic monopoly profits, the relatively efficient ones would be domestic market leaders which could push the relatively inefficient ones to export markets mostly to less developed economies.

In case of AE variable, the expected causality depends on whether AEi or AEii is used in the equation. In case of AEi, b_3 was expected to be negative. This was because AEi is measured based on the price of capital to be 12 per cent interest rate, which was assumed to be far lower than the shadow price of capital in the capital-scarce and labour-abundant Indian economy. The firms which were allocatively efficient on the basis of AEi adopted relatively capital-intensive techniques and deviated from the country's comparative advantage. In case of AEii, it was measured based on the interest rate of 2l per cent that was assumed to be closer to the shadow price of capital. Thus, it captures comparative advantage of labour intensity. Therefore, b_3 was expected to be positive. The expected signs of the parameters associated with the interactive terms were, again, based on the firm size dimension operating through the market structure argument.

$$\text{V.2. } TIE = a + b_1(ZS) + b_2(ZS)^{**}2 + b_3(IM/S) + b_4(VK) + i.$$
$$b_1 < 0;\ b_2 \gtrless 0 : b_3 \gtrless 0 : b_4 > 0 :$$

The previous equation specified the relationship between exports and technical efficiency. Equation V.2 demonstrates the explicit relationship between technical 'inefficiency' and firm size and the other variables which could be explained through the firm size variable. It was necessary to take into consideration that TIE was technical inefficiency, (1/TE).

$$TE = \left(\frac{Y^*}{Y}\right)$$
$$TIE = (Y^*/Y)$$
$$Y = \text{actual output}$$
$$Y^* = \text{the predicted (or optimal) output}$$

The quadratic relation specified with respect to TIE and firm size was based on the argument of technological threshold size. The argument was that small firms had to reach a minimum technological threshold size in order to be technically efficient. In other words, very small firms which operated with outdated technologies would not be able to realize relative technical efficiency in an industry. In such a case, b_1 was expected to be negative and b_3 negative or positive. The TIE should decrease until a critical firm size. After the critical firm size, it would increase if large firms turned out to be technically inefficient. On the other hand, b_2 could turn out to be negative if large firms which had higher access to imported and latest vintage technology were the ones which were determining the efficient technology frontier in the industry.

The IM/S variable was taken to capture the extent of imported technology of firms. The IM/S and VK (vintage of technology) variables were taken to capture the arguments regarding technological gap or distance between firms within an industry and its implications on the measured technical inefficiency. If it was the imported technology which was determining the efficient technology frontier in the industry, then b_3 should be negative. Higher the extent of imported technology, lower should be TIE. On the other hand, if imported technology and its process resulted in higher costs and technological rigidities, b_3 could be expected to be positive. The relationship between VK and TIE, irrespective of the analytical arguments, could be a result of incomplete specification of the measured capital. As TE was measured relative to a single industry frontier, firms employing older vintage technologies would appear inefficient even if they were achieving maximum output for a given vintage of capital. Apart from this, VK variable should also capture the argument regarding technological threshold size. Firms operating with very old and outdated technologies would be technically inefficient.

V.3 $$AE = a + b_1(ZS) + b_2(IM/S) + i$$

In case of AEi, b_1 was expected to be positive. This was because the larger firms had access to capital at lower private price than S&M firms. In case of AEii, the parameter was expected to be negative for the reason argued before. Similarly the sign of b_2 with respect to imported technology variable (IM/S) was expected to be different for AE_i and AE_{ii} under the assumption that imported technologies were capital-intensive, the sign should be positive in case of AE_i where capital price was lower.

Results: Production and Cost Functions Estimated for the Sample of Seventy-Six Firms

1. Cobb–Douglas Production Function

$$\text{Log}\, y = 1.87 + 0.62\log(LS) + 0.26\log K$$

$$(7.0)^{*} \quad (2.75)^{*}$$

$$R\ squared\ 0.92, \quad F = 465 \quad N = 76$$

Multiple correlation coefficient = 0.96

2. The Trans Log Production Function

$$\text{Log } Y = 5.4 + 1.12 \log(LS) - 1.02 \log K$$
$$(2.68)^{*} \qquad (2.22)^{*}$$
$$+0.33(1/2)(\log LS)^{**} +$$
$$(2.68)^{*}$$
$$+0.42(1/2)(\log LS)^{**} 2$$
$$(2.22)^{*}$$
$$-0.32 \log(LS)^{*} \log(K0)$$
$$-(2.12)^{*}$$

R *squared* $= 0.94 \quad F = 220 \quad N = 76$

Multiple correlation coefficient = 0.96

Figures in the brackets are 't' values.

*Significant at 0.01 level.

The estimated trans log function had shown higher explanatory power than the Cobb–Douglas function. Apart from this, the estimated coefficients of the interactive terms were significantly different from zero.

The partial derivatives of the estimated function are:

$$\frac{dY}{dK} = \frac{Y}{K}(-1.02 + 0.42 \log K - 0.30 \log LS) \tag{1}$$

$$\frac{dY}{d}(LS) = \frac{Y}{LS}(1.12 + 0.33 \log LS - 0.3 \log K) \tag{2}$$

The estimated function was checked at all the data points for monotonicity and the function was observed to be well-behaved. The trans log function does not fulfil the requirements of quasi-concavity (convex isoquants) and monotonicity globally. But if the conditions are met over enough of the observed levels of inputs and outputs, the function is considered well behaved (Little, Majumdar, and Page, 1987). These results supported the choice of trans log production function to estimate the production frontier for the sample of seventy-six firms consisting of very large and small firms.

Cobb–Douglas production function for the sub-sample of forty-one S&M firms

Since the trans log function was not appropriate to estimate TE for the sub-sample which consisted of only S&M firms, the Cobb–Douglas functional form was utilized.

$$\text{Log}Y = 2.38 + 0.57\log(LS) + 0.21\log(K)$$

$$(2.16)^{*} \quad (1.58)^{*}$$

$R\ squared = 0.4 \quad F = 9.9 \quad N = 41$

Figures in the brackets are ‘t’ values.

*Statistically significant at 0.05 level.

3. The Trans Log Cost Function.

To estimate AEii, the trans log cost function is estimated with: $Y\sim = Y + Q$ and $r = 21$ per cent of interest rate by *OLS.*

$$\text{Log}C = 1.26 - 0.32\log Y \sim + \ 0.07(1/2)\ (\log Y \sim)**2$$

$$-(4.78)* \quad (6.39)*$$

$$-0.13\log w + 1.48\log r$$

$$-(2.4)*(2.5)*$$

$$+0.07(\log Y \sim)(\log w) - 0.05(\log Y \sim)\ (\log r)$$

$$(4.2)* -(7.6)*$$

$$-0.071(\log w)(\log r)$$

$$-(4.73)*$$

$R\ squared = 0.98 \quad F = 34477 \quad N = 76$

Multiple correlation coefficient $= 0.98$

Figures in the brackets are ‘t’ values.

*Statistically significant at 0.01 level.

Due to multi-colinearity between TE and AE indices, their respective explanation of exports is tested separately.

The Results for Technical Efficiency

V.1.1.a. $E = 953 + 13(ZS) + 681(TE) + 11(ZS)(TE).$

$$(1.99)^{*} \quad (0.10) \qquad (0.4)$$

$$R\ squared = 0.29 \quad F = 10$$

V.1.1.b. $(E/S) = 0.1 + 0.0001(ZS) + 0.239(TE)$

$$(0.77) \qquad (1.62)^{***}$$

$$-0.00093(ZS)\ (TE)$$

$$(1.92)^{**}$$

$$R\ squared = 0.12\ F = 3.5\ N = 76$$

Figures in the brackets are 't' values.

* Statistically significant at 0.025 level

** Significant at 0.05 level.

*** Significant at 0.10 level.

$d(E/S)/d(TE) = 0.259 - 0.00093(ZS)$

The critical turning point, $(ZS)te^{*}$ = INR 1,782 lakh.

Firm-level relative TE explained export propensity significantly rather than absolute exports. The TE explained export propensity positively. But, as in the case of *X* in the previous chapter, there was a critical firm size after which the firm was associated with export propensity negatively. The critical turning firm size in this case was about INR 18 crore sales turnover. The low turning point was expected given the size distribution in the sample.

The results implied that before the critical firm size of INR 18 crore, the relatively technically efficient firms were the ones which were more export-intensive and after the critical size, within the size group, it was the relatively technically inefficient firms which were more export-intensive. These results indicate it was mostly firms in the size range of about INR 1 crore to INR 20 crore sales turnover that were able to realize comparative advantage in exports. This was in terms of employing the appropriate choice of production techniques and realizing high TE in accordance with the country's comparative advantage. But, at this stage, this did not mean that all the firms above the critical size did not realize this efficiency. The most likely reason for the negative association between TE and (E/S) after the critical size could be that, based on the market structure argument, the relatively efficient firms in the size group attained certain degree of domestic market power and performance. As a result, they did not have the pressure to export at higher intensity and did not transmit the efficiency into exports. As argued in case of the result obtained for *X* in the previous chapter, within the size group of large firms, the relatively inefficient would be pushed to the export markets due to the oligopoly rivalry in the domestic market. Among the small firms (below the critical size), it were the relatively efficient ones which were more export-oriented. This supported the argument in Chapter 3 that small firms faced severe competitive pressures and expansion barriers in the domestic market and those small firms which adopted themselves as efficient producers could branch out into export markets.

$$TIE = 4.0 - 0.003(ZS) + 0.00000183(ZS)^{**}2$$

$$-(1.8)^{**} \ (2.10)^{*}$$

$$+2.15(IM/S)$$

$$(0.78)$$

$R\ squared = 0.10 \quad F = 1.9 \quad N = 76$

The figures in the brackets are 't' values.

* Statistically significant at 0.01 level.

** Statistically significant at 0.05 level.

The critical turning point of ZS = INR 50 crore in the results presented above showed the explicit relation between TIE and firm size (see Table 5.1). The results had interesting implications. They indicated that until the firm size of INR 50 crore sales turnover, the (estimated) TIE was declining. But after the critical firm size of INR 50 crore sales turnover, TIE was increasing as firm size increased. It could be seen, if one ignored a few observations in the middle,

Table 5.1 Technical Efficiency (TE) by Firm Size Group

Firm size group by sales (in millions)	Average value	Minimum value	Maximum value	Number of firms in the group
INR 1,592 to INR 330	0.288 (0.108)	0.144	0.463	8
INR 290 to INR 108	0.423 (0.139)	0.312	0.767	8
INR 97 to INR 4	0.40 (0.245)	0.101	1	18
INR 4.13 to INR 2	0.379 (0.192)	0.192	0.92	11
INR1.85 to INR 1	0.307 (0.148)	0.089	0.59	22
INR 1 to INR 0.7	0.208 (0.115)	0.09	0.5	9
Total sample	0.338 (2.2)	0.089	1	76

Note: Figures in brackets are standard deviations.
Source: Computed by author.

that the relationship between firm size and technical inefficiency was 'U'-shaped. The result supported the argument regarding the technological threshold size to realize relative TE in the industry. Very small firms which operated with older and outdated technologies would not be able to be relatively technically efficient. Large firms which had access to imported technology should have determined the frontier. However, this was not the case, as shown by the results. Very large firms due to X-inefficiency and technological rigidities would be relatively technically inefficient. Given the high domestic market power large firms had, they might not have enough pressure to operate on the most efficient path possible.

It was established in Chapter 3 that it was the larger firms which had higher access to imported technologies and inputs. Although it was not statistically significant, the estimated parameter of IM/S, indicated imported technology was not explaining TE. This result suggested that greater access to (latest) imported technology was not giving any additional advantage in realizing relative technical efficiency. In other words, the interpreted result could be that higher technical efficiency was realized by those firms which could realize high total factor productivity based on indigenous technological conditions.

Technical Efficiency

The Results for the Sub-sample of Forty-One S&M Firms

As mentioned in the data section, for this sample, the information collected covered additional factors. This facilitated the use of some additional variables in explaining exports and TE.

V.1.1.i.a
$$E = 905 + 480(ZS) - 1568(TE) - 61(ZS)(TE)$$
$$(7.0)^{*} - (1.0) - \quad (0.43)$$
$$+62\ (YEX)$$
$$(1.75)^{**}$$
$$R\ squared = 0.79 \quad F = 34 \quad N = 41$$

V.1.1.i.b
$$(E/S) = 0.05 + 0.056(ZS) - 0.12(TE)$$
$$(3.43)^{*} - (0.38)$$
$$-0.026\ (ZS)\ (TE) + 0.002\ (YEX)$$
$$-(0.77) \qquad (2.380)^{*}$$
$$R\ squared = 0.47 \quad F = 8.1\ N = 41$$

The figures in brackets are ‘t’ values.

*Statistically significant at 0.025 level.

**Significant at 0.05 level.

In these results for the sample, *TE* was not explaining exports. But the important aspect of the results was the significant positive association between export propensity and firm size. As the sample consisted of only small firms, this result supported the argument regarding the threshold or minimum efficient size in exports. In the estimations, other variables such as skilled labour intensity, number of years of experience of managers, and permanent labour were tested for their explanation of exports. However, none of them were statistically significant. As presented in the results, only the variable of number of years of export activity turned out to be significant. This variable was taken to capture the dynamic learning-by-doing cumulative economies in export activity. The statistically significant positive sign of the estimated coefficient of the variable indicated the presence of these economies.

V.1.2.i. $$TE = 0.16 + 0.028(ZS)$$
$$(3.7)^{*}$$
$$R\ squared = 0.26 \qquad F = 13.9$$

V.1.2.ii. $$TE = 0.50 - 0.024(Vk)$$
$$-(1.88)^{**}$$
$$R\ squared = 0.08 \quad F = 3.5\ N = 41$$

The figures in the brackets are 't' values

*Statistically significant at 0.025 level.

**Significant at 0.05 level.

In the estimations for this sample, only ZS and VK variables were explaining TE. Because of strong multi-collinearity between ZS and VK, they were tested separately for their explanation of TE. The results showed positive association between relative technical efficiency and firm size. The result was expected because the sample consisted of only small firms. This result supported the argument that firms had to reach a technological threshold to realize technical efficiency. The result obtained with respect to the capital vintage variable (VK) reconfirmed the argument regarding the minimum efficient size. The statistically significant positive sign of the estimated coefficient of the variable VK indicated that among the small firms, the firms with older vintage and outdated technologies were not technically efficient.

In the preceding equation the variables such as skill intensity and managerial and labour experience were used as the explanatory variables. But none of them gave statistically significant results.

From these results, it was obvious that firm size and TE were highly correlated. Due to this reason the TE variable in Equation

V.1.1.i. did not explain exports as statistically significant. The equation was re-estimated by removing ZS as a separate variable (for the sample of forty-one firms).

V.1.1.ii.a $$E = 1120 - 5472(TE) + 717(ZS)(TE)$$
$$-(3.0)^{*}(5.1)^{*}$$
$$+ 92\ (YEX)$$
$$(1.76)^{**}$$
$$R\ squared = 0.51 \qquad F = 12.8$$

V.1.1.ii.b $$(E/S) = 0.29 - 0.579(TE) + 0.064(ZS)(TE)$$
$$-(1.8)^{**}(2.59)^{*}$$
$$+0.023\ (YEX)$$
$$(2.46)^{*}$$
$$R\ squared = 0.3 \quad F = 5.3 \quad N = 41$$

The figures in the brackets are ‘t’ values.

* Statistically significant at 0.025 level.

** Significant at 0.05 level.

a. The critical turning firm size (*ZS*)*te** = INR 49 lakh.
b. The critical turning firm size (*ZS*)*te** = INR 58 lakh.

These results had significant implications. Unlike in the previous estimations, the coefficient associated with the TE variable was statistically significant. But the interesting aspect of the results was the non-linearity and the turning points. Only after the critical firm size of INR 58 lakh sales turnover was relative technical efficiency contributing positively to export propensity. This result had to be interpreted based on the previous result in Equation V.1.1.i, of the positive association between technical efficiency and firm size for this sample of small firms. The result gave support to the argument that firms had to reach a technological minimum threshold size in order to ‘produce’ the exportable products on a vertical product differentiation (product quality difference) plane. Firms below the threshold size appeared to be not relevant to exports.

In this context, it was important to take into notice that in both the samples of seventy-six firms (including large and small firms) and forty-one small firms, we had included ten small firms that were indirect exporters. The value of their indirect exports was considered. Some of the small firms tended to be indirect exporters because they could not break the marketing barriers involved in export activity. Generally, there was a certain minimum firm size involved to break the marketing barriers. The preceding results were obtained despite the inclusion of the small firms which undertook indirect exports, in the sense that the extent of the indirect exports coming in the left hand side of the equations gave support to the argument of technological minimum efficient size in order to 'produce' the exportable products.

Results for Allocative Efficiency

AEi: $r = 12$ per cent interest rate
$W =$ an average fixed wage rate

The following show the results without the interactive term of AE_i and ZS, on the right hand side.

V.1.2.i.a $$E = 1942 + 16.4(ZS) - 1429(AE_i)$$

$$(5.4)^* - (0.32)$$

$$R\ squared = 0.29 \quad F = 15$$

V.1.2.i.b $$(E/S) = 0.32 - 0.00017(ZS) - 0.21(AE_i)$$

$$-(2.39)^* - (1.98)^*$$

$$R\ squared = 0.11 \quad F = 4.7$$

The following show the results with the interactive term.

V.1.2.i.c $$E = 799 + 24.2(ZS) + 1901(AE_i)$$

$$(4.23)^* \ (0.31)$$

$$-23.9(ZS)(AE_i)$$

$$(1.61)^{***}$$

$$R\ squared = 0.31 \ F = 11.2$$

$$\text{V.1.2.i.d} \quad (E/S) = 0.32 - 0.00016(ZS) - 0.20\,(AE_i)$$
$$-(1.14) - \qquad (1.76)^{**}$$
$$-0.000033\,(ZS)(AE_i)$$
$$-(0.092)$$

$R\ squared = 0.11\ F = 3.09\ N = 76$

The figures in brackets are ‘t’ values.

*Statistically significant at 0.025 level.

**Significant at 0.05 level.

***Significant at 0.10 level.

In the above results, the estimated coefficient of the allocative efficiency variable (AE_i) was consistently of negative sign. The coefficient was statistically significant in (*b*) and (*d*), where export propensity was used as the dependent variable. The result implied that higher the firm-level allocative efficiency (AE_i) lower the export propensity. The explanation for the negative association lay in the factor price line used in estimating AE_i. The price of capital that the rate of interest of 12 per cent used in estimating AE_i had been argued to be far below the shadow price of capital in the capital-scarce Indian economy. The firms which obtained access to capital at this rate of interest would tend to adopt the production techniques in favour of capital intensity and might use excess capital than (optimally) necessary as the private cost of capital was lower than its opportunity cost. Consequently, the production techniques of these firms could deviate from the country's comparative advantage, reflected in the relative shadow prices of the factors of production.

Therefore, the allocative efficiency measure (AE_i) represented a point like *a* in Figure 5.4. If the relative shadow price line was SL_1W_1, the point *a* was (systematically) allocatively inefficient to the extent of *ca*, based on the country's comparative advantage in the relative factor endowments. This, in turn, explained the negative association between AE_i and export propensity.

As argued in Chapter 3, the large firms in the industry obtained access to capital at a relatively cheaper price than S&M firms and paid higher wages to labour. The AE_i measure represented the allocative efficiency point biased in favour of the large firms. Although the relationship between AE_i and firm size was not established here, the established relationship between firm size and exports showed that the export propensity of larger firms was lower than that of S&M firms as shown by the negative sign of the estimated coefficient associated by the firm size variable (ZS). The negative association between AE_i and export propensity explained the export behaviour of large and small firms from the supply-side factors in terms of the factor market segmentation and factor price differentials. In the capital-scarce and labour-abundant Indian economy, the large firms which obtained access to capital at lower price than small firms might adopt the production techniques deviated from the country's comparative advantage.

Although the estimated coefficients with respect to the interactive terms of AE_i and firm size (ZS) were of negative sign in (*c*) and (*d*), they were not statistically significant to make any reliable interpretations. The explicit relationship between AE_i and firm size would be observed at a later stage.

Results of Systematic Allocative Efficiency (AE_{ii})

$R = 21$ per cent interest rate
$W =$ variable wage rate. $I \ldots\ldots n$

The following shows the results without the interactive term of AE_{ii} and ZS on the right hand side.

V.1.2.ii.a $$E = -10{,}970 + 16.3(ZS) + 1{,}22{,}286(AE_{ii})$$
$$(5.4)^{*} \quad (0.6)$$
$$R\ squared = 0.29 \quad F = 15$$

V.1.2.ii.b $$(E/S) = 0.59 - 0.00017(ZS) + 0.83(AE_{ii})$$
$$-(2.4)^{*}(1.65)^{***}$$
$$R\ squared = 0.10 \quad F = 4.06$$

The following show the results with the intereactive term.

V.1.2.ii.c
$$E = -5423 - 146\,(ZS)$$
$$-(0.75)$$
$$+6696(AE_{ii}) + 162(ZS)(AE_{ii})$$
$$(0.3) \qquad (0.08)$$
$$R\ squared = 0.3 \quad F = 10.4$$

V.1.2.ii.d
$$(E/S) = -0.68 + 0.0024(ZS) + 0.92(AE_{ii})$$
$$(0.5) \qquad (1.72)^{**}$$
$$-\ 0.002(ZS)(AE_{ii})$$
$$-(0.55)$$
$$R\ squared = 0.10\ F = 3.0\ N = 76$$

The figures in brackets are 't' values.

*Statistically significant at 0.025 level.

**Significant at 0.05 level.

***Significant at 0.10 level.

Contrary to the results with AE_i, in this case the estimated coefficients associated with the systematic allocative efficiency variable (AE_{ii}) were consistently of positive sign. The estimated coefficients of AE_{ii} were statistically significant only in (*b*) and (*c*) where export propensity was the dependent variable. The positive association between AE_{ii} and export propensity obviously implied that higher the systematic AE based on the shadow factor prices, higher the export propensity. This result supported the argument regarding the domestic comparative advantage in relative factor endowments reflected by the relative shadow factor prices of factors of production. The 21 per cent interest rate which was used to estimate AE_{ii} was argued to be close to the shadow price of capital.

The firms which were relatively allocatively efficient based on AE_{ii} would be able to minimize costs by adopting the optimum combination of the factors of production on the basis of their true opportunity costs at the country level on the given production frontier. As a result, they would be in a better position to reap the country's comparative advantage in the relative factor endowments and incomes.

As argued in Chapter 3, 21 per cent of interest was what the S&M firms, which had lower access to capital compared to large firms, would pay for capital. Although the relationship between AE_{ii} and firm size was not established here, on the basis on the given relationship between E/S and ZS, one could say that it was the S&M firms' production techniques which were closer to the country's comparative advantage under the segmented factor market conditions.

This observation did not necessarily mean that only the small firms would be able to attain the comparative advantage reflected by AE_{ii}. The comparison of the results obtained with AEi and AE_{ii}, demonstrated that the firms, irrespective of size, which were maximizing the systematic allocative efficiency of AE_{ii} were able to export at higher propensity.

The following results showed the explicit relationship between firm size and AE_i and AE_{ii} (estimated).

V.3.i $$AE_i = 0.36 - 0.00007(ZS) + 1.04(IM/S)$$

$$(0.56) \qquad (3.4)^*$$

$$R\ squared = 0.16\ F = 4.6$$

V.3.ii $$AE_{ii} = 1.0 - 0.000007(ZS) - 0.13(IM/S)$$

$$-(0.26) - (1.92)^{**}$$

$$R\ squared = 0.09\ F = 1.7\ N = 76$$

The figures in brackets are 't' values.

*Statistically significant at 0.025 level.

**Significant at 0.05 level.

In the above results, in both cases of AE_i and AE_{ii}, the estimated coefficients associated with firm size were of negative sign but were not statistically significant. This indicated that there might not be a systematic relationship between firm size and the AE measures. But if one observed Figures 5.5 and 5.6, where the AE_i and AE_{ii} measures are fitted against firm size (reduced to logs), there was a systematic pattern in the cluster of observations of AE_i and AE_{ii} (on the Y-axis) with respect to the size groups (on X-axis). The maximum values of

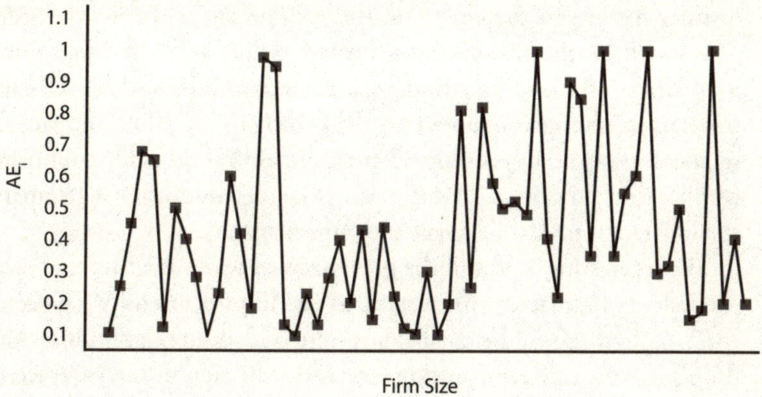

Figure 5.5 AE$_i$ and Firm Size
Source: Derived from estimation of econometric equations.

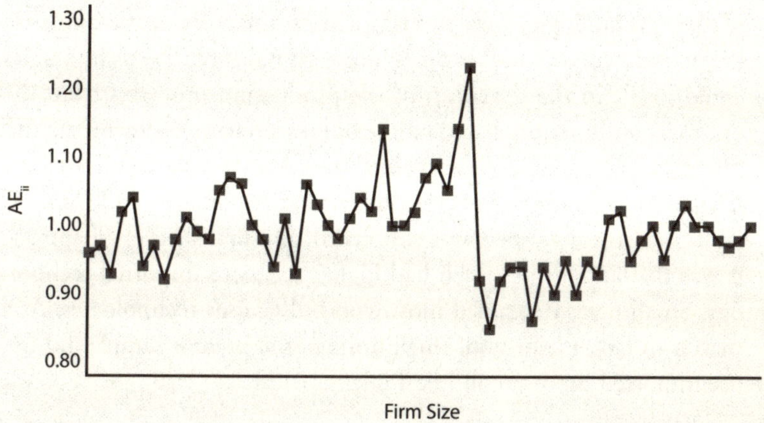

Figure 5.6 AE$_{ii}$ and Firm Size
Source: Derived from estimation of econometric equations.

AE$_i$ and mostly at the larger size group, which was argued to be the expected outcome as the factor price of capital, used in this case is in favour of large firms. There was a clear pattern in the case of AE$_{ii}$ where the separate size groups were striking. The S&M firms had the distinct cluster of the higher AE$_{ii}$ points. And after the maximum point, there was a sudden dip after which the large firms had the distinct pattern in the cluster of the AE_{ii} points at the lower level. This could be the major reason behind the very low R squares in the earlier estimated equation with respect to AE_{ii} variable. These patterns in the figures supported the argument regarding the factor segmentation and its possible effect on the realization of the country's comparative advantage in the relative factor endowments (relative shadow factor prices) by small and large firms.

The interesting aspect of the previous results was the nature of the coefficients estimated with respect to the import intensity variable, *IM/S*. In both cases, the coefficients were statistically significant. But the signs were different. In Equation V.3.i the sign of the parameter was positive and in Equation V.3.ii it was negative. These results supported the argument put forward in Chapter 3, that the firms which obtained capital at far lower price than its shadow price, as in case of AE_i, would tend to adopt capital-intensive imported technologies. If these technologies were not adapted on the basis of the domestic factor endowments and incomes, these capital-intensive technologies could result in the deviation of the production processes from the optimal combinations based on the domestic factor endowments and incomes. This observation explained the negative association between AE_{ii} and *IM/S* and the positive association between AE_{ii} and *IM/S*. As far as the firm size aspect was concerned, as established in Chapter 3, it was the large firms which had higher access to imported technology. Small firms depended mostly on indigenous technologies. As a matter of fact, majority of small firms in the present sample did not use imported inputs at all (see Table 3.2B).

PART 2

International Trade and Investment Behaviour of Firms: The Post-reform Era

6 Introduction to Part 2

Part 1 of the study focused on international trade behaviour and ignored international investment because in most industries TNCs were not allowed to operate. As mentioned before, theoretically international trade and investment are interrelated. The theories of international trade lay the basic foundation for international economics and business, starting from theories of Adam Smith, Ricardo, Heckscher, and Ohlin, to intra-industry theories and theories of multinational firms initiated by Hymer's (1960) intangible assets theory. International investment can expand international trade (inter-industry trade) and could be a substitute for international trade (intra-industry). In this part of the book, we demonstrate how the reforms improve the market imperfections in the product and factor markets, discussed in Part 1, and cause domestic market dynamics and consequent international trade and investment behaviour of firms. In the post-reform era, TNCs started playing an important role in industry dynamics and internationalization of firms in response to opening up of the economy and liberal trade policies.

As is well-known about India, certain internal reforms such as removal of industrial licensing policies and restrictions on the size of firms, reform of reservation policies for small firms, reduction in import tariffs and controls, and partial entry of transnational corporations were initiated in the mid-1980s and major internal and external reforms were initiated in the early 1990s. A detailed discussion of the reforms was made in several studies (Ahluwalia, 2002, 1999; Dossani, 2008; Forbes, 2002; Delong, 2001; Srinivasan, 2000; Das, 2000). Therefore, we do not replicate them in this study.

In response to the reforms, India had been able to augment its annual economic growth rate to 6 to 7 per cent. Reforms, in general, could be considered to have led to positive outcomes unlike the cases of countries in Eastern Europe, Africa, and Latin America. This was because, as demonstrated in Part 1, India had a critical level of initial conditions of capitalist institutions, industrial and technological base, entrepreneurial class, and skilled labour acquired right from the British Raj to the import substitution regime (Patibandla, 2006b). Furthermore, India had comparative advantage in low-cost semi-skilled and skilled labour in several industries. However, the policy regime distorted the price mechanism both in the factor and product markets; furthermore, exchange rate was overvalued. The reforms on these fronts initiated the process of firms realizing comparative advantage and intra-industry trade factors such as technologies and scale economies, consequently augmenting export growth rate. India presents an interesting duality of a combination of technological sophistication with low-cost skilled labour and international competitiveness. Several industries such as electronics and automobiles and components required technological capabilities to be export competitive. Therefore, both inter-industry and intra-industry trade takes place.

Increase in economic growth implies increase in output, employment, and decline in prices of manufactured goods (through increased competition) which result in increase in per capita incomes and market size, scale economies, product differentiation, and technological dynamics. As the incomes, especially of the middle class and the rich, increase, intra-industry trade of export and import of differentiated goods takes place. For example, at present, India exports small cars and imports luxury cars. One of the important outcomes of the reforms had been the expansion of service sectors such as software and services, telecommunications, and certain financial services because the previous policies generated a large base of skilled manpower through heavy subsidization of English-based higher education (Dossani and Patibandla, 2010; Patibandla and Petersen, 2002), a critical level of infrastructure, and the legal system for capitalism. This, in turn, resulted in increase in scope for both inter-industry (comparative advantage) and intra-industry trade (scale economies and product differentiation). Apart from this, trade through firm-level heterogeneity of the 'New' New Trade Theory was in terms of increase in number and types of firms such as TNCs, new entrant Indian firms, and internal and global supply chains between both local and multinational firms. Furthermore, transaction costs of business to business and business to consumers, such as information and search costs and contractual and distributional costs, started to decline on average. This, in turn, led to expansion of economic activity, both internally and externally. As a consequence of the reforms, India started to reap benefits of globalization and rapid technological change and inflows, becoming one of the fastest-growing emerging economies (Spence, 2011).

One of the most important outcomes of the reforms is the increasing presence of TNCs in most industries through vertical and horizontal investments. This has implications on domestic competition and consequent international trade and investment behaviour of firms. To recapitulate, international trade and investment are interrelated. The TNCs may set up operations in developing economies to make use of comparative advantage in low-cost semi-skilled and skilled labour, thereby expanding international trade. The TNCs' operations could be a substitute for intra-industry trade. In the initial phase, a firm may produce in and export from the home market. Later, it would substitute exports by investing in overseas markets to overcome tariff and transport barriers and to be close to the consumers.

The dominant theory of multinational firms is the intangible asset theory (Hymer, 1960), especially in the case of horizontal investments that are undertaken to cater to foreign markets. The theory shows how a firm can become a multinational if it has intangible assets in technology (knowledge), patents, blueprints, trademarks, and brand names. Without these, it will not able to compete with local firms.

Following from this was Dunning's (1988) Ownership–Location–Internalization (OLI) framework, which demonstrated the trade-offs a multinational firm has to take into account in making choices of internalization versus trading an intangible asset across countries. Setting up in multiple locations is determined by trade-offs between multi-plants and scale economies, and transport and tariff barriers (Markusen, 1995). Higher the market imperfections in terms of protection of technology and brand names and transaction costs of formulating and enforcing contracts, higher the need for internalization of an intangible asset. In the case of vertical investment, it is mainly to take advantage of factor and technological endowments of different countries for global operations. As mentioned earlier, a good example is India's software industry in which there has been a high degree of presence of TNCs (Patibandla and Petersen, 2002). Global supply chains have become important sources of international trade and multinational operations as developing countries opened their economies. As a matter of fact, global supply chains are a major source of world trade. For example, Walmart accounted for 30 per cent of China's exports. As China transforms into a middle-income country, some of the global supply chains are moving to countries such as India, Vietnam, and Indonesia (Spence, 2011).

In response to reforms, there had been significant increase in new entrants in several industries. However, most new entrants are incumbent large corporations branching out into different areas on their own and through joint ventures with TNCs and greenfield TNCs except for a few industries such as software and services. This is because India's capital markets remain imperfect (Khanna and Palepu, 2000; Patibandla, 2006a). Nevertheless, this significantly increased competitive conditions, consumer choice, and product diversity. As mentioned before, TNCs enter developing economies with an advantage in technology and international brand names. If local firms were unable to compete with them, they would be eliminated from the market. The response of the Indian corporations to competition from TNCs was to upgrade their technology, improve organizational efficiency (both internal and supply chain with supplier firms), and distribution and marketing. Technology was upgraded by importing and adapting it to local conditions. This was complimented with internal R&D investments (Patibandla, 2002).

Organizationally, as discussed in the previous part, large family-based corporations adopted the top-down approach of having large number of hierarchies and high degree of internal X-inefficiency as there were no competitive pressures to be efficient in the protected markets. In a typical large firm, the number of hierarchy levels ranged between fifteen and twenty. This changed significantly in the post-reform era. Several large corporations started to improve organizational efficiency by adopting a bottom-up approach to improve informational flows internally, which will be discussed later. Furthermore, family businesses started to combine family control and employing professional managers.

One more organizational change was improvements in buyer–supplier (subcontracting firms) relations through better contractual arrangements, both internally and internationally. As discussed in the previous part, subcontracting S&M firms in several engineering industries were in a disadvantageous position in relative bargaining with large final goods producers owing to inefficient contractual relations. This changed significantly with the entry of TNCs, especially the Japanese and South Korean firms in industries such as automobiles, two-wheelers, and electronics, which will be discussed later.

On the capital market front, during the pre-reforms era, diversified family groups were able to build family empires with better access to industrial licensing and capital from the public financial institutions (Tripathi, 2004; Patibandla, 2006a). By the year 2000, most of these public financial institutions were saddled with large sums of non-performing assets, which prompted the government to reform them. For example, ICICI Bank was made into a private merchant bank. In response to the stock market scandal of 1992, the Government of India implemented reforms such as the setting up of the National Stock Exchange, which reduced the monopoly position and insider trading practices of the Bombay Stock Exchange, and the Securities and Exchange Board of India for monitoring corporate governance practices of listed firms. Furthermore, foreign institutional investors were allowed to operate in Indian stock markets. Emergence of financial intermediaries such as mutual funds, investment banks, and foreign institutional investors resulted in improvements in corporate governance practices of listed companies and decline in costs of capital by reducing transaction and information costs of the markets (Shaw and Thomas, 2002). Furthermore, Indian corporations were allowed to tap global capital markets such as the global depository receipts; they were also allowed to list in foreign stock markets. Apart from this, Indian corporations were allowed to invest in overseas markets. These developments helped the better-governed Indian corporations to be able to raise capital and compete with TNCs that have better access to global capital markets. Although there have been improvements in the functioning of capital markets, they remain imperfect in the sense that the market still involves high transaction costs for absolute new entrants to raise capital and compete with incumbent large corporations. For example, large corporates had better access to debt markets of the public sector banks. The Bankruptcy Code was implemented only recently. In the case of S&M firms, those firms that got into the global supply chains of multinationals were able to overcome working capital constraints and technology transfer and other benefits of reducing informational imperfections of the markets.

One of the important developments on the capital market front is the emergence of venture capital and start-up activities during the last decade. The total venture investment in start-ups during the decade 2005–15 has been estimated at INR 1,117 billion. The average annual growth rate in investment flow during the same period was about 42 per cent and more than 10,000 start-ups have received venture funding.

Most of these entrepreneurs come from a middle-class background and are first-generation entrepreneurs. While family and friends can contribute to a part of the initial seed capital, serious investment has to be from external sources. Given the nature of the business—technology- and innovation-driven, and characterized by intangible assets—access to bank funding is limited. It is here that venture investors play an important role by providing equity funding in the seed and growth stages of the venture.

The software and internet services industry has received the maximum rounds of funding (and also the quantum). This is followed by consumer products and services and fintech and payments category. The average investment per round in the fintech and payments sector is higher than that of other sectors, as most of the rounds are concentrated at the top end of the spectrum (Bagchi, 2018). A major part of the risk capital flows in from overseas, from countries such as the USA and Japan.

One of the great success stories of start-ups in India is the case of Flipkart, an online business started by two entrepreneurs in 2007. Its market value increased rapidly even though it was not making profits. In 2018 it was sold to Walmart for USD 19 billion.

One of the differences between the start-ups in India and the USA is that in the USA a start-up can go to the IPO stage even without being profitable whereas in India it has to be profitable. As we gathered from our interviews with a couple of entrepreneurs in Bangalore, customers in India are more price-sensitive than those in the USA, which delays the time for succeeding in the market. Furthermore, Khanna and Palepu (2018) observe that trust between investors and entrepreneurs is an important institutional feature of difference between emerging economies and the USA.

Dossani and Desai (2009) observe that over 90 per cent of the money invested in late-stage initiatives is by mature firms. Even the remainder mostly finances new firms replicating proven business ideas. Therefore, very few innovative start-ups are funded. They observe, as we did earlier, that SMEs account for 45 per cent of employment, 40 per cent of gross domestic product, and 50 per cent of exports. Investments in SMEs could promote overall economic growth and international trade. However, the ability of SMEs to receive risk capital is limited, which requires government institutional support mechanisms. They show the barriers for SMEs, which include regulatory barriers that raise transaction costs and ineffective policy mechanisms for reducing the risk of early-stage risk capital. Nevertheless, we could say that this process is the beginning of emergence of innovative activities of firms in the context of a developing economy.

In the case of labour markets, as discussed in the previous part of the book, labour markets were segmented into the organized and unorganized markets, with large organized sector firms and S&M firms paying different wages and benefits with implications on their respective ability to benefit from comparative advantage. The following issue is whether the segmentation of labour markets decreased or increased in the post-reform era such that large firms could play an important role in inter-industry trade. With the entry of a large number of large-scale firms, both local and TNCs, labour market segmentation declines as these firms have to pay government-stipulated minimum wages and benefits to workers.

One of the important practices that large firms started implementing to overcome government policy regulation of permanent (organized) employees was employment of contractual labourers through the emergent contract labour suppliers and employment agencies. They recruited semi-skilled and unskilled labour across the country and supplied them to the large firms. This provided certain degree of flexibility to large firms in labour management. Nagaraj (2004) showed that between 1995/96 and 2000/01 about 1.1 million workers in the organized sector lost their jobs. Employment and wage levels of supervisors increased. He observed that some of the jobs shed might have reappeared in the unorganized sector with growing subcontracting of production and shedding auxiliary services, such as transport, security, cleaning, and provision of food at workplace. He demonstrated significant decline in wage/capital cost. This could be a result of large firms adopting capital- and technology-intensive production processes to compete with TNCs and in the world markets. In the small-scale sector, despite minimum wage and benefits regulations of the government, about 80 per cent of labour markets remain unorganized and the workers are paid low wages.

The final goods market dynamics in terms of domestic and export markets competition has implications on the labour markets. Increase in number of final goods producers reduces monopsony power in labour markets which, in turn, should result in increase in employment and productivity-enhancing practices of workers and better wage levels. Labour markets, in general, have been tilting in favour of highly skilled labour owing to rapid technological changes (Spence, 2011).

In the post-reform era, large firms started to play an important role in international trade with both inter-industry and intra-industry trade possibilities. Furthermore, large number of TNCs entered the Indian markets both for catering to local market and for utilizing comparative advantage in semi-skilled and skilled labour-intensive endowments. Because of the structural dynamics in the product and factor markets in the post-reforms era, India started to produce large corporations with investments in advanced technologies and high knowledge intensity with cutting-edge strategies and organizational modes (Hansen, 2009), along with the traditional semi-skilled intensive industries. This, in turn, augmented the inter- and intra-industry pattern of international trade and led to the emergence of Indian multinational firms on the global scene. This outcome supports the arguments of the previous part that the domestic market structural dynamics determine international trade and investment behaviour of firms. The process is illustrated in the chapters that follow.

7 The Model

The following model is an extension of the model presented in Part I by introducing firm-level asymmetries in terms of time of entry (the pre-reform and post-reform eras) and firm-level costs of production. The home market is taken to be oligopolistic and the world market competitive. The new entrants in the post-reform era are taken to be TNCs with intangible assets.

The linear inverse home market demand function is

$$P = a - b(X)$$
$$X = x_i + x_j \tag{1}$$
$$P \geq P_w(1+t)$$

x_i is incumbent firm, x_j is the new entrant. x_i refers to domestic sales and x_i^* refers to exports of firm *i*. P_w is the world market price and *t* is the tariff rate on imports. *P* refers to the domestic market price. In equilibrium, $P > P_w$. The profit function of firms facing protected domestic market and competitive export market is

$$\prod_i = P()x_i + P_w x_i^* - c_i / 2(x_i + x_i^*)^2 \tag{2}$$

$$\prod_j = P()x_j + P_w x_j^* - c_j / 2(x_j + x_j^*)^2 \tag{3}$$

where c_i is the cost parameter. By equating the first order derivatives with respect to exports to zero, we obtain

$$x_i^* = (P_w / c_i) - x_i \tag{4}$$

$$x_j^* = (P_w / c_j) - x_j \tag{5}$$

The new entrant (follower) firm j takes x_i as given and solves as follows:

$$\prod_j = (a - bx_i - bx_{jj})x_j - c_j / 2(x_j + x_j^*)^2 \tag{6}$$

$$\partial \prod_j / \partial x_j = (a - bx_{i\_} - 2bx_j) - c_j(x_j + x_i^*) = 0 \tag{7}$$

From Equation 5, we know that $x_j + x_j^* = (P_w / c_j)$. By substituting this into Equation 7, we get:

$$x_j = (a - P_w - bx_i) / 2b \tag{8}$$

Equation 8 is the reaction function of a new entrant who believes that the incumbent's capacity choice does not change to its capacity decision, a la Cournot. As the incumbent firm behaves like a Stackelberg leader, the reaction function of j enters the profit function of firm i. By solving for the profit function of firm i, we obtain:

$$x_i = (a - P_w) / 2b \tag{9}$$

By substituting Equation 9 into Equation 8, we obtain the equilibrium home market sales of the new entrant:

$$x_j = (a - P_{wi}) / 4b \tag{10}$$

The exports of firms in equilibrium are as follows:

$$x_i = (P_w / c_i) - (a - P_{wi}) / 2b \tag{11}$$

$$x_j^* = (P_w / c_j) - (a - P_w) / 4b \tag{12}$$

$$a > Pw$$

The implications of asymmetric advantages across domestic firms and new entrant TNCs on their competitive behaviour can be traced by the following cases:

1. asymmetry in time of entry and $c_i = c_j$;
2. asymmetry in time of entry and $c_i < c_j$; and
3. asymmetry in time of entry and $c_i > c_j$

In case 1, from Equations 11 and 12, the new entrant has higher export orientation than the incumbent. The incumbent *i*, by the sheer advantage of entering first, is able to capture a higher share of the protected domestic market. However, when the incumbent's costs are sufficiently lower than the new entrant's ($c_i << c_j$), the outcome can be reversed. The reason is as follows. When the new entrant has high costs, its domestic market share is a lot lower than the incumbent's. (This would be true even in a Nash–Cournot setting.) Consequently, the new entrant is less restrained in expanding its sales at home as the perceived impact on the domestic price is correspondingly lower. The new entrant becomes more like a perfectly competitive firm, and hence there is less incentive to withhold sales to prop up the price. This could lead to the follower having a lower export orientation than the leader.

Even in case 3, where the new entrant has lower costs than the incumbent firm, it has a lower domestic market share and exports more than the incumbent. The intuitive explanation for this is that it takes time for a new entrant to dislodge an incumbent in the domestic market. Exports, at the initial stage, help a new entrant to realize minimum efficient scale in production. This outcome may be more applicable to a new entrant TNC because the relative advantage of intangibles associated with international markets is with TNCs rather than domestic new entrants. Asymmetries in production costs across firms have implications only on exports but not on domestic sales. The explanation is that as firms face oligopolistic competition in the protected domestic market and are price takers in the export market, exports are undertaken to restrict domestic supply at higher price as part of the price discriminatory behaviour.

In case 3, if the incumbent's costs are sufficiently higher than a new entrant's such that it can operate only in the domestic market, which means its marginal cost of production is higher than the world price, the new entrant will have higher domestic market share.

We can safely assume that profits associated with domestic market are higher than international markets initially as it is oligopolistic. Both the incumbent and new entrant compete rigorously for domestic market shares. There could be cases when first entrants (the incumbents) are in a disadvantageous position than later entrants if they are saddled with outdated technological and organizational assets (Dixit and Nalebuff, 2010; Patibandla, 2002). The optimal response of incumbents is to replace these assets with better practices of international standards in response to competition from new entrant TNCs. However, not all assets acquired in relation to the institutional environment of the pre-reform era were redundant. Institutional knowledge of the Indian economy, dealer networks, and political connections could buy some time for incumbents to be able to compete with TNCs. Although TNCs had an advantage in intangible assets, they lacked experience in dealing with India's institutions and consumers and know-how of the established dealer network. They have to adapt their advantages in intangible assets to local conditions. Their response could be to acquire these assets by forming short-term joint ventures with local firms with institutional knowledge of India and its dealer networks. Once they acquired the institutional knowledge and knowledge of dealer networks, they broke the joint ventures. Both the local firms and TNCs have to make rational expectations regarding changes and growth of the market (increase in economic growth rates), both in the short and long term, in order to undertake investments in what type of differentiated products they invest in in the present. Wrong expectations could result in failures.

The competitive processes and outcomes, in turn, can result in convergence of best practices in technology and organization, which augments international competitiveness (Spence, 2011). There are several case studies of this process, such as Bajaj in the two-wheelers and Mahindra and Mahindra and Tata Motors in automobiles (Patibandla, 2016). Furthermore, if TNCs realize economies of scale with a large host market base, they could undertake exports. A good example is the South Korean car producer Hyundai, which exports small cars from India.

The entry of new firms, especially TNCs, increases the number of firms but also results in technology and organizational heterogeneity such as the 'New' New Trade Theory. This, in turn, increases possibilities for benchmarking and increases the opportunities for imitation by relatively inefficient firms. Furthermore, the relative advantages of TNCs in intangible assets could be diverse, differentiating TNCs within an industry. For example, the unique intangible assets and organizational practices of managerial and vendor development of the Japanese and South Korean firms might be distinct from the American and European practices. Local firms had to assess which practices were more suitable for them to accomplish domestic and international competitiveness.

Costs of production is a function of technology, organization, economies of scale, and economies of specialization of value chains and externalities, as discussed in Part I. Furthermore, international trade and investment activities could result in externalities to firms because intangible assets, no matter how well-protected, still have public goods properties. International trade exposes local firms to best practices in the world markets.

Technology

As discussed in Part 1, in the Schumpeterian world of 'creative destruction', competition among firms is through innovation for monopoly profits. In the case of developing economies, technological change is more of imitative kind rather than innovative. The cases of Japan and South Korea demonstrate the case of achieving high growth rates by imitating new products and processes of developed countries and adopting export-led growth strategies (Amsden, 1989). For the last forty years, China presents similar strategies. In India's case, the process started in the late 1980s and the early 1990s with gradual opening up of the economy to freer international trade and investment. As discussed before, globalization and rapid technological changes and their multi-speed flows across countries have been playing an important role in causing a few developing economies to start converging in economic development with developed economies (Spence, 2011)

When a firm innovates in technology, products, and practices, it generates turbulence in the market by taking away market share from rivals. The optimal response of the competitors is either to imitate or innovate. Incentives for innovation emanate from the market and institutional conditions to realize monopoly profits. Institutional protection in terms of intellectual property rights is necessary for firms to invest in R&D for innovation. On the other hand, even in the absence of intellectual property rights, firms may compete through innovation if there is time lag for imitation by the rivals.

For the competition process, if two agents play the Cournot–Nash game, firms take each others' output choices and maximize their own profits. There is no unilateral incentive for any agent to move away from equilibrium unless there is an exogenous shock. An agent's incentive to invest in R&D and innovate has to be introduced by ad hoc assumptions. One way we can resolve this is by considering that under the Nash–Cournot game, firms compete with R&D investments instead of quantity of output (Dasgupta & Stiglitz, 1980). The R&D race goes on until a discovery is made. If we consider the innovation as process innovation, the firm that makes the discovery will have lower costs and will have higher market share and profits in equilibrium. We consider that the innovative firm is from a developed economy which enters a developing economy with the superior practice as a TNC. Therefore, the innovation comes to a developing economy exogenously. The kind of sophistication and vintage levels of technologies that TNCs bring into developing countries depend on the development level of local firms' capabilities (in order to compete) and macro conditions such as availability of skilled manpower, protection of property rights, and potential growth of the market. Given the technologies TNCs bring in, incumbent local firms have to make efforts to replace the older technological assets with superior practices to compete with new entrant TNCs in the second period (the post-reform era). The adoption of new technologies involves adjustment and adaptation costs (Parente and Prescott, 1994). These costs could range from low to high depending on the firm-level capabilities, product market developments, and macro level conditions.

The R&D investments of local firms would be mostly to adapt imported technology and technology purchases.

For developing economy firms to be able to catch up with TNCs, they need to possess a critical level of conditions of technological endowments, both at the micro level of firms and at macro level of an economy. On the basis of the initial conditions or endowments, the reforms determine how they cause further development of technology through changes in competitive dynamics, product market developments, market opportunities, and institutional conditions. At the macro level, the endowments required are the public stock of knowledge, scientific and knowledge-generating universities, human capital, government funding of R&D, the linkages of private firms with scientific institutions, and investing in knowledge, development of financial institutions and industrial clusters and externalities, and protection of intellectual property rights. India can be considered as an emerging economy possessing a critical level of these conditions to be able to catch up with developed economies. The overall combination of these conditions of a country is called 'National Innovation System' (NIS). A reasonably well-developed NIS reduces the technology lags of imitation and adoption and adaptation costs of new technologies by local firms. In India's case its NIS can be observed to be at a nascent stage.

There are two elements to technological adaptation: codified and tacit knowledge. Codified elements are embedded in blueprints which can be easily tradeable nationally and internationally. New technologies can be characterized by non-rivalrous and non-excludability conditions (Romer, 1990). Non-excludability implies new technologies have some public property characteristics and spillovers (externalities) to other firms. Non-rivalry implies that use of a new technology or a blueprint (or a new idea) does not preclude other users. More the users, the larger is its aggregate value. International trade and investment increase the number of users. Purchase of a blueprint is only part of technological adaptation.

A firm can master tacit elements with close interactions with the sellers' technological operations. Indian firm Bajaj Auto is a good example. Until the mid-1980s only a few local players dominated the two-wheeler industry. In response to the reforms of the mid-1980s, TNCs such as Honda and Suzuki entered the Indian market and introduced technologically superior motorcycle models and grew rapidly in the Indian market, posing a threat to Bajaj's leadership in scooters. As a response, Bajaj sourced technology and licences from countries such as Austria, Italy, and Japan. It augmented in-house R&D. It took its engineers to the onsite manufacturing outlets of technology providers for a few months to master tacit elements of the technology. It combined this with organizational restructuring of adopting lower number of hierarchies and bottom-up approach of information flows. Consequently, Bajaj was able to catch up with Honda's superior technology (Bhudhiraja et al., 2003; Patibandla, 2016). After successful adaptation of imported technologies, local firms might be able to innovate in product features and production processes that are amenable to local conditions. For example, in the two-wheeler industry, which is one of the largest in the world, Indian firms started to undertake incremental innovations in the products and processes, such as hybrids of scooters and motorcycles that combine the best features of the two products to cater to the changing preferences of Indian consumers.

In the case of TNCs, they have to adapt their products and processes in relation to Indian market conditions of infrastructure, changing consumer incomes and preferences, geographical conditions, and building dealer networks and value chains. In general, it is observed that Indian consumers are price-sensitive (price-elastic). If TNCs fail to take this into account, they could fail in the market. South Korean TNC Hyundai presents a success story. It introduced latest technology for producing both small- and middle-size cars and adapted the technology to local conditions. Consequently, it was able to compete with Maruti Suzuki in the small car segment and started to undertake exports from India.

India's NIS in the post-reform era evolved based on the past investments in science and technology and industrial capabilities in the pre-reform era of the import substitution regime. For import substitution objectives, the Indian government heavily subsidized higher education in science and technology and set up several government research institutions and the public sector firms. By the end of the 1990s, there were 229 universities of national importance, 7,199 undergraduate and postgraduate colleges for general education, 162 medical colleges, and 325 pharmacy colleges, in addition to numerous engineering colleges, including the Indian Institutes of Technology (IITs). Furthermore, in response to the boom in the software and services industry, a large number private engineering colleges came into the market. In the 2000s, the Indian government started setting up a large number of IITs and Indian Institutes of Management (IIMs). Apart from this, there are several institutes that are of international repute. The government of India set up several research institutions such as the Center for Scientific and Industrial Research (CSIR), the Department of Science and Technology, the Defence and Research Development Organization, the Indian Space Research Organization (ISRO), the Indian Council of Medical Research (ICMR), and the Indian Agricultural Research Institution (IARI), which generated about a thousand R&D institutions and laboratories across the nation. India's prior investments have enabled new industries to emerge and traditional industries to restructure themselves effectively in the post-reform era. Good examples of this are India's software and services industry, pharmaceutical industry, and the electronics industry.

In terms of skill endowments, about 7,00,000 students were enrolled in undergraduate degree courses in engineering (all fields) in 2003. This rose rapidly, and as of 2008 it was estimated to be 1.25 million. According to Nasscom (2006), the number of new undergraduates in engineering was expected to be 2,64,000 in 2006. The information technology (IT) workforce was further bolstered by those with engineering diplomas (usually a two-year course) and those with master's degrees in computer applications (about 35,000 in 2006). However, the quality of the degrees differ significantly depending on the institutions—IITs, regional engineering colleges, or private providers. Dossani and Patibandla (2010) observe that the private providers focused on the more lucrative fields such as engineering and management education. As a result of their presence, the Indian higher education system became increasingly differentiated. The private providers tend to specialize in only a few fields for which demand is high. By contrast the state providers offer a wide range of studies. Furthermore, the faculty of the private educational institutions tend to be of poor quality as compared to the state institutions. The state can play a critical role in regulating the private institutions with regard to faculty selection and compensations.

For a vibrant national innovation to evolve, the state has to play a role in correcting market failures in research in pure science and promote linkages between technological institutions. For example, in the USA, the government funds pure science with grants from the National Science Foundation. Apart from this, the investments in defence research has been a major source of technological innovations. Even in an environment in which private provision thrives, as in the USA, the state's role is critical. It includes the financing of education for efficiency and equity, directing science and engineering courses towards problem solving and creative thinking, and organizing the policy environment, governance structures, and institutional administration to produce high quality training (Martinez, 2002).

Some of the important aspects of the NIS are the linkages between private firms and the public institutions and inter-firm linkages for cooperative technological innovation. Linkages could be at the higher or lower end of technologies. The former causes a higher degree of technological spillovers than the latter. This is determined by technological capabilities of firms and their ability to find complementarity at the higher end of technology.

Organization

The neo-classical theory takes the firm as a 'black-box' or simply a production function. In reality, a firm is an organization. In Part 1, we examined organizational efficiency in terms of X-efficiency and vertical integration and number of hierarchies within a firm and diversification behaviour of firms. X-efficiency was examined in terms of managers' involvement in maximization of internal efficiency with human resource management, hierarchies, and internal information flows. Furthermore, we observed that when markets were non-competitive there were no incentives for firms with market power to be efficient organizationally. X-efficiency of managers of large Indian corporations improved significantly in the post-reform era owing to increased competitive conditions through the entry of a large number of TNCs in several industries.

In the case of vertical integration, there has been a vibrant field of 'Theory of the Firm', pioneered by Coase and Williamson and their followers. Coase (1937) argued that a firm as an organization comes into existence to economize on transaction costs of markets. The firm internalizes economic activity until marginal internal bureaucratic costs of hierarchy are equal to the marginal transaction costs of the market (boundaries of the firm). Once an economic activity is internalized by a firm, it is hierarchy which governs resource allocation rather than price mechanism. Williamson (1985) in his theory of governance makes behavioural assumptions of bounded rationality and opportunism. Bounded rationality refers to behaviour intended to be rational but limitedly so owing to informational imperfections and cognitive abilities. Opportunistic behaviour is conceptualized in terms of self-interest with guile. Transaction costs differ in three critical dimensions; frequency, uncertainty, and asset specificity. All contracts are incomplete. It is not possible to incorporate all possible contingencies into a contract. Given the differential dimensions of transaction costs, agents choose different governance structures; markets, hierarchy (vertical integration), and hybrids (such as franchisees, to some extent joint ventures) with implications on internal costs and economies of specialization between firms. For investments with high degree of asset specificity, the preferable governance is integration. Higher the internalization of economic activity, higher is the internal organizational inefficiency. The choice between internalization of an economic activity is a matter of trade-offs between economies of specialization and transaction costs of formulating and executing contracts such as possible opportunistic behaviour under incomplete contracts. Developing countries are generally observed to be characterized by high transaction costs. This aspect is discussed later in the case of value chains.

Japanese firms adopted the lean production practices and developed the concept of outsourcing and supplier firms (vertical disintegration). Cost and quality advantage arising out of these practices made the Japanese automobile and electronic companies shake up the world markets in the 1980s and 1990s, forcing companies in the USA and Europe to adopt some of the Japanese practices. Consequently, most companies in the USA and Western Europe have become focused companies, with their focus on not just innovative investments but also on improving production floor practices of organizations. As mentioned, the entry of Japanese companies, such as Suzuki and Honda, and South Korean companies, such as Hyundai, into India led to the development of supplier firms through subcontracting. Indian firms such as Mahindra and Mahindra, Bajaj, and Tata imitated these practices to reduce costs (Okada, 2004; D'Costa, 1995). However, most of India's large family businesses are still diversified business groups like the Japanese and South Korean corporations. Khanna and Palepu (2000) extend the transaction cost logic to rationalize that diversification into unrelated areas in developing countries takes place for economizing on transaction costs of capital and labour markets. In several cases, restructuring of Indian family businesses tend to be based on splitting them among family members rather than adopting focused lines (*Business Today*, 1999).

As discussed in Part 1, India's family-run businesses tended to have large number of hierarchies internally. Larger the number of hierarchies and centralization of management, higher the organizational inefficiency in terms of information overload at the top and high levels of imperfect transfer of information. This type of organizational inefficiency of Indian firms led to substantial improvements in terms of decentralization and the bottom-up approach to managing in the post-reform era.

We present the case analysis of organizational restructuring of Bajaj corporation based on our field interviews of a few executives of Bajaj and the article by Bhudiraja et al (2003). The case analysis provides us with interesting underlying mechanisms of organizational change. Bajaj sourced technology and licences from Austria, Italy, and Japan. It augmented in-house investment in R&D. In order to deal with the tacit elements of technology transfer, it took a group of its engineers to plants abroad to get first-hand knowledge of the new advanced technologies. It undertook organizational restructuring for adaptation of the technology and achieving operational efficiency. The new organizational approach shifted from a top-down approach, typical of a family-run highly centralized organization, to a bottom-up approach. On the shop floor, workmen and section managers were grouped into cells and the members were guided by the self-management approach. All the cells were interlinked for smooth information flow and coordination system. Nearly 5,000 workers were given voluntary retirement. Manpower productivity in terms of the number of vehicles produced per man-year improved by 88 per cent between 1988 and 1998 (Bhudiraja et al., 2003; Patibandla, 2016). The company developed selective vendor firms for the supply of specific components with long-term contracts and facilitated joint ventures with overseas firms for technology development. In the early 1990s, when consumer preferences shifted away from scooters to motorcycles, the company was able to adjust by developing motorcycle models. By the early 2000s, Bajaj was able to catch up with the technological advantage of the TNCs.

Joint Ventures between TNCs and Local Firms and Technological and Organizational Diffusion

One of the mechanisms of transfer of technology and efficient organizational practices for local firms is joint ventures with TNCs. Joint ventures take the form of technology collaborations and equity-based arrangements. In the case of China, at the time of its opening to international investment, the government made the policy that TNCs could enter China with joint ventures with the public sector firms, which were operationally inefficient but possessed valuable assets owing to patronization by the government. This suited TNCs as they could get access to the valuable assets of the public sector firms. This also could be viewed as an attempt to privatize the public sector firms (Huang, 2002). The motive of the Chinese government was that the technology and organizational practices of TNCs should diffuse to local firms. In the long run, technology and best practices diffused to local firms and they were able to produce and export labour-intensive products without the alliances with TNCs.

In India's case, when the policy opened to TNCs in the mid-1980s in a few sectors, it stipulated that TNCs had to form joint ventures with local firms in industries such as two wheelers and automobiles. The examples are Maruti Suzuki, Hero Honda, and TVS Suzuki.

Joint ventures between TNCs and local firms can be viewed as the entry mode strategy of TNCs, especially in developing economies where institutions are complex and beset with high transaction costs. The basic theory of joint ventures is that there is an incentive for two firms to form a joint venture if there is a complementarity between the physical and human assets (or technology) possessed by the firms and if they combine them they produce higher value of output compared to going alone. The issue that follows is bargaining about sharing profits in accordance with assets invested and calculations about the future break-up of the venture. Joint ventures are basically temporary agreements. Once one party's motive of diffusion of the advantage of the other party takes place, it breaks up the venture to realize higher profits. In the case of developing countries, TNCs have an incentive to form joint ventures with local firms to gain access to institutional knowledge of local firms and to gain access to distributional assets. Therefore, a TNC brings in a technology or brand name while a local firm brings forth its established networks and distributional channels and institutional knowledge. Once a TNC gains the specific knowledge and distributional network, it has the incentive to break up. Similarly, if a local firm gains the technological knowledge of TNCs, it has the incentive to break up. If a local firm realizes this at the ex ante stage of formation of the ventures, it makes strategies to gain other advantages, which, in turn, results in diffusion of the best practices to local firms (Patibandla, 2012).

The basic theory of joint collaborations can be drawn from the incomplete contract theory of Williamson (1985) and Grossman and Hart (1986). It is impossible to form a complete contract because of possibilities of contingencies both in static and dynamic terms. Because of this, firms have to invest contractual safeguards for the possibility of breaking up. In the case of Williamson's governance logic, once two firms form a joint collaboration it becomes a bilateral monopoly. The parties have to invest in asset-specific investments once they form the contract. If one party realizes that the other party is locked into asset-specific investments, it could behave opportunistically. High degree of asset specificity requires a firm to internalize the economic activity and avoid joint collaborations. Joint ventures are formed when the costs of hold-up and opportunism are low. In the case of Grossman and Hart's approach, the firm is a set of property rights and focuses on the role of physical assets in a contractual relationship. Two parties possess different assets a priori. If there is a complementarity on vertical lines between the assets, they have an incentive to form a joint collaboration. As contracts are incomplete, there are residual or control rights of the assets that are not specified in the contract. In dynamic terms, even if one party desires to expand its output and mutual investments, if the other party does not have the same incentives or has the fear of opportunism or hold-up, it could refuse. In such cases, the contract could break or there could be merger possibilities. The issues become complex if we consider cross-border mergers and acquisitions because of institutional and (managerial) cross-country cultural differences. It is necessary for an Indian firm buying a foreign corporation to make rational calculations at the pre-merger stage. These are assessing synergies and value of the assets, due diligence, and bidding and post-merger stage of adoption of incentives to managers and workers, and cross-cultural factors of management. An example from India is the Tata corporation buying the British steel company Corus. It was considered a relative failure because of mistakes at the pre-merger stage and difficulties in adopting efficient managerial practices after takeover. On the other hand, the Tata Group's purchase of the British luxury car companies Land Rover and Jaguar was considered a relative success because Tata was able to merge them into one, restructure the company, and make it profitable by adopting right managerial incentives, efficient technology, and organizational practices.

A few examples of joint ventures in India were the collaboration between Japanese TNCs Honda and Suzuki with Indian firms Hero and TVS respectively in the two-wheeler industry. In the case of Hero Honda, Honda kept its R&D at the home base and did not allow it to pass on to Hero. Hero was not able to gain technological knowledge of Honda effectively. At the time of the break-up, it faced difficulties to compete with Honda as an independent entity. In the case of TVS Suzuki, TVS made careful calculations of investing in R&D since the beginning of the venture to gain the technology advantage of Suzuki. After the break-up, it was able to compete effectively (Patibandla, 2012).

As the markets develop and institutions become more efficient, the TNCs with strong intangible asset advantage have low incentive to form joint ventures to reduce the possibilities of leakage of their technology. As the reforms progressed, the Indian government relaxed the policies allowing TNCs to set up fully owned greenfield ventures in most industries. As mentioned before, even in the case of greenfield ventures, the intangible assets of TNCs have public goods properties benefitting the local firms that are able to invest in R&D for internalization of the externalities.

Scale Economies and Differentiated Products

Economies of scale could be internal to a firm (learning-by-doing), or external to firms but internal to the industry. According to Kaldor, for firms to realize dynamic economies of scale, industries have to grow at a sustained rate. To recall, market size defined by income levels of a country determines the scope for economies of scale and number of differentiated products a country can produce. Since the early 1990s, the Indian economy experienced growth rates of 6 to 7 per cent as compared 3 per cent in the pre-reform era. At present, India is considered the fifth largest economy consisting of a sizeable middle class and rich consumers although income distribution remains skewed. This provides both for trade determined by comparative advantage (inexpensive semi-skilled and skilled labour) and intra-industry trade factors (of scale economies and product differentiation).

To provide qualitative evidence, in the automobile sector almost all the major small car producers of the world entered the Indian market. They were able to realize economies of scale and undertake exports from India. In the case of luxury cars, the market can be considered not large enough for them to realize minimum efficient scales with high fixed costs. This market is catered mostly by imports. Similar outcome can be observed in other industries such as electronics and consumer durable goods industry.

In the case of product differentiation, there had been increase in the number of differentiated goods on vertical and horizontal lines in the consumer durable and non-durable goods industries with world-class brands introduced into the Indian markets. This has led to intra-industry trade possibilities.

A large market provides scope for economies of scale and economies of scale, in turn, expand market size if firms adopt long-run average cost pricing. This is illustrated in Figure 7.1. *P* is price, *Q* is quantity. *D* and D_1 are demand curves which represent the market

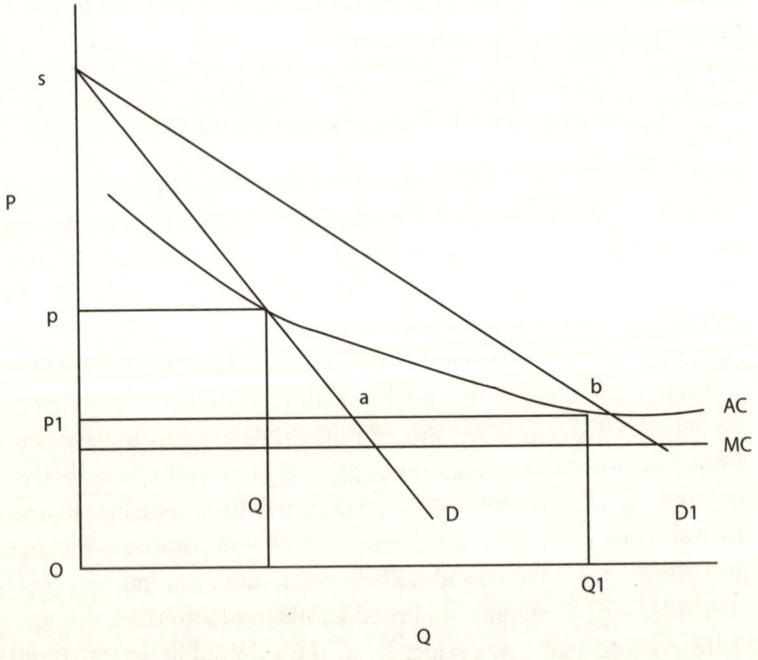

Figure 7.1 Market Size and Scale Economies
Source: Author's representation.

size. *AC* and *MC* are long-run average and marginal costs of a large firm respectively. D_1 represents increase in market size which helps a large firm realize minimum efficient scale. With demand curve *D*, the firm produces at suboptimal scale and produces at *Q* and charges a price *P*. Let us take the case that demand curve shifts to D_1 for some exogenous reasons. With D_1, the firm produces at optimal scale (minimum efficient scale given the fixed costs in production) of quantity of Q_1 and charges a price of P_1. Decline in price increases real income, consumer surplus increases by *P1Sab* which is like increase in income levels. This, in turn, increases market sizes in general by increasing consumption and savings.

Value Chains (Subcontracting) and Economies of Specialization

Value chains (supply chains) producing a product between firms is a matter of trade-offs between economies of specialization and costs of formulating and enforcing contracts. The boundaries of firms determined at marginal costs of specialization are equivalent to marginal contractual costs and also internal costs of bureaucracy (hierarchy) (Coase, 1936). Contracts could be formal or relational. In the case of formal contracts, firms have to incorporate contractual safeguards in the case of disputes that may have to be resolved by courts. However, the transaction costs of enforcement by courts are high in India. Therefore, firms resort to informal or relational contracts. Japanese corporations developed the practice of relational contracts of long-term relations of cooperative behaviour with respect to suppliers.

Part 1 demonstrated widespread subcontracting practices on vertical value chains between S&M firms and large final goods producer firms in several industries. This relation was based on inefficient contractual arrangements. The S&M subcontractor firms were made to wait long periods for payment of deliveries which significantly increased working capital costs to them. Apart from this, costs of market fluctuations were passed on to S&M firms. We showed that a few S&M firms which were able to reach a critical level of technological sophistication and size branched out to export markets as they were paid with letters of credit, which reduced working capital constraints. These types of inefficient contractual conditions changed significantly in the post-reform era with the entry of TNCs, especially the Japanese and South Korean ones. Apart from this, the new entry final goods producers increased the number of final goods producers, which resulted in decline in monopsony power and drove firms to search for productivity-enhancing practices, such as efficient value chains, based on cooperative long-term contracts rather than myopic competition of the 'prisoners dilemma' type.

A good example is Suzuki which entered the Indian market with collaboration with the Indian government (Maruti Suzuki) in the early 1980s. Within a small period, it became the largest producer of small cars, owing to protection from the government. It is well-known in the literature on value chains that the Japanese engendered significant changes in organization of value chains, which consists of transformation of design, restructuring of assembler–supplier relations, reorganization of production along the lines of just-in-time delivery, and total quality management. Suzuki brought in these practices to India. It derived a cost advantage by indigenizing close to 70 per cent of the production of components, meticulously developing local vendor (subcontractor) firms through technology transfer, long-term commitment to contracts and encouraging spatial concentration of vendor firms around its plant in the state of Haryana (Okada, 2004). This became possible because there was already presence of component producers with a certain degree of technological competence. Maruti Suzuki encouraged supplier firms to locate their plants close to its own plant. This could result in opportunism in contracts as suppliers could get locked-in with Maruti Suzuki. This outcome was reduced with long-term contracts of transfer of technology and organizational practices on cooperative lines. As reforms eliminated entry barriers further, global multinationals such as Honda, Hyundai, and so on entered the Indian markets, which reduced monopsony power of large final producers. Indian large corporations started to adopt efficient supply chain practices with respect to S&M supplier firms.

Tata Group's TELCO, which is a major player both in the production of components and final goods, was a vertically integrated firm with 'arm's length' relations with suppliers. TELCO started to change its supplier relations in 1996 by creating a special unit called Supplier Quality Improvement Group to provide technical assistance to suppliers and improve product quality for its indigenous development of a small car (Patibandla, 2006b).

Mahindra and Mahindra (M&M) was a leading producer of commercial vehicles and tractors. It achieved high cost efficiency within a short period by adopting practices of outsourcing. In 1994, the company undertook a major restructuring and increasingly adopted outsourcing of its components and sub-assemblies to local suppliers. It undertook indigenous development of the Scorpio van by purchasing the Italian design. The company developed a network of 110 local suppliers and pushed the outsourcing policy to the limit, virtually outsourcing a major part of the component requirements. Consequently, it was able to launch the van at a competitive price and with a great degree of market success (Sutton, 2004).

The case of Hyundai and Ford is interesting. They located their plants in the coastal region of south India in Chennai in Tamil Nadu. Their location led to the development of a vibrant cluster of component producers. The location of the plants close to the port of Chennai facilitated their long-term objective of using India as a base for exports.

Hyundai adopted outsourcing practices and was able to indigenize the production of the components to the extent of 70 per cent by developing supplier firms in and around Chennai. There are around seventy suppliers in the vicinity of Chennai, out of which sixteen are Korean component suppliers of Hyundai who set up their plants jointly with local partners. Hyundai facilitated technology transfer to the suppliers to enhance quality and cost efficiency. Within a short period, it was able to achieve a high degree of local market success and undertook exports from the Indian plant to the home market and markets in other developing and developed economies. The TNCs such as Ford entered the Indian industry by encouraging some of their home (international) supplier firms, such as Visteon, to locate their plants in India. General Motors and Daimler Chrysler also brought in a few of their supplier firms from overseas. Unlike Hyundai, Ford undertook development of local supplier firms in a slow manner to maintain quality standards for supplying in local market and for exporting from India (Patibandla, 2006b).

The evolution of the outsourcing practices of both TNCs and local assembler firms led to the emergence of a three-tier system of supplier firms. The first tier includes the large TNCs' joint ventures and local firms supplying to the assemblers. The second tier comprises the S&M firms supplying to the tier 1 firms. At the bottom are the small firms supplying to the tier 2 firms. Diffusion of best practices permeated quickly to the first-tier firms but not to the ones at the bottom. In order to realize high quality standards and cost efficiency, the first-tier firms increased capital and skill intensity of production thereby gradually eliminating bottom tier suppliers.

One of the elements of institutional change is the improvement in the bargaining position of the supplier firms. Tewari (2005), based on her field study of supplier firms, observed that first-tier suppliers had become discriminatory towards getting into a supply relation with assemblers by taking into account volume, size and nature of investment, and the price range of assemblers. It is interesting to note that it was the larger firms within the component industry who could adopt capital-intensive technologies in a labour-abundant country, and were able to improve their bargaining position with respect to assemblers. Furthermore, adapting to the inefficient local infrastructure conditions required the TNCs to develop supplier firms' agglomeration into clusters. Cluster activity can result in collective efficiency and reduce transaction costs of contract formulation and enforcement through repeated interactions.

Since the late 1990s, India's exports of auto components started to grow in a rapid manner. Out of the top component exporters, ten were TNC joint ventures while three formed part of a single domestic group, the TVS group (Sutton, 2004).

India and Global Value Chains

One of the important aspects of globalization is global value chains of TNCs on vertical chains of value creation with implications on volume of international trade and employment, especially in developing economies in the recent times (Spence, 2011). They can be intra-firm (within a large TNC) and inter-firm (between a large number of inter-linked firms globally). The theoretical basis is differences in labour costs in different locations and economies of specialization between firms. The value chains could be based on upstream and downstream linkages in value creation. The percentage of developing countries in the global chain of value creation was 15 per cent in 1996, which increased to 34 per cent in 2009, with China accounting for 17 per cent, mostly at the low-end. High-end value chains are concentrated within the USA, Germany, Japan, Taiwan, and South Korea. India's share was low (OECD, 2009; Banga, 2017) owing to constraints in infrastructure, logistics, and transaction costs.

One of the positive outcomes of increase in international trade and employment for the entry of TNCs in industries such as software and services, electronics and automobiles, and chemicals was generation of global value chains. India's participation in manufacturing global value chains is in general due to the sourcing of intermediates from abroad. India also shows a high participation in the services sector business, mainly driven by the use of Indian intermediates in the exports of other countries. Most of the final demand for manufactured goods and market services in India represents value-added that has been created domestically. The foreign value-added share was about 26 per cent in 2009. Market services demonstrate the largest domestic value-added, especially direct domestic value-added (OECD, 2009).

In recent times, Vietnam has been able to take advantage of labour cost arbitrage in global value chains in the electronics industry, which is a semi-skilled and skilled labour–intensive industry. Although India has strong advantage in the level and magnitude of semi-skilled and skilled labour, as mentioned earlier, the constraints in logistics and high transaction costs of contracts and business are major sources of the constraints for realization of the potential at present.

Externalities

Externalities can be positive and negative. As discussed in the case of scale economies, economies of scale external to a firm and internal to industry which cause downward shifts of cost curves of firms can be treated as externalities to firms. This takes place if an industry produces large amounts of intermediate goods. As mentioned before, international activities themselves could result in externalities to firms because intangible assets and new technologies, however well-protected, still have public goods properties. In the case of international trade, exports could result in externalities as it exposes firms to best practices at the global frontiers.

On the other hand, there could be negative externalities associated with international trade. We discussed in Part 1 how small firms played a prominent role in exports. Most small firms tend to be in the labor-intensive areas, in which India has a natural comparative advantage. Apart from this, several of these industries were also pollution-intensive, such as dyes and pigments manufacturing and leather industries. Several of these products were reserved for small-scale firms, for example, leather processing up to the semi-finished state. The trade policy reforms, especially devaluation of the rupee in 1991, enhanced the comparative advantage of labour-intensive goods produced by small firms and there was a rapid growth of exports by the small-scale sector. In 2003, the small-scale industry accounted for 40 per cent of the industrial production, employed about 17 million people, and accounted for 35 per cent of India's total exports. Small-scale firms, belonging to a specific industry, tend to form geographically concentrated clusters (Cawthorne, 1995). To give a few examples, there are textile dyeing industries in the states of Gujarat and Rajasthan, the leather industry is in Tamil Nadu, the diamond cutting industry is in Surat, and hosiery and garments are found in Ludhiana and in Tirupur. Several of these clusters resulted in significant pollution of river and ground water and agricultural lands in the nearby regions. For example, in Tamil Nadu, leather industry in the Palar Valley and garment industry cluster in Tirupur have resulted in vast tracts of agricultural land becoming unfit for agricultural use and a large section of the local population was deprived of their sources of drinking water. However, in a few cases, such as leather tanning, foreign governments such as that of Germany banned imports from India because of chemical content. This forced both large and small firms to come to cooperative agreement to set up chemical treatment plants.

It is well illustrated in the literature on China that it violated environmental and labour standards in order to achieve high growth rates through export promotion. If one accounts for the negative externalities, China's growth rate would be lower than it was generally shown. In recent times, China has started to adopt environmentally friendly policies. For example, Walmart imparts training to supplier firms to adopt environmentally friendly practices.

Industrial Clusters and Internationalization of Firms

We can observe that there is a relationship between formation of industrial clusters and internationalization of firms owing to externalities of international trade and investment activities in information, transaction costs, and inter-firm linkages and cooperation. In India's case the examples are the Bangalore cluster in IT industry, Chennai, Gurgaon, and Pune in automobiles, Tirupur and Ludhiana in garments, and Surat in diamond polishing and cutting. Most of these clusters are highly internationalized.

The original theory of agglomeration by Marshall showed that industrial clusters form with an aim towards minimizing transportation costs, free mobility of labour across firms, and intellectual spillovers. The agglomeration economies or externalities tend to be more significant in technology-intensive industries such as the IT industry. The most important element of hi-tech industry clusters is skilled manpower: a network of relations between skilled people supported by universities, high technology public institutions, effective financial (venture capital) institutions, and small and large companies determine the dynamics of a high-technology cluster. The emergence of the IT cluster of Silicon Valley in the USA could be traced to the defence industry–related activity of the US government. At the time of World War II, the US armed troops were based in the Bay Area of California. The demand for electronics for military use by the federal government caused the generation of a technical base in the Bay Area. The electronic products found a commercial market in due course. Subsequently, the setting up of Hewlett-Packard also created a semi-conductor industry, which gave a strong initial impetus to the formation of the cluster.

As mentioned before, the most important element of success of a cluster is local availability of skilled labour. Bangalore supplied a large pool of skilled labour and it has the elite Indian Institution of Science as well as a number of the largest and most prestigious public sector firms in the fields of electronics, aeronautics, and machine tools. Skilled manpower of these institutions became a major source of a pool of skilled labour for private firms to draw upon. Entry of local firms and, later, TNCs made Bangalore a vibrant and internationally oriented cluster.

In a developing economy, the industry clusters that are international trade–oriented contribute more to local development than inward-oriented clusters. This is because, as mentioned earlier, most of the technological innovations and new ideas are generated in developed economies, and trade with them is a source of technology transfer and externalities. The technological and information externalities get magnified and spread faster locally through external economies of cluster activity. Cluster activity also promotes effective networking between local firms and multinationals and thereby causes technological diffusion. As mentioned earlier, the diffusion to local firms in general will be more rapid in a cluster than a geographically diffused industry. In essence, international orientation has made the software cluster of Bangalore develop its technological dynamism. As the local industry grows and generates a highly skilled workforce, necessary market institutions such as venture capital emerge. Bangalore and other dynamic clusters may become generators of innovations and new ideas.

The TNCs played a significant role in the dynamics of the Bangalore software cluster. The location of the subsidiary of Texas Instruments (TI) in Bangalore in 1984 gave a further boost to the cluster. It was the first offshore software development facility, using satellite-based telecommunications links, which provided significant technological and information externalities to local firms. At that time, the government of India did not allow private firms to own and operate satellite technology. Satellite equipment was brought in by TI and given to the government. It took the satellite link from the government. The excess capacity of the equipment allowed local firms to make use of it and move from onsite projects to offshore activities. The successful operation of TI in Bangalore demonstrated the effect to other major American corporations to set up operations to draw upon a large pool of low-cost English-speaking skilled manpower from Bangalore for their international operations. The developments in IT and telecommunications make global diffusion of ideas and new technologies very rapid with little cost.

The TNCs cause significant externalities to local firms and skilled manpower if they build both forward and backward technology linkages. Backward linkages are with local educational institutions for generation of skilled manpower, and joint collaborations with local firms and R&D institutions. As the Bangalore cluster became vibrant, TNCs such as Hewlett-Packard, Oracle, Microsoft, Motorola, Nortell, Cisco, and several others built backward and forward linkages generating significant externalities (Patibandla and Petersen, 2002). Forward linkages are with their international operations. Movement of skilled manpower to overseas operations and back is a major source of externalities of rapid flow of ideas and technologies. Linkages at the higher end of technology have higher degree of externalities (Patibandla and Petersen, 2002). A large number of firms operating in a cluster with diverse technology increases diversity of skill base of the cluster. There are roughly 300 major TNCs operating from Bangalore, doing high-end R&D, programming, coding, and software development. Second, mobility of skilled and experienced workers across firms facilitates effective diffusion of ideas and technologies, which, in turn, increases aggregate human capital formation (Saxenian, 1996).

TNCs and Labour Market Dynamics of Software Industry

We could make the proposition that TNCs entered the Indian market to make use of initial endowment of skilled manpower, and as the number of TNCs increased they provided incentives for local manpower to acquire technical skills, which, in turn, increased employment levels. The second effect was improvements in productivity of skilled workers. Prior to opening of the Indian economy to TNCs, local firms used skilled manpower mostly for mundane tasks, paying low wages owing to their monopsony power. Entry of a large number of TNCs tilted the market more in favour of labour markets by reducing monopsony power of local firms. The TNCs entered the Indian market for utilization of skilled manpower for their global operations rather than serving the small Indian market. This relaxed the market size constraint as the world market presents infinite elasticity of demand. This had two effects in the labour market: increase in employment levels and improvements in productivity and corresponding wage rates.

It is well established in development economics that workers' productivity is a function of capital accumulation and technology (Solow, 1988; Romer, 1990). Capital can be separated into physical and human capital. The TNCs bring in physical capital and employ local human capital. If they bring in latest technologies and train the local technical manpower on how to use them, it further increases productivity and corresponding wage rate. Furthermore, learning economies in the IT industry are significant because the production activity itself embodies technological learning (Patibandla and Petersen, 2002). As the wage rate went up, it forced local firms to make improvements in productivity of skilled labour employed. As industry dynamics improved the quality ladder, India's labour markets failed to supply necessary skilled manpower (Dossani and Patibandla, 2010). This made both local firms and TNCs start investing in internal training of skilled manpower as an endogenous process of sustaining comparative advantage.

8 Empirical Analysis

The econometric exercises were based on firm-level panel data for three industries for the post-reform era. These industries are two-wheelers (TW), automobiles (AM), and auto components (AC). The AC industry consists of a large sample as it includes both large and small firms. As discussed before, it consists of firms belonging to three tiers. As a result, technological heterogeneity of firms in the industry is high. These industries were chosen because they have maximum exposure to international trade and investment. The data was collected from the Prowess Database of the Centre for Monitoring Economy. The time period covered 2007 to 2018. Panel data analysis has several advantages as it captures the dynamics of change because of inclusion of both cross-sectional and time-series dimensions. It utilizes information on both inter-temporal dynamics and individuality of entities being investigated which controls for the effects of missing or unobserved variables (Cheng, 1986). We adopted a fixed effects model to control for firm-level effects. This methodology also reduces the bias caused by omitted variables. One can treat some of the variables as exogenous without violating the underlying theory with the panel data analysis. All the results are presented in log-linear terms in order to capture non-linearity in causations and reduce multi-collinearity among independent variables. The estimated co-efficient is elasticity.

Variables

S = sales
E = exports
SW = salaries and wages. This variable is taken to capture both labour intensity of production and as an input in the production function
GF = gross fixed assets. It is taken to capture firm size dimension
NF = net fixed assets
RM = raw materials consumed
IM = imports
RD = research and development expenditure
RTF = royalties and technical fees. It captures overseas technology purchases by firms
TE = relative technical efficiency of firms (the methodology was discussed in Chapter 5)
VA = value-added (*S* – *RM*)
VI = vertical integration (*VA*/Sales)

Export intensity is taken to be a function of firm size (GF), relative firm-level technical efficiency (TE), labour intensity (SW), and capital intensity (NF). Table 8.1 provides the results. The results show that in general there is a positive relation between exports and firm size, which is contrary to the results of the pre-reforms era of the first part. This can be interpreted both in terms of relevance of scale economies and competitive conditions for explanation of firm-level exports. This is supported by the positive association between relative technical efficiency and exports. The interpretation here could be that markets have become more competitive in the post-reform era. Furthermore, in the case of AC and TW industries there is a positive association between labour intensity and exports, which implies that comparative advantage in labour intensity became germane for exports. It is important to note here that labour intensity was taken in terms of salaries and wages, which captured skill intensity of labour employed by firms. As discussed in Part 1, this captures the human capital dimension in the production function. In the case of AC, as discussed earlier, there are three tiers of firms, with the first-tier firms

Table 8.1 Econometric Explanation of Exports (Dependent Variable: Log *E*)

Industry	Constant	Log *GF*	Log *TE*	Log *SW*	Log *NF*	R^2	F-Value	N
AM	1.46	0.55	0.66	0.04	−0.05	0.1	0.3	443
	(0.42)	(0.90)	(0.15)	(0.10)	(0.10)			
AC	0.01	0.32*	0.32*	0.24*	−0.01	0.20	12.21	5792
	(1.2)	(30.6)	(2.68)	(3.79)	(0.01)			
TW	0.08	1.06	0.73*	0.53*	−1.03	0.54	2.5	140
	(0.03)	(0.43)	(2.0)	(2.6)	(0.47)			

Notes: Figures in brackets are 't' values.
* Significant at 0.10.
Source: Computed based on data from Prowess Database of the Center for Monitoring the Indian Economy.

being technologically advanced and of larger size and with linkages to TNCs and global supply chains (original equipment manufacturers). The positive association between firm size and TE with export intensity supports this observation.

TE is taken to be a function of *RDV* (research and development intensity), *IMV* (import intensity), *RFS* (royalties and technical fees intensity), and *VI* (vertical integration). Table 8.2 presents the results. The results are rather mixed. In the case of AM and AC industries,

Table 8.2 Econometric Explanation of TE (Dependent Variable: Log *TE*)

Industry	Constant	Log *RD*	Log *IM*	Log *RTF*	Log *VI*	R^2	F-Value	N
AM	−3.5*	0.04*	−0.02*	−0.01	0.85*	0.13	30.98	443
	(19.3)	(2.6)	(2.3)	(0.46)	(5.3)			
AC	−5.4*	0.02*	0.01	0.03*	0.97*	0.12	39	5792
	(65)	(5.01)	(1.2)	(3.5)	(10.27)			
TW	−0.92*	0.01	0.01	0.02*	0.64*	0.10	86.5	140
	(19.4)	(1.2)	(0.52)	(4.26)	(15.48)			

Notes: Figures in brackets are 't' values.
* Significant at 0.10.
Source: Computed based on data from Prowess Database of the Center for Monitoring the Indian Economy.

Table 8.3 Econometric Explanation of Externalities (Augmented Production Function: Dependent Variable Log *VA*)

Industry	Constant	Log *SW*	Log *NF*	Log *RD*	Log *E*	Log *IM*	Log *RTF*	R^2	F-Value	N
AM	4.33*	0.30*	0.26*	0.04*	0.03*	0.04*	–0.02	0.70	19.30	443
	(7.42)	(2.6)	(3.40)	(2.6)	(2.1)	(2.3)	(1.30)			
AC	3.88*	0.11*	0.36*	0.02*	0.02*	0.01*	0.02*	0.76	54.3	5792
	(17.70)	(4.63)	(8.90)	(4.30)	(3.95)	(3.43)	(3.0)			
TW	2.50*	0.89*	–0.06	0.01	0.02*	–0.01	0.04	0.87	20.83	140
	(3.0)	(6.40)	(0.08)	(1.12)	(2.6)	(0.82)	(1.34)			

Notes: Figures in brackets 't' values.

* Significant at 0.10.

Source: Computed based on data from Prowess Database of the Center for Monitoring the Indian Economy.

the estimated coefficient of *RDV* variable is positive and statistically significant, which implies it is important for firms to undertake in-house R&D for realizing higher relative technical efficiency to be competitive. In the case of the AC industry, overseas technology purchase variable's (*RTF*) estimated coefficient is positive and statistically significant. As discussed before, in this industry, firms' linkages with final product manufacturer TNCs for technology transfer is a common practice. The result is similar in the case of TW industry. In the case of AM industry, it is statically insignificant. The results associated with the imports variable (IM) are in general statistically insignificant to draw any inferences. One general result for all the industries is that vertical integration (VI) explains TE positively and as statistically significant. The interpretation here can be that the Indian economy is still a high-transaction-cost one and firms prefer in-house control of economic activity, especially technology-intensive processes.

Externalities of international trade and investment are explained through the estimation of augmented Cobb–Douglas production in which, apart from labour and capital, we introduce RD and E, IM, and RTF variables. This captures externalities associated with international trade and technological inflows and their explanation of externalities (Aitken and Harrison, 1999). The results are presented in Table 8.3. One strong result across all industries is that the estimated coefficients associated with export (E) and import (IM) variables are of positive sign and statistically significant. This implies that international trade activities appear to result in strong positive externalities. The greater promotion of international trade by the government results in overall productivity gains for the economy. The results with respect to technology purchase variable (RTF) is positive and significant in the case of AC industry, providing support to our arguments of global value chains. The other results are not statically significant for making any generalizations.

9 Indian Multinational Firms

One of the important features of globalization during the last decade or more has been the emergence of emerging economy multinationals onto the global stage from countries such as China, India, Brazil, Mexico, Taiwan, Argentina, Russia, and South Africa. This is expected to play an important role in shaping the world economy (Guillen and Garcia-Canal, 2013). Table 9.1 presents a few cases. Some of the examples from India are TCS, Wipro, and Infosys in software and services, and outsourcing, Reddy Labs and Ranbaxy in pharmaceuticals, Bharat Forge in metals, and Tata Group in tea, automobiles, and steel. Major investors from India are in the service sector unlike other developing economies. For example, Asia's economic growth was driven by manufactured goods' exports. Dossani and Patibandla (2010) show that, as of 2008, the service sector in India was both driving economic growth and posing to be a global competitor. The Indian success with remote services provision disproves a widespread belief that Asia is better at manufacturing than services. This shibboleth was based on the evidence that even the advanced economies of Asia, that is, Japan, Singapore, Taiwan, Hong Kong, and South Korea failed to create globally competitive service industries. One of the reasons behind this was that the internet and lower digital storage costs combined to reduce the capital costs associated with remote service provision. India's endowment of large-scale

Table 9.1 Global Leaders from Emerging Economies (by Sector)

Firm	Country	Industry	Global Position
Arcor	Argentina	Confectionery	No. 1 in candy
Bimbo	Mexico	Food processing	No. 1 in bread and bakery
JBS	Brazil	Food processing	No. 1 in meat
Modelo	Mexico	Beverages	No. 1 in import beer
Vale	Brazil	Mining	No. 3
Tenaris	Argentina	Steel	No. 1 in seamless tubes
Bharat Forge	India	Metals	No. 2 in forgings
POSCO	South Korea	Steel	No. 4
Cemex	Mexico	Cement	No. 1 in ready-mix concrete
Braskem	Brazil	Bioplastics	No. 1
Acer	Taiwan	Personal computers	No. 2
Lenovo	China	Personal computers	No. 4
BYD	China	Electronics	No. 1 in Ni-Cd batteries
Haier	China	Household appliances	No. 1
Samsung Electronics	South Korea	Consumer electronics	No. 1
Embraer	Brazil	Aircraft	No. 1 in regional jets
Gazprom	Russia	Energy (excluding oil)	No. 1
Cosan	Brazil	Biofuels	No. 1
DP World	Dubai	Port operator	No. 4
Infosys	India	Information services	Top 5
Wipro	India	Outsourcing services	Top 5

Source: Guillen and Garcia-Canal, 2013.

skilled manpower (human capital) provided comparative advantage both for exports and international investments. As mentioned before, major software firms undertook exports from the home base. As they grew, they started to set up greenfield ventures overseas to be closer to customers with strong linkage with home base operations.

In 2003 alone Indian companies acquired about seventy-five foreign companies. In 2004, there were 714 overseas joint ventures, and 1,043 wholly owned subsidiaries operating in the overseas markets (Hansen, 2009). To recapitulate, this has become possible because the highly competitive domestic market in the post-reform era made several Indian corporations acquire technological, organizational, and managerial capabilities to be able to compete in the world markets. The investments have been both horizontal and vertical lines. As mentioned before, horizontal foreign direct investment is generally undertaken as a substitute for intra-industry trade of market-seeking nature and vertical investments are mostly a substitute for inter-industry trade of resource- and asset-seeking nature.

In the case of software and services, which had been one of the prominent sectors for outward investments in the initial phase, Indian firms exported to developed economies by taking advantage of low-cost skilled labour. Later, they started substituting exports with foreign direct investment that had both forward and backward linkages. As observed by UNCTAD (2004), 'The success of Indian firms as service providers in the outsourcing of IT services, BPO and call centres by developed-country companies has exposed them to knowledge and methods for conducting international business and induced outward FDI [foreign direct investment] through demonstration and spillover effects.' This pattern of investment is basically foreign direct investment as a substitute for inter-industry trade. This helped Indian firms to be able to compete with local firms in developed economies. Global giants in this industry, in turn, started setting up their operations in India to take advantage of low-cost skilled manpower in order to compete with Indian firms in their home markets and globally (Patibandla and Petersen, 2002).

One of the underlying factors for Indian corporations (generally emerging economy multinational firms) investing in developed countries is to develop linkages with the world market in order to leverage strategic resources that, in turn, promote learning within the firm (Mathews, 2006). This is a means of augmenting domestic competitive advantage into the international markets. We have to combine this with the intangible asset theory to understand Indian firms' ability to compete with local firms in developed economies. The important question is: what are the intangible assets of Indian corporations in manufacturing industries? Several manufacturing industries are capital- and knowledge-intensive. Therefore, low-cost advantage of semi-skilled and skilled labour is not a dominant advantage for global operations. Hansen observes that the advantages of Indian firms are their flexibility, low overhead cost-effective business models, and ability to draw on linkages with other firms and establish networks and relationships. Access to debt capital from the public and private banks and internal funds of diversified business groups were also one of the advantages of Indian corporations (Nayyar, 2008; Khanna and Palepu, 2000; Nagaraj, 2004). Guillen and Garcia-Canal (2013) observe that one of the advantages of emerging economy multinationals is their ability to execute a strategy effectively rather than wasting resources in formulating grand strategies.

The main governance choice of most Indian firms had been through global mergers and acquisitions. Most of them had been in developed economies such as the USA and Western European countries (Nayyar, 2008; Hansen, 2009). This can be considered as a form of 'inverse internalization': an Indian corporation acquires technology and brand name of corporations in developed economies. A good example was India's Tata Group acquiring the British luxury automobile companies Land Rover and Jaguar, merging them into one, and turning it around to be internationally competitive. However, the Tata Group was not very successful in the acquisition of the British company Corus in the steel industry. A considerable number of cross-border mergers fail in the post-acquisition phase. To understand this, one has to assess the different phases of the mergers and acquisition: experience and competencies in the specific activity or industry, location and the target, assessing synergies, raising finance, conducting due diligence, bidding, managing moral hazards, and carrying out merger and the post-merger administration of the company in terms of handling and incentivizing managers and workers and cross-cultural management. Mistakes in these spheres result in failures (Grossman and Hart, 1986).

Conclusion

During the last forty years, globalization and rapid technological changes and their multi-speed flow across countries resulted in structural changes in the world economy, especially in the developing world (Spence, 2011). The developing economies that had been able to take advantage of this phenomenon are those that established certain initial endowments in technology and skills, income levels, and institutional conditions of free markets before opening up to international trade and investments and technological inflows. The examples are South Korea, Taiwan, several East Asian countries, China, and India in the recent times.

South Korea was a poor country in the 1960s. President Park, the benevolent dictator, played a crucial role in setting up the initial conditions. He implemented land reforms which generated the middle class, broke up the trade unions, and forced the rich to convert their assets into productive ones. The state adopted selective intervention. The state identified potential winners in the international markets and provided the conglomerates with concessional capital, access to imported technology, and infant industry protection. The corporations were forced to undertake exports from the initial stage. The state adopted a 'carrot and stick mechanism' towards industrialists (Amsden, 1989; Evans, 1995). With this mechanism, South Korea achieved rapid economic growth. However, TNCs did not play any major role in its growth dynamics. On the other hand, Taiwan achieved its rapid growth by exporting labour-intensive goods through S&M firms rather than large corporations.

Until 1978, China was one of the most autarkic economies in the world. Although the communist state caused some degree of industrialization and spread of literacy to the masses, its economy stagnated. The cultural revolution of the 1970s put China twenty years backward in science and technology. This prompted the Chinese government under the leadership of Deng Xiaoping to open its economy to the outside world in the late 1970s. At the time of the reforms, the initial conditions were widespread literacy and health of the masses, and widespread electrification of the rural areas. Apart from this, in the early 1980s the state undertook land reforms for allotting land to rural households as a form of social security and village officials were provided with incentives under decentralization to perform (Bardhan, 2012). Although the Chinese government sought advice from the World Bank at the time of implementing the reforms (Spence, 2011), it did not follow the typical structural adjustment and stabilization policies. The Chinese state, in its attempts to retain the communist philosophy of state ownership of capital, undertook external reforms of opening up to foreign capital and trade first and kept the internal structure unreformed. Public sector firms remained important players. It denied property rights to native Chinese until 1998 (Huang, 2002).

For many years, much of Western investment into China was channelled through intermediaries in Hong Kong, who dealt with the Western investors on the basis of formal rules that were common to Hong Kong and US/British legal systems, and dealt with producers in mainland China on relational basis (guanxi) (Shaomin, Li, and Zhang, 2000). This was done to take advantage of the Western system of capitalism by retaining its basic socialistic framework. As is well known, China flooded the world market with cheap manufactured goods and achieved an annual growth rate of 8 to 10 per cent. At present, China's private sector has started playing an important role in China as well as the world markets. China exports both low-end and highly sophisticated manufactured goods to the rest of the world (Rodrik, 2006).

In India's case, it acquired certain basic institutions of capitalism and democracy from the British rule from 1857 to 1947. Furthermore, it had a dynamic local entrepreneurial class. After its independence in 1947, it adopted federal democracy. The state donned the mantle of a development state with pervasive intervention into economic activity. Under import substitution regime, it heavily subsidized higher education. It failed to implement universal primary education, public health, and land reforms, which restrained it from adopting labour-intensive export strategies like China's (Dreze and Sen, 2013). Furthermore, the Indian economy is generally observed to be a high-transaction-cost one.

Private agents were given property rights, but these were modified by several controls. The policies, in general, created a large industrial base with both large- and small-scale sectors playing a role in its industrialization. Although the policies generated pervasive inefficiency, they also generated initial conditions for the emergence of a strong local entrepreneurial class. It also generated institutional infrastructure for private capital: the well-developed capital markets, endowment of skilled workers, and a functioning legal system, although with high transaction costs. In order to overcome the inefficiencies, certain internal reforms, as mentioned before, were initiated in the mid-1980s. Further major reforms were initiated in the early 1990s sponsored by the World Bank and IMF. These reforms started the process of India's economy being integrated into the world economy through international trade and investment with significant improvements in the industrial structure.

The basic hypothesis of this study, in the context of India, is that it was domestic market dynamics which determined international trade and investment behaviour of firms. The study was divided into two parts: the pre-reform and the post-reform behaviour of firms. The pre-reform era covered the 1980s and ignored international investment because in most industries TNCs were not allowed to play a role. The TNCs started to play an important role since the late 1980s. The discussion of the pre-reform era also demonstrated the initial conditions prevalent for the internal and external reforms to take effect on domestic market dynamics and economic growth and consequent international trade and investment behaviour in the post-reforms era. The study systematically identified different economic factors and their implications for determining firm-level international trade and investment behaviour. This has policy implications of filling up gaps of economic and institutional conditions and improving underlying factors for augmenting international trade and investment for generation of economic growth and productive employment opportunities.

The theories, conceptual framework, and empirical analysis of the first part were extended in the analysis of the second part of the post-reform market dynamics and consequent international trade and investment behaviour of firms. The theoretical framework introduced asymmetries into the model in terms of time of the pre-reform and post-reform eras and sources of costs efficiencies for their implications on international trade and investment behaviour of firms. The new entrants were taken to be TNCs with intangible assets' advantages. This, in turn, augmented domestic market competition between Indian corporations and TNCs, resulting in lower (real) prices, increase in output, and consequent increase in real income levels and increase in availability of differentiated products of both Indian and foreign brands.

One of the important features of the Indian economy during the pre-reform era was economic duality. On the one hand there was a well-developed economy and the rest was characterized by factor market segmentation, high transaction and information costs, and outdated technologies and techniques of production. The product market structure in terms of firm-size asymmetry and heterogeneity along with factor market distortions (segmentation) determined the conduct of large and small firms and their consequent international trade behaviour. The empirical results showed that there was a systematic negative association between firm size and export intensity. One of the reasons was that the policies bestowed long-run monopoly power to the large-scale organized sector firms in the domestic market. One of the interesting econometric results was that within the size group of large firms, the relatively inefficient and capital-intensive firms undertook exports. This could be because domestic leaders remained focused on deriving excess profits in the domestic market and pushed the relatively inefficient to export markets.

The factor market duality resulted in S&M firms adopting labour-intensive technologies and techniques which aligned them to be on par with India's comparative advantage in labour abundance. Apart from this, the small-scale sector faced high transaction costs in selling and raising working capital. There was widespread sub-contracting activity between small- and large-scale firms in several engineering industries. However, the contractual relations resulted in high transaction costs to small firms. These conditions drove small firms that reached a critical size and efficiency levels to branch out to exports, which presented lower transaction costs of payments through letters of credit thus reducing working capital costs. As discussed earlier, this improved significantly with the entry of Japanese and South Korean TNCs which adopted efficient supplier relations in the post-reform era.

The intra-industry trade possibilities were minimal as income distribution segmented product differentiation and restricted large firms to realize scale economies. However, the insights of the 'New' New Trade Theory of firms' heterogeneity in technology and organization of firms was quite prevalent in many industries. This, in turn, explained differences in international trade behaviour of large and small firms. The S&M firms within industries were able to take advantage of comparative advantage in labour intensity after reaching a minimum efficient scale.

The highly skewed income distribution fragmented the economy, resulting in product differentiation on vertical lines. Consequently, large-scale firms were unable to realize economies of scale advantage of exports. In the case of S&M firms, economies of specialization and high levels of X-efficiency resulted in the small-scale sector playing significant role in exports. As the Indian economy grew in the post-reform era, increased per capita incomes generated possibilities for realization of scale economies in a few sectors and introduction of high-quality differentiated products, thereby increasing consumer welfare. This, in turn, provided the basis for scale economy advantages in exports in sectors such as small cars, motorcycles, and electronics goods. For example, in 2015, figures showed that Bajaj sold 2,76,000 two-wheelers on average every month. It exported about 1,33,000 bikes.

The empirical exercises for the post-reform era examined the cases of three industries—AM, AC, and TW—because these industries have high degree of exposure to TNCs. The results for the firm-level panel data for these three industries demonstrate interesting implications. Unlike in the case of the results of the pre-reforms era discussed in Part 1, in the post-reform era firm size variable and relative technical efficiency of firms explain exports positively. The interpretation here can be that the markets in the post-reform era have become more competitive, making larger firms undertake exports. The results also indicate that in-house R&D investments are necessary for achieving higher TE. One common and strong result across all the industries under consideration is that there are strong externalities associated with international trade activity. Exports make firms gain access to world standards and qualities, and information externalities thereby promote productivity gains. Imports imply technology inflows with implications on productivity. Promotion of international trade results in significant productivity gains associated with positive externalities to the economy. The other general result of vertical integration was explaining TE positively. Here, the interpretation can be that the Indian economy remains a high transaction cost one (with low levels of ease of doing business), constraining potential gains of economies of specialization of greater degree of local and global supply chains.

In a few areas, India was able to leapfrog in exporting technology and human capital–intensive goods and services, such as software and related services. For a long period, Indian firms had been able to derive comparative advantage in the large pool of English-speaking engineering graduates for programming, coding, and software development. However, in recent times, technologies are changing rapidly and flowing across the globe at great speed (Spence, 2011). This has posed significant challenge for Indian software firms to move up on technology value chain. One can argue that there is a market failure on the part of India's higher educational institutions to produce high-quality graduates (Dossani and Patibandla, 2010). One possible response of Indian firms is investing in skill training internal to the firm and setting up greenfield ventures in developed economies to employ highly skilled workforce. We can term this as 'endogenous comparative advantage'.

There is increasing evidence of local firms from countries such as China, India, and Brazil competing effectively with TNCs from advanced countries, and they themselves becoming multinational players in the global market (Guillen and Garcia-Canal, 2013). It can be said that the domestic market structural dynamics, in response to global integration, made the large corporations from emerging economies be able to compete with global giants.

However, in India's case it has not been able to achieve export success in labour-intensive goods similar to China owing to several factors such as factor market distortions, infrastructure bottlenecks, substandard primary and secondary education to the masses, and clearing of large-scale investments subject to high transaction costs. China is transforming into a middle-income country (Spence, 2011), which implies that it is losing advantage in low-labour costs for exporting manufactured goods. Apart from this, the one-child policy followed by China caused a gradual decline in the young population, which implies its labour-intensive exports policy would not be sustainable. On the other hand, India is supposed to have demographic dividend of large endowment of young population, which can be the basis for labour-intensive manufacturing exports. India can take advantage of this by attracting international and domestic investments in producing and exporting labour-intensive manufactured goods. However, this requires substantial investments in good-quality primary and secondary education and reducing transaction costs of doing business and investments in critical infrastructure.

It is interesting to note that due to increased employment opportunities in the post-reform era owing to economic growth and increasing presence of TNCs there are incentives for both the middle class and the lower-middle class, and even the poor (Tooley, 2000) for investing in education for their children, especially in English-medium institutions. This is especially prominent in southern India. However, a major part of the north remains poor in this dimension.

This is where the state has to play an important role, especially for attracting labour-intensive foreign direct investment and global value chains for employment generation and increase in volume of trade and consequent economic growth. Furthermore, income distribution still remains skewed, which makes the domestic demand and market segmented for differentiated goods. This, in turn, constrains scale economies' advantage and potential expansion of intra-industry trade and international investments.

Bibliography

Afriat, S.N. 1972. 'Efficiency Estimation of Production Functions'. *International Economic Review* 13 (3) (October): 568–98.

Ahluwalia, I.J. 1985. *Industrial Growth in India: Stagnation since the Mid-Sixties*. New Delhi: Oxford University Press.

Ahluwalia, M.S. 1999. 'India's Economic Reforms: An Appraisal'. In Jeffrey Sachs, A. Varshney, and N. Bajpai (eds), *India in the Era of Economic Reform*. Delhi: Oxford University Press.

———. 2002. 'Economic Reforms in India Since 1991: Has Gradualism Worked?' *Journal of Economic Perspectives* 3: 67–8.

Aigner, D.J. and S.E. Chu. 1968. 'On Estimating the Industry Production Function'. *American Economic Review* 84 (58).

Aigner, D.J., C.A.K. Lovell, and P.J. Schmidt. 1977. 'Formulation and Estimation of Frontier Production Function Models'. *Journal of Econometrics* 6 (1) (July): 27–37.

Aigner, D.J., T. Amemiya, and D.J. Poirier. 1976. 'On the Estimation of Production Frontiers: Maximum Likelihood Estimation of Parameters of a Discontinuous Density Function'. *International Economic Review* 17 (2) (June): 377–96.

Aitken, B. and A. Harrison. 1999. 'Do Domestic Firms Benefit from Foreign Direct Investment? Evidence from Venezuela'. *American Economic Review* 89 (3): 605–18.

Akerlof, G. 1970. 'The Market for Lemons: Qualitative Uncertainty and the Market Mechanism'. *Quarterly Journal of Economics* 84 (3) (August): 488–500.

Allam, G. 1988. 'India's Technology Policy: Its Influence on Technology Imports and Technology Development'. In Ashok V. Desai (ed.),

Technology Absorption in Indian Industry, pp. 136–55. Wiley Eastern Limited.

Amsden, A. 1989. *Asia's Next Giant: South Korea and Late Industrialization.* Oxford University Press: New York.

Annavajhula, J.C.B. 1989. 'Japanese Sub-Contracting Systems'. *Economic and Political Weekly* 24 (8) (25 February).

Anthony, P. 1987. 'Export Competitiveness: India's Bicycle Industry'. Working paper, ICRIER, New Delhi.

Arrow, K.J. 1962. 'The Economic Implications of Learning by Doing'. *The Review of Economic Studies* 29 (3): 155–73.

Arrow, K.J., H.B. Chenery, B.S. Minhas, and R.M. Solow. 1961. 'Capital Labour Substitution and Economic Efficiency'. *Review of Economic and Statistics* 43 (August): 225–50.

Auquier, A. 1980. 'Sizes of Firms, Exporting Behaviour and the Structure of French Industry'. *The Journal of Industrial Economics* 29 (December): 203–327.

Bagchi, A. 2018. 'Foreword'. In *India Venture Capital and Private Equity Report.* Madras: Indian Institute of Technology.

Banga, K. 2017. 'Impact of Linking into Global Value-Chains on Indian Employment'. CEP Working Paper.

Bardhan, P. 1984. *The Political Economy of Development in India.* New York: Basil Blackwood.

———. 2012. *Awakening Giants, Feet of Clay.* Princeton: Princeton University Press.

Baumol, W.J. 1982). 'Contestable Markets: An Uprising in the Theory of Industry Structure'. *American Economic Review* 72 (1): 1–15.

Bell, M., B. Ross-Larson, and Z.E. Westphal. 1984. 'Assessing the Performance of Infant Industries'. *Journal of Development Economics* 16: 1–2; 101–28.

Bhaduri, A. 1988. 'Comparative Advantage, External Finance and the Vulnerability of Industrialization'. *Industry and Development*, Vol. 23, pp. 45–56. UNIDO.

Bhagwati, J.N. and P. Desai. 1970. *India: Planning for Industrialization.* London: Oxford University Press.

———. 1980. *Indian Planning for Industrialization and Trade Policies since 1951.* Delhi: Oxford University Press.

Bhagwati. J.N. and T.N. Srinivasan. 1975. *Foreign Trade Regimes and Economic Development: India.* New York: National Bureau of Economic Research and Colombia University Press.

Bharadwaj, R. 1962. 'Structural Basis of India's Foreign Trade'. i.d., 'Factor Proportions and the Structure of Indo-US Trade'. *Indian Economic Journal* (October).

Bharadwaj R. and J.N. Bhagwati. 1967. 'Human Capital and the Pattern of Foreign Trade: The Indian Case'. *Indian Economic Journal* 2 (2) (October).

Bhudhiraja, S., G. Piramal, S. Ghoshal, and R. Bauman. 2003. 'Bajaj Auto'. In S. Ghoshal (ed.), *World Class in India*. New Delhi: Penguin.

Blair, J.M. 1972. *Economic Concentration: Structure, Behaviour and Public Policy*. New York: Harcourt Brace Jovanovich.

Brahmananda. P.R. 1982. *Productivity in the Indian Economy: Rising Inputs for Falling Outputs*. New Delhi: Himalaya Publishing House.

Brander, J.A. 1981. 'Intra-Industry Trade in Identical Commodities'. *Journal of International Economics* 2 (9): 1–14.

Brander, J.A. and Barbara J. Spencer. 1983. 'International R&D Rivalry and Industrial Strategies'. *Review of Economic Studies* 50 (163): 707–22.

———. 1985. 'Export Subsidy and International Market Share Rivalry'. *Journal of International and Economics* 18: 83–100.

Brander, J.A. and P. Krugman. 1983. 'A Reciprocal Dumping Model of International Trade'. *Journal of International Economics* 15 (3–4) (November): 313–21.

Broeck, J. Vanden, F.R. Forsund, L. Hjalmarsson, and W. Meeusen. 1980. 'On the Estimation of Deterministic and Stochastic Frontier Production Functions: A Comparison'. *Journal of Econometrics* 13 (1) (May): 117–38.

Bruch, M. and Z. Urick Hiemen. 1983. *Small and Medium Scale Manufacturing Establishments in Asian Countries: Perspectives and Policy Issues*. Report No. 9, Economics Office Report series. Asian Development Bank.

Business Today. 1999. Cover story: 'Fathers, Sons and CEOS'. June.

Caves, R.F. 1981. 'Intra-Industry Trade and Market Structures in the Industrial Countries'. *Oxford Economic Papers*, Vol. 33, pp. 203–23. Oxford University Press.

Cawthorne, P.M. 1995. 'Of Networks and Markets: The Rise and Rise of a South Indian Town, the Example of Tirupur's Cotton Knitwear Industry'. *World Development* 23 (1): 43–56.

Chakraborty, D. 1983. 'Translog Production Function: A Review of Literature'. *Artha Uirnana* 25 (2) (June): 115–46.

Chakravarty, S. 1979. 'On the Question of Home Market and Prospect for Indian Growth'. *Economic and Political Weekly*, Special Number (August): 76–108.

Chakravarty, S. 1985. 'Methodology and Economics'. *Journal of Quantitative Economics* 1 (9): 1–9.

Chandler, Alfred D., Jr. 1977. *The Visible Hand: The Managerial Revolution in American Business*. Cambridge: Harvard University Press.

Chatterjee, R. 1989. *The Behaviour of Industrial Prices in India*. New Delhi: Oxford University Press.

Cheng, H. 1986. *Analysis of Panel Data*. Cambridge: Cambridge University Press.

Christensen, L.R., D.W. Jorgenson, and L. Lau. 1971. 'Conjugate Quality and the Transcendental Logarithmic Production Function'. *Econometrica* 55 (1) (February): 28–45.

———. 1973. 'Transcendental Logarithmic Production Frontiers'. *Review of Economics and Statistics* 55 (1) (February).

Christensen, Laurits R. and William H. Greene. 1976. 'Economies of Scale in U.S. Electric Power Generation'. *The Journal of Political Economy* 84 (4), Part 1: 655–76.

CII (Confederation of Indian industries). 1985. *Confederation of Indian Industries Year Book 1985*.

Coase, R.H. 1937. 'The Nature of the Firm'. *Economica* 4: 386–405.

———. 1960. 'The Problem of Social Costs'. *The Journal of Law and Economics* 3: 1–40.

Corden, W.M. 1965. *Recent Developments in the Theory of International Trade*. Princeton: Princeton University.

———. 1970. 'A Note on Economies of Scale, the Size of the Domestic Market and the Pattern of Trade'. In I.A. McDougall and R.H. Snape (eds), *Studies in International Economics*. Amsterdam.

———. 1974, *Trade Policy and Economic Welfare*. Oxford: Oxford University Press.

Das, Gurucharan. 2000. *India Unbound*. New Delhi: Penguin.

Dasgupta, P. and J. Stiglitz. 1980. 'Uncertainty, Industrial Structure and Speed of R&D'. *Bell Journal of Economics* 11 (1): 1–28.

D'Costa, A.P. 1995. 'The Restructuring of the Indian Automobile Industry: Indian State and Japanese Capital'. *World Development* 23 (3): 485–502.

Delong, B.J. 2001. 'India since Independence: An Analytic Growth Narrative'. Berkeley: Department of Economics, University of California.

Demsetz, H. 1973. 'Industry Structure, Market Rivalry and Public Policy'. *Journal of Law and Economics* 16 (1): 1–10.

Desai, L.M. 2003. 'India and China: An Essay in Comparative Political Economy'. Paper for IMF Conference.

Desai, V. Ashok. 1980. 'The Origin and Direction of Industrial R&D in India'. *Research Policy* 9 (1): 20–44.

———. 1982. 'Market Structure and Technology: Their Interdependence in Indian Industry'. Mimeo. New Delhi: NCAER.

———. 1984. 'The Slow Rate of Industrialization: A Second Look'. *Economic and Political Weekly* 19 (31–3): 1267–72.

———. 1988. 'Technology Absorption in Indian Industry', ed. Wiley Eastern Limited (conference paper), pp. 1–29.

Dixit, A. and B. Nalebuff. 2010. *The Art of Strategy.* New York: W.W. Norton and Company.

Dixit, A. and G. Stiglitz. 1977. 'Monopolistic Competition and Optimum Product Diversity'. *American Economic Review* 67 (3): 297–308.

Dixit, A. and V. Norman. 1984. *Theory of International Trade*. Cambridge: Cambridge University Press.

Diwan, R. 1989. 'Small Business and the Economics of Flexible Manufacturing'. *Small Business Economics* 1 (December): 10–9.

Dossani, R. 2008. *India Arriving: How This Economic Powerhouse Is Redefining Global Business.* New York: Amacon.

Dossani, R. and A. Desai. 2009. 'Assessing Early-Stage Risk Capital in India'. In Rajesh Kumar and Murali Patibandla (eds), *Institutional Dynamics and the Evolution of the Indian Economy*. New York: Palgrave and MacMillan.

Dossani, R. and M. Patibandla. 2010. 'Technology and Educational Challenges in a Globalizing World: A Case Study of India'. In H. Bidogli (ed.), *The Handbook of Technology Management*. New Jersey: John Wiley and Sons.

Dreze, J. 1960. 'Ouelquer Reflexions serirner Sur 1' adaptation del' Industries belge an March'e Commun'. Complete rendus Travaux de la society Royale d' Economic Plitique de Belgique, no. 275.

Dreze, J. and A.K. Sen. 2013. *An Uncertain Glory: India and Its Contradictions*. New Delhi: Penguin.

Dunning. J.H. 1985. *Industrial Structure, MNE's and International Competitiveness*. New York: John Wiley and Sons.

——— (ed.). 1988. *Explaining International Production*. London: Unwin.

Ethier, W. 1979. 'Internationally Decreasing Costs and World Trade'. *Journal of International Economics* 9 (1): 1–24.

———. 1982. 'National and International Returns to Scale in the Modern Theory of International Trade'. *American Economic Review* 72 (4): 389–405.

Evans, P. 1995. *Embedded Autonomy: States and Industrial Transformation.* Princeton: Princeton University Press.

Fare, R. and C.A.K. Lovell. 1978. 'Measuring the Technical Efficiency of Production'. *Journal of Economic Theory* 19 (4) (October): 150–62.

Farrell, M.J. 1957. 'The Measurement of Production Efficiency'. *Journal of the Royal Statistical Society* A.120 (Part 3): 253–81.

Forbes, N. 2002. 'Doing Business in India: What Has Liberalization Changed?'. In A. Krueger (ed.), *Economic Policy Reforms and the Indian Economy.* New Delhi: Oxford University Press.

Forbes, N. and D. Weild. 2002. *From Followers to Leaders: Managing Technology and Innovation in Newly Industrializing Countries.* New York: Routledge.

Forsund, F.R. and E.S. Jansen. 1977. 'On Estimating Average and Best Practice Homothetic Production Functions Via Cost Functions'. *International Economic Review* 18 (2) (June): 463–76.

Forsund, F.R., C.A. Knox Lovell, and Peter Schmidt. 1980. 'A Survey of Frontier Production Functions and of Their Relationship to Efficiency Measurement'. *Journal of Econometrics* 13 (12): 5–25.

Frankel, J. 1971. 'On the Domestic Demand and Ability to Export'. *Journal of Political Economy* 79 (7): 668–72.

Frankena, M. 1973. 'Marketing Characteristics and Price of Exports of Engineering Goods from India'. *Oxford Economic Papers,* New Series, Vol. 251, pp. 127–32.

Freeman, C. 1997. 'The "National System of Innovation" in Historical Perspective'. In D. Archibugi and J. Michie (eds), *Technology, Globalization and Economic Performance.* Cambridge: Cambridge University Press.

Friedman, J.W. 1983. *Oligopoly Theory.* New York: Cambridge University Press.

Fuji, S. 1971. 'Japan's Small Enterprises and Export Trade'. In T. Yamanaka (ed.), *Small Business in Japan's Economic Progress,* pp. 65–73. Tokyo.

Glejser, H., K. Goossens, and E.M. Vanden. 1982. 'Inter-Industry versus Intra-Industry Specialization in Exports and Imports'. *Journal of International Economics* 12 (3): 363–70.

Greene, W.H. 1980. 'On the Estimation of a Flexible Frontier Production Model'. *Journal of Econometrics* 13 (1): 101–15.

Grossman, S. and O. Hart. 1986. 'The Costs and Benefits of Ownership: A Theory of Vertical and Lateral Integration'. *Journal of Political Economy* 94 (4): 691–719.

Grubel, H. 1967. 'Intra-Industry Specialization and the Pattern of Trade'. *Canadian Journal of Economics* 33 (August): 374–88.

Grubel, H.G. and P.J. Lloyd. 1975. *Intra-Industry Trade*. London: Macmillan.

Guillen, Mauro and Esteban Garcia-Canal. 2013. *Emerging Economy Rule*. New York: McGraw Hill.

Haberier, G. 1936. *The Theory of International Trade with Its Applications to Commercial Policy*. London: William Hodge.

Hansen, M.W. 2009. 'The Rise of Indian Multinationals: Explaining Outward Foreign Direct Investment from India'. In Rajesh Kumar and Murali Patibandla (eds), *Institutional Dynamics and the Evolution of the Indian Economy*. New York: Palgrave and MacMillan.

Hay, Donald and M. Morris Derek. 1979. *Industrial Economics: Theory and Evidence*. Oxford: Oxford University Press.

Hazari, R.K. 1986. *Essays on Industrial Policy*. New Delhi: Concept Publishing Company.

Helleiner, G.K. 1973. 'Manufactured Exports from Less-Developed Countries and Multinational Firms'. *Economic Journal* 83 (9): 21–47.

———. 1976. 'Industry Characteristics and the Competitiveness of Manufacturers from Less Developed Countries'. *Welt Winscheftlicher Archiv* 112 (3): 507–24.

———. 1981. *Intra-Firm Trade and Developing Countries*. London: MacMillan.

Helpman, E. 1981. 'International Trade in the Presence of Product Differentiations: Economies of Scale and Monopolistic Competition; A Chamberlin-Heckscher-Ohlin Approach'. *Journal of International Economics* 2 (30): 305–40.

Helpman, E. and P.R. Krugman. 1985. *Market Structure and Foreign Trade: Increasing Returns. Imperfect Competition and the International Economy*. Cambridge: MIT Press.

Helpman, Ellhanan, Mark J. Melitz, and Stephan Ross Yeaple. 2004. 'Export versus FDI with Heterogenous Firms'. *American Economic Review* 94 (1): 300–16.

Hirsch, S. and Azvi Adar. 1974. 'Firm Size and Export Performance'. *World Development* 2 (7) (July): 41–6.

Hotelling, H. 1929. 'Stability in Competition'. *Economic Journal* 39 (153) (March): 41–57.

Huang, Y. 2002. *Selling China: Foreign Direct Investment during the Reform Era*. New York: Cambridge University Press.

Hufbbauer, G.C. 1965. *Synthetic Materials and the Theory of International Trade*. London: Gerald Duckworth and Company.

Hufbauer, G.C. 1970. 'The Impact of National Characteristics and Technology on the Commodity Composition of Trade in Manufactured Goods'. In R. Vernon (ed.), *The Technology Factor in International Trade*. New York: Columbia University Press.

Hymer, S.H. 1960. 'The International Operations of National Firms: A Study of Direct Foreign Investment'. PhD dissertation, MIT (published in 1976).

ICICI Bank. 1985. *Export Performance of ICICI Financial Companies: 1978–79 to 1980–81*.

Joshi, Vijay and I.M.D. Little. 1994. *India: Macroeconomics and Political Economy 1964–1991*. Washington, D.C: The World Bank and Oxford University Press

Khanna, T. and D. Melito. 1997. 'Modern India'. HBS Case-797-108. Harvard Business School.

Khanna, T. and K. Palepu. 2000. 'Is Group Affiliation Profitable in Emerging Markets? An Analysis of Diversified Indian Business Groups'. *The Journal of Finance* 55 (2): 86.

———. 2010. *Winning in Emerging Markets: A Road Map for Strategy and Execution*. Cambridge: Harvard University Press.

Kaldor, N. 1966. *Causes of the Slow Rate of Economic Growth of the United Kingdom*. Cambridge: Cambridge University Press.

Kamien, M.I. and N.L. Schwartz. 1982. *Market Structure and Innovation*. London: Cambridge University Press.

Katrak, H. 1969. 'An Empirical Test of Comparative Cost Theories: Japan, Peru, the United Kingdom and the United States'. *Economica* 3 (18): 103–18.

———. 1973. 'Human Skills, R&D and Scale Economies in the Exports of the United Kingdom and the United States'. *Oxford Economic Papers* (November).

———. 1985. *Imported Technology, Enterprise Characteristics and R&D in a Newly Industrializing Country: The Indian Experience*. Guilford: University of Surrey.

Keesing, D.B. 1965. 'Labour Skills and International Trade: Evaluating Many Trade Flows with a Single Marketing Device'. *The Review of Economic and Statistics* 47 (3): 287–94.

———. 1966. 'Labour Skills and Comparative Advantage'. *American Economic Review* 56 (3): 249–58.

Kemp, M.C. 1969. *The Pure Theory of International Trade and Investment.* New York: Prentice Hall.

Kemp, M.C. and T. Negishi. 1970. 'Variable Returns to Scale, Commodity Taxes, Factor Market Distortions and Implications for Trade Gains'. *Swedish Journal of Economics* 772 (12): 1–11.

Klein, R. Lawrence. 1965. *An Introduction to Econometrics.* New Delhi: Prentice Hall of India.

Kmenta, Jan. 1971. *Elements of Econometrics.* New York: MacMillan Publishing Co. Inc.

Kopp, R.J. 1981. 'The Measurement of Productive Efficiency A Reconsideration'. *Quarterly Journal of Economics* 96 (3) (August): 477–503.

Kravis, I.B. 1956. 'Availability and Other Influences on the Commodities Composition of Trade'. *Journal of Political Economy* 44 (April): 143–55.

Krugman, P. 1979. 'Increasing Returns. Monopolistic Competition and International Trade'. *Journal of International Economics* 9: 469–79.

———. 1980. 'Scale Economics, Product Differentiation and the Pattern of Trade'. *American Economic Review* 70: 950–9.

———. 1981. 'Intra-Industry Specialization and the Gains from Trade'. *Journal of Political Economy* 39: 959–73.

———. 1984. 'Import Protection as Export Promotion: International Competition in the Presence of Oligopoly and Economies of Scale'. In Henryk Kierzkowski (ed.), *Monopolistic Competition and International Trade.* Oxford: Clarendon Press.

———. 1987. 'Is Free Trade Passe'. *Journal of Economic Perspectives* 1 (2): 131–44.

Krugman, P. and Maurice Obstfeld. 2003. *International Economics: Theory and Policy.* Boston: Addition-Wesly.

Lall, Deepak. 1980. *Prices for Planning: Towards the Reform of Indian Planning.* London: Heinemann.

Lall, Sanjay. 1973. 'Transfer Pricing by Multinational Firms'. *Oxford Bulletin of Economics and Statistics* 35 (6): 173–95.

———. 1982a. 'The Emergence of Third World Multinationals'. *World Development* 10 (8): 127–46.

———. 1982b. *Developing Countries as Exporters of Technology.* London: Macmillan.

———. 1984. 'Exports of Technology by Newly Industrializing Countries: An Overview'. *World Development*: 471–80.

———. 1987. *Learning to Industrialize.* London: Macmillan Press.

Lall, Sanjay and R. Kumar. 1981. 'Firm-Level Exports Performance in an Inward-Looking Economy: The Indian Engineering Industry'. *World Development* 9 (5): 453–63.

Lancaster, K.J. 1971. *Consumer Demand: A New Approach*. New York: Columbia University Press.

———. 1980. 'Intra-Industry Trade Under Perfect Monopolistic Competition'. *Journal of International Economics* 10 (3): 151–76.

Lancaster, R. 1979. *Variety, Equity and Efficiency*. New York: Columbia University Press.

Le Craw, D.J. 1977. 'Direct Investment by Firms from Less Developed Countries'. *Oxford Economic Papers*, Vol. 29, pp. 442–57.

Lee, L. and William G. Tylee. 1978. 'The Stochastic Frontier Production Function and Average Efficiency'. *Journal of Econometrics* 7 (9): 385–9.

Leibenstein, H. 1980. *Inflation. Income Distribution and X-Inefficiency.* New York: Harper and Row.

Leontief, W.W. 1953. 'Domestic Production and Foreign Trade: The American Capital Position Re-examined'. *Proceedings of the American Philosophical Society* 97 (4): 332–49.

Li, D.D. 1996. 'A Theory of Ambiguous Property Rights in Transition Economies: The Case of the Chinese Non-State Sector'. *Journal of Comparative Economics* 23 (1): 1–19.

Linder, S.B. 1961. *An Essay on Trade and Transformation*. Stockholm: Almquist and Wiksell International.

Little, I.M.D., D. Majumdar, and J. Page. 1987. *Small Manufacturing Enterprises: A Comparative Analysis of India and Other Economies*. New Delhi: Oxford University Press.

Markusen, J. 1981. 'Trade and the Gains from Trade with Imperfect Competition. *Journal of International Economics* 2 (4): 531–51.

Markusen, J. and J. Melvin. 1981. 'Trade, Factor Prices and Gains from Trade with Increasing Returns to Scale'. *Canadian Journal of Economics* 14 (3): 450–69.

Markusen, R.M. 1995. 'The Boundaries of Multinational Enterprise and the Theory of International Trade'. *The Journal of Economic Perspectives* 9 (2): 169–89.

Martinez, M. 2002. 'Understanding State Higher Education System: Applying a New Framework'. *Journal of Higher Education* 73 (3): 349–75.

Mathews, J.A. 2006. 'Dragon Multinationals: New Players in 21st Century Globalization'. *Asia Pacific Journal of Management* 23 (1): 5–27.

McAleese, D. 1979. 'Intra-Industry Trade: Level of Development and Market Size'. In H. Giersch (ed.), *On the Economics of Intra-Industry Trade*, pp. 137–54. Tubingen: J.C.B. Mohr.

Mead, C.D. 1984. 'Of Contracts and Sub-contracts: Small Firms in Vertically Disintegrated Production/Distribution Systems in LDCs'. *World Development* 12 (11–12): 1095–106.

Melitz, Mark J. 2003. 'The Impact of Trade on Intra-Industry Reallocations and Aggregate Industry Productivity'. *Econometrica* 71 (6): 1695–725.

Meesen, W. and J. Van der Broeck. 1977. 'Efficiency Estimation from Cobb–Douglas Production Functions with Composed Error'. *International Economic Review* 18 (2) (June): 435–44.

Miroudot, S., R. Lanz, and A. Ragoussis. 2009. 'Trade in Intermediate Goods and Services'. OECD Trade Policy Working Papers, No. 93.

Mitra, A. 1977. *Terms of Trade and Class Relations*. London: Frank Publications.

Myint, H. 1971. *Economic Theory and the Underdeveloped Countries*. Oxford: Oxford University Press.

Nagaraj, R. 1984. 'Sub-Contracting in Indian Manufacturing Industries: Analysis, Evidence and Issues'. *Economic and Political Weekly* 19 (31–3): 1435–52.

———. 1985. 'Some Aspects of Small-Scale Industries in India: Findings Based on Two All-India Surveys'. *Economic and Political Weekly* 20 (41): 65–95.

———. 2004. 'Fall in Organized Manufacturing Employment: A Brief Note'. *Economic and Political Weekly* 39 (30): 3387–90.

———. 2006. 'Indian Investments Abroad: What Explains the Boom?' *Economic and Political Weekly* 41 (46): 4716–18.

Nasscom. 2006. *Strategic Review*. New Delhi: Nasscom.

Naya, Seiji. 1985. 'The Role of Small-Scale Industries in Employment and Exports of Asian Developing Countries'. *Hitotsubashi Journal of Economics* 26 (3): 147–63.

Nayyar, D. 1976. *India's Exports and Export Policies in the 1960s*. Cambridge: Cambridge University Press.

———. 1978. 'Industrial Development in India: Some Reflections on Growth and Stagnation'. *Economic and Political Weekly*, Special Number (August): 201–40.

———. 2008. 'The Internationalization of Firms From India: Investments, Mergers and Acquisitions'. *Oxford Development Studies* 36 (1): 111–31.

Nishimizu, Mieke and John M. Page. 1982. 'Total Factor Productivity Growth, Technological Progress, and Technical Efficiency Changes

Dimensions of Productivity Change in Yugoslavia: 1965–1978'. *Economic Journal* 92 (December).

OECD. 2009. *Global Value-Chains: India.*

Okada, A. 2004. 'Skills Development and Inter Firm Learning Linkage under Globalization: Lessons from the Indian Automobile Industry'. *World Development* 32 (2): 1265–88.

Olson, M. 1965. *The Logic of Collective Action.* Massachusetts: Harvard University Press.

Pack, H. 1981. 'Fostering the Capital Goods Sector in LOCs'. *World Development* 9 (3): 227–50.

Page Jr., J.M. 1984. 'Firm Size and Technical Efficiency: Applications of Production Frontiers to Indian Survey Data'. *Journal of Development Economics* 16 (1): 125–52.

Panchamukhi, V.R. 1978. *Trade Policies in India: A Quantitative Analysis.* New Delhi: Concept Publishing Company.

Panzar, C. John and Robert D. Willig. 1981. 'Economies of Scope'. *American Economic Review* 71 (2) (June): 268–72.

Patibandla, M. 1988a. 'Import Liberalization and Engineering Industry: Some Issues of Short-Term Adjustment'. *Economic and Political Weekly* 23 (52–3): 24–31.

———. 1988b. 'Role of Large and Small Firms in India's Engineering Exports'. *Economic and Political Weekly* 23 (22): 105–24.

———. 2002. 'Policy Reforms and Evolution of Market Structure in an Emerging Economy: The Case of India'. *The Journal of Development Studies* 38 (3): 95–118.

———. 2006a. 'Equity Pattern, Corporate Governance and Performance: A Study of India's Corporate Sector'. *Journal of Economic Behavior and Organization* 59 (1): 29–44.

———. 2006b. *Evolution of Markets and Institutions: A Study of an Emerging Economy.* New York and London: Routledge Taylor and Francis.

———. 2012. 'Dynamics of Joint Ventures between Multinational Enterprises and Local Firms in Emerging Economies'. *Jindal Journal of Business Research* 1 (2): 127–37.

———. 2016. 'Divergence and Convergence of Firm-Level Best Practices: The Case of Bajaj and Hero-Honda in India's Two-Wheeler Industry'. *Journal of East–West Business* 22 (4): 351–68.

Patibandla, M. and B. Petersen. 2002. 'Role of Transnational Corporations in the Evolution of a High-Tech Industry, the Case of India's Software Industry'. *World Development* 30 (9): 1561–77.

Parente, S.L. and E.C. Prescott. 1994. 'Barriers to Technology Adoption and Development'. *Journal of Political Economy* 102 (2): 298–321.

Park, R.E. 1966. 'Estimation with Heteroskedastic Error Terms'. *Econometrica* 34 (4).

Piramal, G. 1996. *Business Maharajas.* New Delhi: Penguin Books India.

Porcelli, F. 2009. *Measurement of Technical Efficiency: A Brief Survey on Parametric and Non-parametric Techniques.*

Posner, M.V. 1961. 'International Trade and Technical Change'. *Oxford Economic Papers*, Vol. 13 (October): 323–41.

Porter, M.E. 1979. 'The Structure within Industries and Companies Performance'. *Review of Economics and Statistics* 61 (2): 627–34.

Richmond, J. 1974. 'Estimating the Efficiency of Production'. *International Economic Review* 15 (2) (June): 515–21.

Rodrik, D. 1988. 'Imperfect Competition, Scale Economies, and Trade Policy in Developing Countries'. In R.E. Baldwin (ed.), *Trade Policy Issues and Empirical Analysis.* National Bureau of Economic Research, The University of Chicago Press.

———. 2006. 'What's So Special about China's Exports?' *China & World Economy* 14 (5): 1–19.

Romer, P.M. 1990. 'Endogenous Technological Change'. *Journal of Political Economy* 98 (5): S71–102.

Saxenian, A. 1996. *Regional Advantage: Culture and Competition in Silicon Valley and Route 128.* Cambridge: Harvard University Press.

Scherer, F.M. 1980. *Industrial Market Structure and Economic Performance*, 2nd edition. Chicago: Rand McNally.

Schmalensee, R. 1989. 'Inter-industry Studies of Structure and Performance'. In Schmalensee R. and R. Willig (eds), *Hand Book and Industrial Organization*, Vol. II. North Holland.

Schmidt, P. 1976. 'On the Statistical Estimation of Parametric Frontier Production Functions'. *Review of Economics and Statistics* 58 (2) (May): 238–9.

Schmidt, P. and C.A.K. Lovell. 1979. 'Estimating Technical and Allocative Inefficiency Relative to Stochastic Production and Cost Frontiers'. *Journal of Econometrics* 9 (3) (February): 343–66.

———. 1980. 'Estimating Stochastic Production and Cost Frontiers when Technical and Allocative Inefficiency Are Correlated'. *Journal of Econometrics* 13 (1).

Shaw, A. and S. Thomas. 2002. 'The Evolution of the Securities Markets in India'. Mumbai: Indira Gandhi Institute of Development Research.

Shaked, A. and J. Sutton. 1984. 'Natural Oligopolies and International Trade'. In Henryk Kierzkowski (ed.), *Monopolistic Competition and International Trade*. Oxford: Clarendon Press.

Shaomin, Li, Shuhe Li, and Weiying Zhang. 2000. 'The Road to Capitalism: Competition and Institutional Change in China'. *Journal of Comparative Economics* 28 (2): 269–92.

Siddharthan, N.S. 1986. *Changing Pattern of Exports and Relocation of Industries Lessons from the Indian Experience*. New Delhi: Institute of Economic Growth.

———. 1988a. 'In-house R&D Imported Technology and Firm Size: Lessons from Indian Experience'. *Developing Economies* 26 (3): 212–21.

———. 1988b. 'Technology, Modernization and Growth: A Study of Indian Corporate Sector, 1975–83'. *Economic and Political Weekly* 23 (31) (July): 1587–90.

Solow, R. 1988. 'Growth Theory and After'. *American Economic Review* 78 (3): 307–17.

Spence, M. 1981. 'The Learning Curve and Competition'. *Bell Journal of Economics* 12 (1): 49–70.

———. 2011. *The Next Convergence: The Future of Economic Growth in a Multispeed World*. New York: Farrar, Straus and Giroux.

Srinivasan, T.N. 2000. *Eight Lectures on India's Economic Reforms*. New Delhi: Oxford University Press.

Sutton, J. 2004. 'The Auto-Component Supply Chain in China and India: A Bench-Mark Study'. London School of Economics and Political Science.

Stackelberg, H.V. 1934. *Marketform and Gleichgewicht*. Vienna: Spinger.

Stewart, Frances. 1984. 'Recent Theories of Trade: Some Implications for the South'. In Henryk Kierzkowski (ed.), *Monopolistic Competition and International Trade*. Oxford: Clarendon Press.

Stigler, G.J. 1951. 'The Division of Labour Is Limited by the Extent of the Market'. *Journal of Political Economy* 59 (3): 185–93.

Teece, D. 1976. *The Multinational Enterprises and the Resource Cost of Technology Transfer*. Cambridge, MA: Ballinger.

Teitel, S. 1984. 'Technology Creation in Semi-Industrial Economies'. *Journal of Development Economies* 16 (1–2): 39–61.

Tewari, M. 2005. 'Foreign Direct Investment and The Transformation of Tamil Nadu's Automotive Supply Base'. In Yves-André Faure and Loraine Kennedy et Pascal Labazée (eds), *Local Production Systems and Global Markets in Emerging Economies: Brazil, India and Mexico*. Paris: IRD, Karthala.

Todd, Douglas. 1985. 'Productive Performance in West German Manufacturing Industry 1979–80: A Farrell Frontier Characterization'. *Journal of Industrial Economies* 33 (4) (March): 295–315.

Tooley, J. 2000. 'Private Schools for the Poor in India'. *Economic Affairs*, June.

Tripathi, D. 2004. *The Oxford History of Indian Business*. New Delhi: Oxford University Press.

UNCTAD. 2004. *India's Outward FDI: A Giant Awakening*.

Vernon, R. 1966. 'International Investment and International Trade in the Product Cycle'. *Quarterly Journal of Economics* 80 (2): 190–207.

———. 1970. *The Technology Factor in International Trade*. New York: Columbia University Press.

Viner, J. 1953. *International Trade and Economic Development*. Oxford: Oxford University Press.

White, L.J. 1974. 'Industrial Organisation and International Trade: Some Theoretical Consideration'. *American Economic Review*, December.

Williamson, O.E. 1985. *The Economic Institutions of Capitalism*. New York: The Free Press.

Wolf, M. 1982. *India's Exports*. New Delhi: Oxford University Press.

World Bank. 1984. 'India: Non-Electrical Industrial Machinery Manufacturing—A Sub-sector Study'. Document of the World Bank, Report No. 5095- IN, 2 August.

Index

About the Author

Murali Patibandla is professor at the Indian Institute of Management Bangalore, India, since 2004. He was associate professor at the Copenhagen Business School (1999–2004), Fulbright postdoctoral scholar at University of California, Berkeley, USA (1998–99), and assistant and associate professor at the Indian Institute of Management Ahmedabad, India (1994–8). His book *Evolution of Markets and Institutions: A Study of an Emerging Economy* was published in 2006. He co-edited with Rajesh Kumar *Institutional Dynamics and the Evolution of the Indian Economy* (2009).

He has published academic articles in leading international and national journals such as the *Journal of Development Studies*, *Journal of Economic Behaviour and Organization*, *World Development*, *Economic and Political Weekly*, *Indian Economic Journal*, *International Journal of Management and Decision Making*, *Jindal Journal of Business Research*, *Journal of East–West Business*, and *Productivity Journal*. These are on subjects such as transaction cost economics, international business and economic development, New Institutional Economics and its relevance to emerging economies, India's software industry, India's higher-education institutions, and comparative analysis of institutions in and economic growth of China and India. His research has been influential and been widely cited in works across the world. He was awarded the 'Lifetime Achievement Award for Contributions to Economics' by Venus International Foundation, Chennai, in 2017.

He has also published a book of poems titled *A Garden with a Broken Fence*.